ILLUMINATING TEXTS

Jim Burke
ILLUMINATING TEXTS

How to Teach Students to Read the World

HEINEMANN
Portsmouth, NH

Heinemann

361 Hanover Street
Portsmouth, NH 03801–3912
www.heinemann.com

Offices and agents throughout the world

The author and publisher wish to thank those who have generously given permission to reprint borrowed material:

Fig. 2–1 © 1999 Time Inc. New Media. All rights reserved. Reproduction in whole or in part without permission is prohibited. Pathfinder is a registered trademark of Time Inc. New Media.

Fig. 2–3 reproduced with the permission of AltaVista. AltaVista and the AltaVista logo are trademarks of AltaVista Company.

Fig. 2–4, Iron Eyes Cody public service spot, courtesy of Keep America Beautiful, Inc.

Figs. 5–3, 6–1 reprinted with permission of NWREL. Traits of an Effective Reader is a NWREL Trademark.

Fig. 7–4 courtesy of National Campaign Against Youth Violence and The Ad Council. For more information, write to info@noviolence.net.

Library of Congress Cataloging-in-Publication Data
Burke, Jim, 1961–
    Illuminating texts : how to teach students to read the world / Jim Burke.
        p. cm.
    Includes bibliographical references and index.
    ISBN 0-86709-497-4 (alk. paper)
    1. Reading (Secondary).   2. English language—Computer-assisted instruction.   3. Criticism, Textual.   I. Title.

LB1632 .B82 2001
428.4′071′2—dc21   2001024926

Editor: Lois Bridges
Production: Abigail M. Heim
Cover design: Judy Arisman, Arisman Design
Manufacturing: Steve Bernier

Printed in the United States of America on acid-free paper

14 13 12 11 10   VP   8 9 10 11 12

For Miles Myers,

*whose example and advice have
illuminated my path these many years*

I doubt Dr. Francescue ever read books. One book only, that of the human body, took the place of all others. He never raised his eyes from it. He read it like a printed page as though he knew that in the calligraphy there just beneath the skin were all the secrets of the world.

—Richard Selzer, from *Letters to a Young Doctor*

Every man is a volume if you know how to read him.

—Chinese proverb

We can and do read not only words and pictures but faces, clouds, waves, and even stones.

—Robert Scholes, from *Protocols of Reading*

"What do you like—realistic fiction, fiction, or nonfiction?" asked Gabe. "Medium," said Whitman.

Conversation between my six-year-old son, Whitman, and an older boy while eating their peanut-butter-and-jelly sandwiches

Contents

Appendices

Acknowledgments

More than any of my previous books, this one has been the result of an ongoing conversation with many people, all of whom shared their ideas with me and, in doing so, helped me better understand my own. I am especially indebted to Robert Scholes and his books, particularly *The Rise and Fall of English: Reconstructing English as a Discipline*. Several other authors and their books are central to the premise of this book: Miles Myers' *Changing Our Minds: Negotiating English and Literacy*; Mitchell Stephens' *the rise of the image the fall of the word*; Leonard Shlain's *The Alphabet versus the Goddess*; and Alan Purves' *Scribal Society: An Essay on Literacy and Schooling in the Information Age*. These books and their authors lit the fires that kept me company during the year I wrote this book.

Other colleagues helped me, as they always have, to understand what I think by asking me the essential questions. Carol Jago and Sandy Briggs, my two mentors, responded to many ideas in this book, though they didn't always realize they were doing this. Participants in my online course, Teaching English in a Digital Age, helped me, through the course, to refine the ideas in this book. Drafts of chapters benefited from their feedback; for this and for their friendship, I give thanks. As with my previous books, I found Sam Intrator an essential guide to the world I was trying to understand. He shared not only his intelligence but a wealth of excellent resources and, as always, his unbridled enthusiasm.

Special thanks to Lois Bridges, my editor and good friend, for her continued guidance and support of my ideas; and to Betsy Feldman, editor of my netcourses, and Leigh Peake, for all their efforts to help and for their friendship.

Finally, thanks to my students and my family. Nothing is possible without them; with them, and their support, everything seems possible.

How to Use This Book

This book is more than the sum of its pages. Its accompanying Web site, <www.englishcompanion.com/illuminating>, continues and complements the book by providing additional resources in media other than mere paper. Cross-references to the Web site are indicated throughout the book with an icon in the margin:

WEB SITE

This Web site material seemed an important component of the book, given its argument about reading and creating multiple texts to convey ideas and information. Indeed, central to the idea of textual intelligence is the idea that we should often begin with the question "How should I use this book?" or, if we are writing, "How should I design this book and organize its contents to be used by the reader?"

This book offers both practical and theoretical information on teaching and reading. Each chapter has a clear focus—for example, "Reading Literature," "Reading Information"—and all follow a similar format:

- Background on and rationale for the chapter's focus
- Standards connections
- Questions to ask
- Classroom connections
- Elements of the text
- Additional resources

Thus, teachers seeking guidance in how to use and read the Internet with their students will find specific help in how to do that. The book is also built around a series of arguments, all of which fall under the overarching idea of textual intelligence. This text is appropriate for either college-level classes or teacher study groups to aid discussion about literacy.

My book *Reading Reminders: Tools, Tips, and Techniques* was originally intended to be part of this book's appendix. However, as this book continued to evolve, it became apparent that the material that became *Reading Reminders* would no longer fit here. This book is a companion to *Reading Reminders*, as this book goes into greater depth about the primary academic texts supported by *Reading Reminders*. You do not, however, need one to read or benefit from the other.

You can turn to this book for a five-minute read and find some questions to use in your next period. You can also use it as a tool for reflection, taking time to read an entire chapter and using that chapter to help you better understand what you think. Most of the ideas in this book grew out of an online course I taught through HeinemannU called Teaching English in a Digital Age.

Teachers in all subject areas will find information in this book to support their teaching. I often deliberately chose examples from subjects other than English to make this book more helpful to teachers in other subject areas, especially in the sections about reading textbooks, tests, and the Internet, three types of text common to all subject areas.

In the end, all good readers learn to establish their own use for a book. I hope this book will help you think about the issues most important to your own practice and to our profession at large. This book is one we will create together as you make contributions to the Web site and add your own questions and insights to mine and those of the other teachers and writers included in this text.

1

Introduction: Reading the World

The purpose of education in this society is to bring the kids up to be conversant with the most important ideas and the representation systems that are used to express them.
—Alan Kay

Let us draw closer to the fire so we can hear what we are saying.
—Unknown

My elementary school class huddled in the dark, all our heads angled up toward the small square of light that promised a glimpse into the next world: the first walk on the moon. Our silence and obedience signaled our understanding that this was a sacred moment. Mrs. Baldwin, our fifth-grade teacher, stood by, equally serious. When finally we saw the images and heard Neal Armstrong's voice, we all experienced the same sense of awe, our open mouths spelling out our wonder. None of us questioned whether what we saw was real, whether it had actually happened: in those days, what you saw was real. "I saw it with my own eyes," you heard people say. You also heard people say, when testifying to another's credibility, "He's a man of his word." Despite such events as the McCarthy hearings and the Cuban missile crisis, people had faith in what they read, what they heard, and what they saw.

Television, and before that, radio, transformed our expectations and shaped our tastes, but not our assumptions about authority, credibility, or veracity. If Walter Cronkite said it, it was true. If we read it in *Time*, it was gospel. And if we saw it "with our own eyes," it happened.

Vietnam changed much of that, as did Watergate, as have computers. Chances are after my friends and I left school that day, still talking about the moon walk, we came home to parents who watched the news and its statistics about the war in Vietnam, all of which we now know were false, used to create and maintain a level of support for the war. Speaking years later at an English teachers convention, novelist Tim O'Brien (1996) told a story about Vietnam, drawing us in with his mesmerizing details about his efforts to evade the draft. When he finished, having fully engaged us, the room heavy with silence and respect for the storyteller, he said, "Now that didn't happen. But it's true." And the protagonist of Larry Watson's novel *Montana 1948* says, "So no matter what the historical documents might say, I feel free to augment them with whatever lurid or comical fantasy my imagination concocts. And know that the truth might not be far off . . . For my students I keep a straight face and pretend that the text tells the truth, whole and unblemished" (1993).

Tim O'Brien's comment captures the sense of confusion many readers experience and will face with increasing frequency in the coming years. We read of Pulitzer Prize-winning reporters who write whole articles about "real people" that don't exist, incorporating into the stories sources that are equally false. The reporter might claim the story is nonetheless true; the point is that he offered it as fact. We watch events and see them the way others want us to see them, such as the Gulf War on CNN, when we were told we were seeing Patriot missiles blowing up Scud missiles, only to learn later that Hussein, too, had CNN and so our military had to pretend we were blowing up Saddam's weapons so he would think he was losing. Several years later so many readers of *Time* questioned the authenticity of a cover photograph of President Clinton and Monica Lewinsky—surely it was doctored by Photoshop—that *Time* had to publish a statement in its next issue certifying that the picture was, in fact, real, meaning untouched, meaning authentic. Finally, nearly all major newspapers publish both online and print editions of their paper; the difference is that many include on their digital edition stories they do not want to commit to print yet because the stories might not be true. The point is no longer to be right but to be first when it comes to covering a story; the point too often is not to be right but to sell papers, magazines, and advertisements.

But it's even more complicated than that: there is never one story, or rather, there is one story told by an ever-increasing range of authors, in different media, from different perspectives, with different intents because of the nature of their different audiences. Information, whether it is about a product, an idea, history, or science, has become one more product in a market saturated with texts, each one competing with the other for the title of The Truth or The Best. This era's version of the old *caveat emptor* ("buyer beware") is *caveat lector* ("reader beware").

The Reader's Tool Belt

It becomes the teacher's role, then, to arm the student with a tool belt heavy with strategies and the skill to use them appropriately when reading—and making—texts. I wrote this book in two different media, paper and the Web, and used a wide range of text types, including images, Web sites, and traditional printed texts. I also designed the book to be used/read in several different ways depending on the reader's needs: as a reference book, a netcourse, a workshop, a course for students (i.e., one I propose should exist and which the book helps design), a textbook for a content area reading course, and, of course, just a book for people to read and enjoy. Though disorienting at first, the experience of writing this book—and subsequent research on other projects—revealed a trend I began to see everywhere: writing (and thus reading) texts for multiple media, but also writing them with the following question in mind: Which media is most appropriate for this text? The notion of a tool belt is consistent with the idea that texts are made; moreover, they are made out of a variety of elements and are designed to serve specific, if multiple, purposes. Effective readers in the future will need to recognize the role of design and the function of different elements when they read. They will have to ask themselves how those elements in Figure 1–1 affect the meaning of the text.

Authors' increasing attention to the design, format, and structure of a text, whether on the screen or on the page, will demand that readers know how to skim, scan, screen—and just plain read, of course. Everything in our accelerated society points toward faster living and greater distraction—and, thus, the need to read well on the run:

> All those clamoring activities line up by rank, in order of the power of their claim on your attention. That book looks appealing, but this magazine pulls harder. Even better is that new jazz recording, but then you prefer the exhilarating rush of an on-line session of the game so fittingly called Total Annihilation. It's as if, corrupted by haute cuisine and soft mattresses, we can't go back to the simple pleasure of bread and butter and sleeping under the stars. (Gleick 1999)

NOTE

Add to Gleick's and Stephens' lists emoticons (-: and such Web slang as *LOL* (laughing out loud) or *yr* (your) or *ur* (you are), all of which make communication more visual but also more rapid in the effort to achieve real-time exchanges online.

Gleick writes, "We have learned a visual language made up of images and movements instead of words and syllables. It has its own grammar, abbreviations, clichés, lines, puns, and famous quotations" (1999). In his book *the rise of the image the fall of the word*, Mitchell Stephens (1998)

Author/World

- assumptions
- bias
- culture
- era
- expectations
- ideology
- influences
- intent
- situation

Elements

Expository

- argument
- body text
- caption
- citations
- conclusion
- introduction
- thesis

General

- directions
- genre
- idea
- numbers
- theme
- time
- title (of text)
- URL

Narrative

- action
- character
- climax
- conflict
- ending
- exposition
- names
- narrator
- place
- plot
- point of view
- setting
- story

Visual

- charts
- diagrams
- graphics
- graphs
- illustrations
- maps
- photographs
- tables
- time lines

Credibility

- affiliation
- awards
- byline
- categories
- context (original)
- domain name
- endorsements
- evidence
- means of production
- production quality
- publisher
- signature
- sources
- title (position)

Devices

- abbreviations
- acronyms
- analogies
- animation
- buttons
- color
- date
- embedded media
- footnotes
- hyperlinks
- icons
- intertextual links
- jumplines
- kicker
- lead
- lists
- omissions
- parallelism
- patterns
- pop-up menus
- pullout quotes
- puns
- rhyme
- sequencing
- sidebars
- silence
- sinks
- sound
- special effects
- symbols
- teaser
- transition
- typography
- Web site counter
- white space

Components

- acknowledgments
- afterword
- appendix
- borders
- boxes
- breaks
- columns
- cover
- dedication
- epigraphs
- epilogue
- fonts
- footer
- foreword
- front matter
- glossary
- header
- headings
- index
- introduction
- layout
- margins
- material
- medium
- notes
- page numbering
- preface
- prologue
- section dividers
- shape
- table of contents
- title page

Stylistics

Arrangement

- composition
- indentation
- line breaks
- placement

Conventions

- gestures
- paragraphs
- punctuation
- sentences
- violations

General

- allusions
- ambiguity
- characterization
- homage
- imagery
- intonation
- metaphors
- motifs
- repetition
- sensory details
- tone

Language

- diction
- foreign words
- grammar
- semantics
- special terms
- syntax

Qualities

Experiential

- clarity
- consistency
- emphasis
- movement
- pace
- seduction
- significance
- surprise
- tension
- unity

Structural

- complexity
- condition
- integrity
- length
- multimedia
- shape
- size

FIGURE 1–1   The Elements of a Text. Attentive readers ask, "What is this made from?" and, "How does it work?" This list reminds us of all that is actually happening within any given text.

builds on Gleick's comment: "our eyes are no longer asked to *see;* they are simply asked to interpret the code," a code that is no longer made up solely of *logos* (the word), but of *logos* (icons), which we encounter on the page and the screen, the bodies and the clothing of others, the labels of products, and the various advertisements we encounter everywhere in between. Stephens argues that a skilled videographer can accomplish in three minutes of video what many writers would need thirty pages (or three hundred) to achieve. Digital storyteller Dana Atchley, along with a growing number of video artists, takes these different media tools and, combining them with cultural or corporate artifacts, creates compelling interactive, multimedia texts:

> The best way to understand digital storytelling is to watch Atchley in action. For the past decade, he's done a one-man show called "Next Exit," which traces his life story. The show is a remarkable blend of performance art, memoir, stand-up comedy, and documentary film. Here's how "Next Exit" works: Atchley strides onstage and sits on a tree stump. Beside him is a monitor surrounded by logs. He blows on the screen and—poof—a video campfire begins to crackle. On a wall behind him, tethered to a computer, is a screen of roughly the same size as one that you'd find at a multiplex. Atchley puts on a headset microphone a la Garth Brooks, grabs his wireless mouse, and begins. With the mouse, he opens an on-screen suitcase containing about 70 stories, most of them short digital videos that he has crafted from home movies, still photos, and video tapes. With the audience's help, he selects 12 to 18 stories for the evening. (Pink 1999)

See Dana Atchley's digital story "Shipwrecked" on his Web site, <http://www.nextexit.com>, and visit these digital storytelling Web sites to learn more about this emerging form: Digital Storytelling Festival: <http://www.dstory.com>; Center for Digital Storytelling: <http//www.storycenter.org>. Also see the *Illuminating Texts* companion Web site.

WEB SITE

When I say we need to be different kinds of readers—and judging from Atchley's work, different kinds of audiences—I do not mean just as consumers of commercial texts or news media; I mean as consumers of historical, mathematical, scientific, and literary texts, as well as all video and online texts, regardless of content. As 1999 drew to a close, many textbooks included factual errors, not to mention instances of ideological bias. Moreover, mathematics books used to teach young students included abundant commercial content (e.g., word problems about the number of McDonald's hamburgers eaten, or the number of miles traveled to get to Disney). Finally, more and more films based on novels and historical events appear every year, tempting many students to mistake fiction for fact, a cinematically inspired emotion for a thought that helps them better understand history. Films about Malcolm X and JFK, the Civil War and the American Revolution, just to name a few, require sophisticated textual skills that enable students to discern what is *real* versus what is *true*, to return to O'Brien's terms.

What We Read: Types of Text

WEB SITE

See the companion Web site for a sample sequence integrating multiple types of text into the study of *All Quiet on the Western Front*.

Just imagine what it must be like for students each day: six consecutive periods, each with its own subject matter and text, complete with its own set of conventions, each teacher believing deep down that her subject matter is the key to health, wealth, and happiness. Consider this feasible sequence of textual experiences jammed against one another, then magnify it by fifty minutes, multiplied by six periods a day, five days a week:

- In math, students are given a word problem.
- In history, students read the Gettysburg Address and explain the relationship between the speech and the poem "Oh Captain, My Captain!" by Walt Whitman, after which they will examine why Lincoln meant so much to the nation and to Walt Whitman in particular.
- In health, they are given different labels from products and asked to find the ones that amount to a balanced diet for that day. The texts here include lists of ingredients as well as the standard table of related health information common to all products. The teacher assigns them a diet and asks them, after reading it, to determine which of the different items are acceptable for this person to eat. If they make a mistake, the person could have dire consequences.
- In English, students read speeches and examine the use of various rhetorical devices. The teacher demonstrates the lesson using Lincoln's Gettysburg Address because she knows they were just studying it in their American history class.
- In art, they are shown a series of American paintings on exhibit at the Chicago Institute of Art and available through the virtual tour on the institute's Web site. The teacher asks the class to explain what the artists are saying about America through the paintings and how the different styles and artistic devices help them express their ideas.
- In physics, students receive photocopies of the folktale "Tortoise and Hare" and explain how the story relates to the principle of relativity, which they have been studying lately.

All the while, each teacher, regardless of what he or she teaches, has had to consider only one set of conventions, one type or domain of text. Whether they are literary or scientific, mathematical or financial, artistic or architectural, the texts with which teachers concern themselves are based on closed systems of thought, seen as complete by most teachers and their students instead of related through conventions, themes, and structural elements. The student, on the other hand, pinballs from subject to subject, finding little reason for the differences and hardly a rhyme of commonality between the way texts are taught, how they are read, and what they, as students and readers, must do when they read. Their experience resembles a kaleidoscope filled with shards of shapes in different colors that gather in a new pattern with each twist of the lens. So it is with school for most kids.

Figure 1–2 shows the many possible ways to think about texts. Many of these examples do not fit neatly into their little boxes because they function differently according to their original and current contexts. A sermon from Puritan New England for example, first offered as a sacred and persuasive text, might today be read as either a historical artifact in a United States history class or as early American literature in an American literature class. Additionally, a text such as "Sinners in the Hands of an Angry God" is transformed through performance since to speak a text is to adapt or otherwise change it. Thus, in addition to the ways of looking at text outlined in Figure 1–2, we can also view them in a number of other ways, as illustrated in Figure 1–3.

Visit the companion Web site for a sample of "Sinners in the Hands of an Angry God."

WEB SITE

Where Should I Sit? The Role of the Teacher

Twenty-five hundred years ago, Socrates resisted what the book had to offer, suggesting we would lose our memory if everything could be written down and consulted when we needed to know it. Phaedrus, a student of Socrates, dared to bring a book to class one day; Socrates agreed to listen to him read, at which point Phaedrus asked a question we ourselves ask more and more: "But if I am to read, where would you please to sit?" What about us, the teachers: Are we guides? Experts? Mentors? Directors of experiences we design? Indeed, where *do* I stand if my students turn from me to a screen, a monitor, an image, or a page from a book I have not read (which they have chosen for self-selected reading)? I feel much like I did the day we watched the moon walk in fifth grade: I, along with my peers (i.e., fellow teachers), sit in the dark, overwhelmed by a combination of awe and confusion when I see what we can do now, when I think about where our society is heading. And like

To Inform

- abstract
- annual report
- ballot
- bibliography
- bills
- brochures
- catalog
- executive summary
- financial statement
- flyer
- forms
- gauges
- index
- instruments
- job applications
- labels
- manual
- map
- menu
- meters
- minutes
- multimedia encyclopedia
- obituaries
- pager codes
- pager text messages
- precis
- product labels
- recipe
- report
- schedule
- statistic
- table of contents
- tables
- tax forms
- want ads

To Persuade

- advertisement
- allegory
- blurbs
- broadsides
- buttons
- campaign documents
- clothing
- editorial
- flag

- gestures
- headlines
- letterhead
- pamphlet
- parable
- proposal
- resume
- reviews
- signs
- slogans
- television commercial

To Explain

- affidavit
- annotated text
- caption
- constitution
- contracts
- diaries
- dictionary entries
- directions
- journals
- law
- memoir
- memos
- narratives (slave and Indian captivity)
- policy
- prospectus
- rubric
- rule
- school assignment/ worksheet
- service agreements
- summary
- textbook
- theory
- time line
- travelogue
- warranties
- word problems

Multiple Functions

- autobiography
- biography
- business letter
- cartoon

- chart
- chat room dialogue
- cover letters
- deposition
- diagram
- dialogues
- documentary film
- e-mail
- essay
- event program
- fable
- fairy tale
- film
- flowcharts
- folktale
- graph
- hypertexts
- illustration
- instant messages
- lists
- listserv
- logos
- magazine article
- mixed media (e.g., artwork)
- monologue
- montage
- multimedia product
- myth
- names
- newsgroup postings
- newspaper article
- novel
- online magazine
- oral storytelling
- painting
- personal letter
- photograph
- play
- poem
- popular magazines
- product packaging
- professional journals
- screen capture
- short story
- song lyric
- speech
- symbols
- tattoos

- Web page
- Web site

Miscellaneous

- chapbooks
- eulogy
- graffiti
- history
- icons
- MOO
- MUD
- occasional letter
- sermon
- situations
- television program
- test/examination
- testimony
- tracts

FIGURE 1–2   Types of Text. Good readers always assess what they are reading in order to determine how they should read it. As you can see, there are as many different types of texts as there are purposes to which you can put these texts.

May be copied for classroom use. Jim Burke. 2001. Illuminating Texts. *Portsmouth, NH: Heinemann.*

BY TYPE

- artifact
- commercial
- interpretive
- performative
- personal
- private
- product
- production
- public
- receptive

BY FUNCTION

- descriptive
- financial
- historical
- instructional
- literary
- logistical
- persuasive
- philosophical

- political
- procedural
- reflective
- sacred

BY FORM

- iconic
- interactive
- mixed media
- multitextual
- spoken
- statistical
- symbolic
- visual
- written

BY GENRE

- Drama
  - monologue
  - play
- Expository

- Literature
  - fiction
  - romance
  - science fiction
- Poetry
  - epic
  - lyric

BY MEDIUM

- digital
- face
- mixed media
- paper
- video
- voice

BY PURPOSE

- to arouse
- to clarify
- to describe
- to entertain

- to inform
- to obfuscate
- to persuade
- to sell
- to teach

FIGURE 1–3   **Types of Text II.** This list offers a different way of looking at texts.

May be copied for classroom use. Jim Burke. 2001. Illuminating Texts. Portsmouth, NH: Heinemann.

Mrs. Baldwin, my most memorable of all grade school teachers, we must turn on the lights, return to the classroom after the event is over, and teach our students, even as we learn ourselves, how to read the history we just watched being made, how to make sense of what we hear, how to comprehend what we read as we move along the continuum of complexity that forces us all to learn to read again and again.

Reading Standards Across the Curriculum

As we move along that continuum, we need guidelines and signposts to help us navigate, to give us some idea of how we are doing or what our doing should look like. To find these markers, I traveled across many different standards documents in all subject areas from many states, collecting common traits as I went. I don't offer the following as my own standards but rather as a synthesis of what we are all being asked to accomplish as teachers and as students when it comes to reading. These documents say students should be able to:

IDENTIFY

- conventions that govern the particular text and how those help shape meaning
- the main idea in a text

- the main argument in an expository text
- literary devices used in a text and how they function to convey meaning and affect the reader
- organizational patterns used to convey information
- rhetorical devices and how they are used in different texts
- figurative language (metaphor, simile, analogy) and how it functions within the text
- the genre to which the text belongs
- archetypes and symbols used in the text, and determine how they contribute to its meaning and affect the reader
- subtle differences between words and ideas and how those affect the reader and contribute to meaning

EVALUATE

- stylistic elements and how they contribute to the writer's voice and convey meaning
- an author's ideas for bias and the extent to which this bias affects the integrity of the text
- the author's choice and use of a particular medium to determine its effectiveness
- a document in order to determine how it should be read
- an author's approach to a particular idea and the effectiveness of his perspective, argument, or idea
- the accuracy and clarity of any information
- the philosophical assumptions that underlie the author's ideas or the text itself
- the effectiveness of the point of view from which the text is written
- a particular idea across a range of texts to understand it more fully
- the author's choices in terms of how they contribute to meaning and affect the reader
- the author's style or this text in light of other texts by the same author or within the same genre
- the validity of an argument according to the context in which it is used

INTERPRET

- current information in light of what they have read so far in order to revise their understanding
- the point of view from which the text is written
- the current text in light of other works by that author or from the same era or culture
- a range of types of information—numerical, statistical, graphic, expository—to arrive at a complete understanding of the text in context

- observable patterns within the text in order to arrive at a complete understanding of the text in this context

USE
- a range of strategies to comprehend different texts, choosing the most appropriate one for that particular text
- representational strategies to make abstract material concrete
- a range of strategies to determine the meaning of a particular word in its context
- information from the text they read in order to make a decision
- information provided by the text to solve a problem

EXPLAIN
- how the structural components of the text influence meaning and affect the reader
- the motivations of fictional characters, drawing examples from the text to support the reading
- how an author's use of sensory detail contributes to the form and the function of the text
- the conclusions they draw using information from the text to support their thinking
- the relationship between different elements or parts of a text and how those contribute to meaning and affect the reader
- the process by which they arrived at their understanding of a particular text or solved a problem posed by the text

DETERMINE
- the veracity of information within any text
- whether the information is fact, opinion, or rumor
- the author's intent and the devices used to achieve the desired outcome
- whether this is a document they need to read at all and, if so, which parts of it should be read
- the extent to which the culture, the era, or other factors affect the text's meaning and the reader's response
- the type of text and how it is supposed to be read (according to its textual conventions and genre)

KNOW
- the core terms appropriate to the textual domain (i.e., vocabulary specific to a novel, a legal text, a scientific text)
- the origins and the roots of certain essential words
- the fundamental conventions that govern a text in this particular genre, discipline, or domain

- how a text functions to create a specific response in the reader
- the different types of text or genre within a discipline
- essential background information necessary to read this document successfully
- the defining characteristics of a variety of informational texts
- the principles of grammar, syntax, and semantics as they relate to a particular text

COMPREHEND
- words using the most appropriate strategy (context, roots, connotative or denotative meanings)

INTEGRATE
- information from a variety of sources and types of texts to arrive at a more complete understanding of a subject

ORGANIZE
- information as they read to suit the demands of the reading task

DEVELOP
- an appreciation for the beauty and the power of language as it is used to convey meaning in different types of texts
- their own questions while reading, and use their experience and knowledge as readers to find the answers within the text

NOTE

The Northwest Regional Educational Laboratory studied the traits of effective readers of both nonfiction and fiction texts. Its rubrics and descriptions are shown in Figures 5–3 and 6–1 and provide a very useful device to help teachers assess student performance and their own teaching. You can find out more about its work in this area at its Web site, <http://www.nwrel.org>. For more information on standards in all subject areas, visit <http://www.mcrel.org> to link to Robert Marzano's standards document.

One study (Langer 1999) examined the teaching practices of a set of schools whose students "beat the odds" (i.e., went on to college) despite various obstacles to their academic success. The table in Figure 1–4 provides a useful summary not only of what we might call teaching standards but of how students are able to work if challenged by work that has meaning to them in the context of their lives.

NOTE

For this and other reports, visit the Center for English Learning and Achievement online (<http://cela.albany.edu/reports.htm>).

Issue	Beating the Odds Schools and Teachers	Typical Schools and Teachers
Approaches to skills instruction	Systematic use of separated, simulated, and integrated skills instruction	Instruction dominated by one approach (which varies among schools and teachers)
Approaches to test preparation	Integrated into ongoing goals, curriculum, and regular lessons	Allocated to test prep; separate from ongoing goals, curriculum, and instruction
Connecting learnings	Overt connections made among knowledge, skills, and ideas across lessons, classes, and grades, and across in-school and out-of-school applications	Knowledge and skills within lessons, units, and curricula typically treated as discrete entities; connections left implicit even when they do occur
Enabling strategies	Overt teaching of strategies for planning, organizing, completing, and reflecting on content and activities	Teaching of content or skills without overt attention to strategies for thinking and doing
Conceptions of learning	When learning goal is met, teacher moves students beyond it to deeper understanding and generativity of ideas	When learning goal is met, teacher moves to a new lesson (or activity) with different goals/content
Classroom organization	Students work together to develop depth and complexity of understanding in interaction with others	Students work alone, in groups, or with the teacher to get the work done but do not engage in rich discussion of ideas

FIGURE 1–4   Issues of Concern and Overview of Findings. Based on "Beating the Odds: Teaching Middle and High School Students to Read and Write Well," by Judith Langer (1999). The complete report is available online at <http://cela.albany.edu/reports.htm>.

Classroom Connections

The Web now offers remarkable online teacher support guides to go with films, newspapers, magazines, and television shows. Three exemplary sites are <www.pbs.org>, <www.nara.gov> (the National Archives), and <www.nytimes.com/classroom>.

NOTE

Teachers are increasingly the authors of their own texts despite the constraints imposed upon them by the adopted texts. History teachers bring into the classroom visual texts (e.g., footage of the civil rights protests), primary source documents (via such online sites as the National Archives), and contemporary commentary on the past from a variety of sources to create a collage of perspectives the modern reader must learn to interpret. Consider, for example, the skills needed by students who are asked to research the Holocaust and who, in the course of this research, encounter the Web site of Northwestern University professor (of electrical engineering) Arthur Butz, who argues that the Holocaust is a legend. Butz's article, complete with explanations to support his theory, becomes yet one more text that students must learn to read against the others in order to navigate their way through the minefield of truths that make up the Information Age.

WEB SITE

See the companion Web site and page 28 for more information about Arthur Butz's page. The site <http://www.martinlutherking.org/> offers readers related challenges and further demonstrates why students must have these skills.

Without meaning to carry all this too far, I suggest you can look at a course itself as a text that must be read. While designing an online course for teachers (Teaching English in the Digital Age), I realized that in the absence of a classroom, of my face and my voice, of all the markers that help orient both teacher and student in a traditional classroom, the course syllabus was all the students would have to guide them. And the substance of this course—the selected readings, the assignments students do, the conversations that arise in discussion groups online—creates what feels like an interactive book more than a course as we are used to thinking about it. The course is a text that the readers/users may ask questions of and one to which they can contribute their own writings as part of the course, thus collaborating with the professor in the creation of the text called "Teaching English in the Digital Age." This futuristic speculation might seem irrelevant if it weren't for the predictions of such knowing people (with records for predicting the future with remarkable accuracy—reading the future, as it were) as Ray Kurzweil (1999) saying that most learning will take place online by 2009. The required ability of the reader to draw reasonable inferences from such digital texts without a teacher there to respond to questions suggests the ability to read well will only be more important with every passing semester.

Closing Thoughts

Technology is not the only force driving the form and the function of different texts we encounter. While doing research for the book *The*

English Teacher's Companion (1999), I was amazed by the evolution of books in the previous twenty years. Some books, even such classics as James Moffett's *Teaching the Universe of Discourse* (1987), contained no index and had tables of contents that offered little guidance to the teacher on the run. Moffett's table of contents, for example, offers no guidance to help the harried teacher find his way to the many useful strategies in the book. Moffett himself seems to have understood that readers' needs and expectations changed in the intervening ten years: *Student-Centered Language Arts K–12*, written with Betty Jane Wagner in 1992, includes a very useful table of contents that is organized for easy reference; it also includes subheaders, bulleted lists, and a generous index. All of these features reflect a new relationship between the author and the reader. As the Umberto Eco says, "Every text, after all, is a lazy machine asking the reader to do some of its work" (1995). As Eco's remark suggests, the author's obligation has changed; no longer is it enough to provide good information. Authors, in conjunction with their editors and the production staff (or Webmaster), now have to design the book's form—do I dare say its interface?—with the reader's needs in mind. I designed *The English Teacher's Companion*, for example, for the teacher who might have only five to fifteen minutes at a sitting to find her way to a useful idea she could use that afternoon. I designed *Reading Reminders* (2000) so teachers could use it for as little as one minute and find useful information to help them teach better the next period. For instance, when the readers get to the unit they seek, they find an easily referenced list including bullets or some other means of organizing the information for quick digestion and easy use.

Each discipline comes with its own types of texts that students must learn to read if they are to be literate in that domain. For so long, high school teachers used *reading to learn*, assuming—because it's what they were told—that students *learned to read* in the earlier grades. Of course they did learn how to read in the early grades, and still do, but they do not come to high school knowing how to identify irony or how to discern the organizational patterns used in a particular essay or how to interpret speech that is intended to persuade. The range of texts and their changing nature, not to mention the complexity of some texts, makes it necessary for us to teach students how to read such texts so they can both identify the author's intended meaning and construct their own, more personal meaning.

This book is about teaching students what they need to know and be able to do: read a range of texts in various ways for different purposes. In our world of multiple texts—Web sites, hypertexts, textbooks, and newspapers—many of which incorporate words, images, sounds, visual explanations (e.g., graphs and tables), and even video clips, our students need to graduate able to read these increasingly complicated texts in different media so they can have the textual power needed to be successful in their adult lives.

In England they speak of "reading history," by which they mean studying it. So it should be with all other subject areas: how does it change our role and perception of ourselves if our students speak of reading health or reading science in high school? I don't mean just reading words; I mean reading the entire topography of the subject, its glorious mountains of words, its rivers of meaning, the landscape of its history as a subject insofar as that helps them place the current study of the subject in the larger context of its history. Every subject we teach is essential, and by emphasizing the idea of teaching reading at all levels and in all subject areas, I am not suggesting in any way that English as a discipline be compromised. In fact, it seems liberating to me as an English teacher to get out from under the tyranny of assumptions that English teachers are the only ones who should teach reading and writing. By teaching students to read in the ways I outline here, we will help them understand that "reading is not just a matter of standing safely outside texts, where their power cannot reach us. It is a matter of entering, of passing through the looking glass and seeing ourselves on the other side" (Scholes 1989). To just read, moreover, is an incomplete textual encounter: not until we have come out on the other side and created our own text, in whatever form, have we completed the interaction between ourselves and the author, our own assumptions and his, his ideas and our own. Thus is reading an active, even interactive experience through which we do not fill ourselves up but create ourselves and thereby our world as we understand it.

In this respect I am arguing that through textual studies students can—and should be required to—think and operate as practitioners of the domains they are studying, learning to read as biologists, writers, historians, or craftsmen. This shift in perspective, one that places students in a more active role of reading and writing within a discipline, offers the added benefit of developing their imaginations by requiring them to occupy the role appropriate to each domain. For too long the imagination and its role in education has been dismissed by the public as irrelevant or even dangerous. But what are we doing as teachers if not helping students try on a series of possible selves through our disciplines, while helping them develop the necessary abilities in those subjects in the hope that they will find the ones they wish to become in their adult lives? In this respect we might say our students are engaged in a constant reading of the world and of themselves as they try to figure out what both mean and where they fit into the texts of the world they are busy creating through their own choices.

Further Studies

Myers, Miles. 1996. *Changing Our Minds: Negotiating English and Literacy.* Urbana, IL: National Council of Teachers of English.

Purves, Alan. 1990. *Scribal Society: An Essay on Literacy and Schooling in the Information Age.* Boston, MA: Longman.

Scholes, Robert. 1998. *The Rise and Fall of English: Reconstructing English as a Discipline.* New Haven, CN: Yale University Press.

2

Reading the Internet

We are increasingly entrusting to software the various gathering, sorting, and linking operations that we used to perform for ourselves and that were part of the process of thinking about a subject. We have to ask, not just "What does software do, and what does mind do?" but "What should *software do and what* should *mind do?*
—Sven Birkerts, from "Sense and Semblance"

Schools will change to become more like museums and playgrounds for children to assemble ideas and socialize with other children all over the world.
—Nicholas Negroponte, from *Being Digital*

I work on the Web. I reach for the keyboard as easily as I do for any book at this point, the deciding factors being my purpose, my time, and the ability of a chosen text to satisfy my needs most appropriately and efficiently. I clip text and images out of Web sites to use in lesson plans, presentations, and my own Web site. I run a listserv for a few thousand English teachers; this means I get a pile of e-mail every day from people who sometimes have "hot" news about people, programs, or methods. I teach a course through the Internet, which requires that I search the digital world for sites or texts to use, read messages in chat rooms, and participate in online discussion groups. I also created and continue to maintain my own Web site so I can provide ongoing support for English teachers and those who read my books. My point is that every day, I encounter information from a variety of sources, in different contexts, which I must evaluate according to all the criteria and using all the strategies discussed in this book.

For example, today, a typical day on the Net for me, I:

- Searched the Net for Theodore Kaczynski's "Unabomber Manifesto" to complement a senior English class' reading of *One Flew over the Cuckoo's Nest*, in which students were discussing the Combine and what modern society is doing to us with its machinery.
- Participated in an online discussion group hosted by a university that is using my book *The English Teacher's Companion: A Complete Guide to Classroom, Curriculum, and the Profession* (1999); this required me to read a bunch of different postings and understand what the participants were saying about their teaching experiences.
- Read a batch of contributions to my own netcourse's discussion group, some of which included links to other Web sites or articles the students wanted me and the rest of the class to check out.
- Searched for articles about the components of a Web site and how to determine the validity of information found in online resources. This required me to first scan through the different annotations of the sites that the search engine returned to me and then decide which ones to actually visit.
- Went to Amazon.com to search for books about how to read images. Here I found dozens of titles and read reviews of the books, making my choices according to my own previously established criteria and the reviews of reputable publications like *Kirkus Reviews* or *Booklist* as well as the posted comments of several readers who explained exactly why certain books were so useful.
- Updated my own Web site (<www.englishcompanion.com>) to make it more efficient for readers by clustering the new and most valuable information into easily scannable lists with the key words hotlinked for easy navigation.
- Watched *Fooling with Words*, Bill Moyers' PBS special on poetry, and visited the Web site (<http://www.pbs.org/wnet/foolingwithwords/main_teacher.html>) to evaluate its teacher materials for possible use in my own classroom and my online course, noting that the materials were developed by a woman who won Teacher of the Year in her state and is now working with PBS as part of a fellowship.

Because the Internet is here to stay, my students need to know how to read what they find there. My search for Kaczynski's manifesto led me to sites filled with horrible information published by the lunatic fringe about bombs and hate; it also guided me to the latest online edition of *Time*, which included an interview with Kaczynski conducted by his brother (yes, the one who turned him in). The previous year, when students of mine researched violence in America, they found "fake" Web sites allegedly created by the two boys who killed their classmates at Columbine High School in Littleton, Colorado. They also found sites like the one maintained by Associate Professor Arthur Butz, who asserts that the Holocaust was only a legend. And in the midst of the presidential campaign, I can go right now to two Web sites for candidate George Bush, one of them actually maintained by him and another, which looks very much the same (with content differences), maintained by a man who is dedicated to undermining Bush's candidacy. Both look equally official; in fact, the "fake" site (<www.gwbush.com>) actually uses the very same images and banners as the official site (<www.georgebush.com>).

Types of Texts on the Internet

Out on the infobaun, readers find a wide range of texts, each serving a different audience and purpose:

- Chat rooms
- E-mail
- Listservs
- Multiple user domains
- Newsgroups
- Threaded discussion groups
- World Wide Web

These are all common domains on the Internet. Each serves the needs of its target audience and each demands that readers employ some serious critical reading skills if they are to read the sites successfully. Spend some time talking with students who spend any amount of time on the Internet and they'll tell you that reading messages from e-mail is a lot different from reading a message from a newsgroup, which is a lot different from reading a message on a Web site. The Internet has quickly taught our students what many of us have labored years to teach: different modes of discourse should be—must be—read differently. But how?

Students have quickly figured out how to read e-mail. They not only figured it out but adopted its coded spelling and use that code as quickly and easily as we Smith Corona babies use traditional spelling. They read *g2g* (got to go) and *cu* (see you) and *y r u* (why are you) without pause. They read the subtleties of the text carefully so that they see a difference in *ur* (your) and *u r* (you are). Furthermore, they understand that an e-mail message that appears in all caps probably indicates that someone is a tad upset. They know how to read the words and the intent of their e-mail messages. What they often lack, though, is that same skill when it comes to reading Web sites. Since this is the most common online text and the one where students are mostly likely to encounter information of dubious credibility, I want to spend time discussing how we can help ourselves and our students read those sites.

As Robert Harris reminds us in his article "Evaluating Internet Research Sources," *"Information pretending to objectivity but possessing a hidden agenda of persuasion or a hidden bias is among the most common kind of information in our culture"* (1997). Harris' point is critical for any type of text, but it seems even more pertinent for Web-based texts. Therefore, it is critical that we help students acquire the skills they need to determine a site's validity, aesthetic or literary quality, accuracy, and authenticity. These skills seem especially important for many high school readers, who still believe what they read, subscribing to the idea that if it is written, it is true. For an example of how much information students can encounter in one site, just look at all the different types of content contained in the *Time* Web site, shown in Figure 2–1.

Types of Web Sites

The form and function of different Web sites depends on why we are reading them and why the author is creating them. One way of classifying them is by content, in which case there are five types:

- Commercial (.com or .net)
- Educational (.edu)
- Institutional (.org)
- News/media (.com)
- Personal (.com)

These days, however, Web sites rarely exist to serve one purpose. If a site is not regularly updated or does not have content that merits regular visits, it dies unless its primary purpose is to store information for occasional use. Think about all those eighth-grade boys who are interested in cars. Now they can go to a site on cars that not only sells them but offers discussion areas for its customers, chat rooms for car collectors, an online museum devoted to certain cars, links to other sites, a library of manuals, news of upcoming events, and several different daily features with entertainment value designed to bring the visitor back daily to the site. As Michael Wolf writes in *The Entertainment Economy: How Mega-Media Forces Are Transforming Our Lives* (1999):

> On the Internet, business and entertainment finally converge. With television, the qualities of design, sound, graphics, and personalities all must be arresting in order to keep the viewer's thumb off the remote control. A mouse click is just as fast as a TV remote. Viewers expect no less from Internet content than

FIGURE 2–1   Time.com Web Site. Nearly all magazines and newspapers offer print as well as online editions. The nature of online publishing makes differences between the two versions inevitable—and sometimes crucial. *(©1999 Time Inc. New Media. All rights reserved. Reproduction in whole or in part without permission is prohibited. Pathfinder is a registered trademark of Time Inc. New Media.)*

they have become accustomed to on their other small screen. So when a company decides to stake out a position on the Web, it must also decide, in part, to become an entertainment company.

NOTE

To see how authors now use the Internet to extend the reach and the content of their books, visit Wolf's site at <www.entertainmenteconomy.com.>

Web sites can also therefore be categorized by purpose, such as the following, though the car site, as just mentioned, serves many different purposes.

- To educate
- To entertain
- To inform
- To persuade
- To sell
- To share
- To support

Obviously these purposes are nothing new to the world of writing; what we as teachers can do, however, is show our students how these different purposes can be combined in one site to create a more powerful means of communicating with people. We must also teach them how to read Web sites with these purposes in mind, to fully understand the intended meaning of the site.

Questions to Ask

Students may groan when they discover that we expect them to question what they are about to read before they even turn on the computer. Consider the conversation I had with a student as he sat down to begin a search on mythological characters:

ME: So, what are you searching for today?

BEN: Stuff on mythology.

ME: Yeah? What kind of stuff?

BEN: You know, like gods and goddesses and, and, like, what they were head of and stuff.

ME: How will you know when you've found a good site?

BEN: Huh?

ME: As you are searching, how will you know if you've come to a site that has information you need?

BEN: Uh, I don't know. I guess if it's, like, long or has, like, important stuff. [Pause] I don't know. I'll just keep looking until something looks good.

It's an interesting technique that Ben will use—sort of the "surf till you drop" technique. That technique, though, just doesn't work. We need to teach our students that discerning readers must begin asking questions before they ever log on to the Internet. The prereading questions a reader should ask vary depending on their purpose for reading, but the most obvious ones include:

- What information do I seek? (e.g., information about the war in Vietnam or the Civil War)
- What type of information do I need most? (e.g., facts, personal narratives, news stories)
- What will I use this information for? (e.g., persuasive speech, research paper, creative writing)
- What are the terms I should use to conduct a successful search? (e.g., *war* or *Civil War* will be too broad; *Gettysburg* or *Emancipation Proclamation* are specific)
- What are my criteria for selecting documents to read or information to use? (e.g., How can I tell if the information is valid and if it will also suit my needs for this project?)

NOTE

See the Internet site evaluation form in Appendix B for more detailed and diverse questions.

Once we are out on the Web, scanning through the lists generated by different search engines, we become ruthless, restless readers who read the home page or summary of a site to determine if it has what we seek. People don't read Web sites in the traditional sense, nor are Web sites written to be read; we scan them, bouncing across the bulleted lists and highlighted text to determine if we are the intended audience and this is the sought-after information. Of course our ability to navigate a text depends on how effectively it is organized and how clearly the information is written.

Web readers should use the following observations to help them navigate online texts. Morkes and Nielsen (1997) concluded that the following features help readers most:

- Highlighted **keywords** (hypertext links serve as one form of highlighting; typeface variations and color are others)
- Meaningful **subheadings** (not "clever" ones)
- Bulleted **lists**
- **One idea** per paragraph (users will skip over any additional ideas if they are not caught by the first few words in the paragraph)
- The **inverted pyramid style** (i.e., starting with the conclusion)
- **Half the word count** (or less) of conventional writing

NOTE

For another example of a Web site designed to draw you in (through deception) and convince you of its offensive ideas, see <www.martinlutherking.org>.

Readers can then infer from the quality of the writing that the information on the site *may* be of reasonable quality; we cannot be too sure, however, as such sites as Arthur Butz's show (see page 28 for more on his Web site). Butz writes well-organized prose that lacks any of the generalizations and emotional appeals that quickly signal a site is untrustworthy. The intelligent reader must then look beyond such surface details as the quality of the writing and take into consideration factors that cover several topics. What follows are the topics I consider when checking out a Web site.

SOURCES
- Where does the author get the evidence he uses to support his claims?
- What other sources—experts, publications, institutions—does the author cite?
- Does the author represent himself (e.g., "David Chase, a member of the American Bar Association") or does he represent a larger institution (e.g., The American Bar Association today, represented by David Chase, announced . . .")?
- Who is responsible for the content of the site?
- Is the source of all information clearly identified and properly cited?

TIMELINESS
- When was this written?
- Is this information consistent with our current understanding in this field?
- When was this site last updated?

AUTHORITY
- On what basis is this person or organization qualified to inform people about this subject?
- Is this the author's field of expertise?
- How current is the author's knowledge of this subject?
- Does the author or institution clearly establish or provide links to its credentials, affiliations, and sponsors?
- What awards, if any, has this site won, and are these awarding agencies credible?
- Does this person or institution have a reputation for thorough, accurate, objective work?

AUDIENCE
- Does the author clearly identify his intended audience?
- Do the advertisements, if the site has any, provide further insight into the quality of the content and its intended audience?
- Does the site suggest any bias in favor of its audience's perspective?
- What do the Web site's links tell you about its audience?
- Does the site offer an "About Us" section or an introduction that describes the site's purpose and intended audience?

QUALITY CONTROL
- Are articles published by respected, peer-reviewed journals, newspapers, or reputable magazines prior to or in addition to being published on this site?
- Is the information within the site consistent in terms of point of view, tone, and content? (For example, if the site is described as supporting the study of the Civil War, does it consistently maintain its balanced perspective and present its content in a tone students find appropriate, even supportive?)
- If the site offers a biased perspective on a subject, does it provide an opposing view or an opportunity for readers to respond with other perspectives?
- Are all the site's links internal or do some connect you to outside sources that lend credence to the site's content?
- Is information offered as fact or opinion? Is this clearly stated for the reader?
- Are the authors of all content clearly identified? Are any articles anonymously written?

These areas and questions work for adult readers. However, they are beyond the reach of many middle schoolers. For an evaluation rubric that students might find helpful, see Figure 2–2.

Consider the following list of sites in light of the previous questions. Each site and every text within that site must be evaluated against the matrix of criteria outlined earlier. This list was assembled by Keith Stanger (<keithstanger.com>) at Eastern Michigan University. The entire list is available through his Web site, but it is far too long to include here in its entirety, a sad fact that only emphasizes the importance of the reading skills described in this chapter.

- Welcome to the White House
  - <http://www.whitehouse.gov> (the official site)
  - <http://www.whitehouse.net>

Site Version	Sample Paragraph	Usability Improvement (relative to control condition)
Promotional writing (control condition) using the "marketese" found on many commercial Web sites	Nebraska is filled with internationally recognized attractions that draw large crowds of people every year, without fail. In 1996, some of the most popular places were Fort Robinson State Park (355,000 visitors), Scotts Bluff National Monument (132,166), Arbor Lodge State Historical Park & Museum (100,000), Carhenge (86,598), Stuhr Museum of the Prairie Pioneer (60,002), and Buffalo Bill Ranch State Historical Park (28,446).	0% (by definition)
Concise text with about half the word count as the control condition	In 1996, six of the best-attended attractions in Nebraska were Fort Robinson State Park, Scotts Bluff National Monument, Arbor Lodge State Historical Park & Museum, Carhenge, Stuhr Museum of the Prairie Pioneer, and Buffalo Bill Ranch State Historical Park.	58%
Scannable layout using the same text as the control condition in a layout that facilitated scanning	Nebraska is filled with internationally recognized attractions that draw large crowds of people every year, without fail. In 1996, some of the most popular places were: • Fort Robinson State Park (355,000 visitors) • Scotts Bluff National Monument (132,166) • Arbor Lodge State Historical Park & Museum (100,000) • Carhenge (86,598) • Stuhr Museum of the Prairie Pioneer (60,002) • Buffalo Bill Ranch State Historical Park (28,446).	47%
Objective language using neutral rather than subjective, boastful, or exaggerated language (otherwise the same as the control condition)	Nebraska has several attractions. In 1996, some of the most-visited places were Fort Robinson State Park (355,000 visitors), Scotts Bluff National Monument (132,166), Arbor Lodge State Historical Park & Museum (100,000), Carhenge (86,598), Stuhr Museum of the Prairie Pioneer (60,002), and Buffalo Bill Ranch State Historical Park (28,446).	27%
Combined version using all three improvements in writing style together: concise, scannable, and objective	In 1996, six of the most-visited places in Nebraska were: • Fort Robinson State Park • Scotts Bluff National Monument • Arbor Lodge State Historical Park & Museum • Carhenge • Stuhr Museum of the Prairie Pioneer • Buffalo Bill Ranch State Historical Park	124%

FIGURE 2–2 Morkes and Nielsen Usability Table. This table offers a fascinating parallel study of the different demands texts make on readers. The complete report, as well as other interesting information, is available on <www.useit.com>.

- Hatewatch
  - http://www.hatewatch.net
- A short introduction to the study of Holocaust revisionism
  - <http://pubweb.nwu.edu/~abutz/di/intro/html>
- Statement by Northwestern University President Henry S. Biennia regarding Associate Professor Arthur Butts and his Web page
  - <http://www.nwu.edu/president/news/970107-Butz.html>

As an example, here is Arthur Butz's home page, followed by his "Short Introduction to Holocaust Revisionism," which I have included as they appear on his Web site:

HOME WEB PAGE OF ARTHUR R. BUTZ

**Associate Professor of Electrical and Computer Engineering
Northwestern University, Evanston, Illinois, USA
© A.R. Butz 1996–1999**

I am the author of the book *The Hoax of the Twentieth Century* (1976), a work of "Holocaust revisionism".

This Web site exists for the purpose of expressing views that are outside the purview of my role as an Electrical Engineering faculty member. The material will be continually updated and revised, but will always have an emphasis on Holocaust revisionism.

It is intended to keep this Web site relatively simple, at least as far as this home page appears to the reader. For much more on Holocaust revisionism the reader can start with the Web site of IHR, my publisher.

Images and pictures will be used only when specifically supportive of the exposition, since they slow things down considerably for the reader coming through a modem.

The initial aim of this site, as inaugurated on 7 May 1996, is to present my article *A short introduction to the study of Holocaust revisionism*, published in 1991 in the *Daily Northwestern*, with supplementing commentary and documentation.

A second aim is to present, from time to time, new material likely to be appreciated only by advanced students of Holocaust revisionism. This material was last updated on 24 March 1998.

A third aim is to present news items of particular interest to Holocaust revisionists. This material was last updated on 8 April 1999. last modification of another file at this site: 8 April 1999

Please note that the hyperlink in Butz's home page leads to the following "Short Introduction," which I include here in its entirety.

Article published in the *Daily Northwestern* of May 13, 1991, corrected May 14. The links are to commentary and documentation that did not appear in the original article, and which will be continually updated and elaborated.

A SHORT INTRODUCTION TO THE STUDY OF
HOLOCAUST REVISIONISM,
by Arthur R. Butz.

I see three principal reasons for the widespread but erroneous belief in the legend of millions of Jews killed by the Germans during World War II: US and British troops found horrible piles of corpses in the west German camps they captured in 1945 (e.g. Dachau and Belsen), there are no longer large communities of Jews in Poland, and historians generally support the legend.

During both world wars Germany was forced to fight typhus, carried by lice in the constant traffic with the east. That is why all accounts of entry into the German concentration camps speak of shaving of hair and showering and other delousing procedures, such as treatment of quarters with the pesticide Zyklon. That was also the main reason for a high death rate in the camps, and the crematoria that existed in all.

When Germany collapsed in chaos then of course all such defenses ceased, and typhus and other diseases became rampant in the camps, which quartered mainly political prisoners, ordinary criminals, homosexuals, conscientious objectors, and Jews conscripted for labor. Hence the horrible scenes, which however had nothing to do with "extermination" or any deliberate policy. Moreover the west German camps involved were not the alleged "extermination camps", which were all in Poland (e.g. Auschwitz and Treblinka) and which were all evacuated or shut down before capture by the Soviets, who found no such scenes.

The "Final Solution" spoken of in the German documents was a program of evacuation, resettlement and deportation of Jews with the ultimate objective of expulsion from Europe. During the war Jews of various nationalities were being moved east, as one stage in this Final Solution. The legend claims that the motion was mainly for extermination purposes.

The great majority of the millions allegedly exterminated were east European, not German or west European, Jews. For that reason study of the problem via population statistics has been difficult to impossible, but it is a fact that there are no longer large communities of Jews in Poland. However the Germans were only one of several parties involved in moving Jews around. The Soviets deported virtually all of the Jews of eastern Poland to their interior in 1940.

After the war, with Polish and other Jews pouring out of the east into occupied west Germany, the Zionists moved large numbers to Palestine, and the US and other countries absorbed many Jews, in most cases under conditions making impossible a numerical accounting. Moreover the Polish borders were changed drastically at the end of the war; the country was literally moved west.

Historians generally support the legend, but there are precedents for nearly incomprehensible blindness on the part of scholars. For example throughout the Middle Ages even the Pope's political enemies conceded his false claim that the 4th century Emperor Constantine had ceded rule of the west to the Pope, although all knew very well that Constantine had been succeeded by more emperors. Near unanimity among the academics is especially suspect when there exist great political pressures; in some countries Holocaust revisionists have been prosecuted.

It is easy to show that the extermination legend merits skepticism. Even the casual reader of the Holocaust literature knows that during the war virtually nobody acted as though it was happening. Thus it is common to berate the Vatican, the Red Cross and the Allies (especially the intelligence agencies) for their ignorance and inaction, and to explain that the Jews generally did not resist deportation because they did not know what was in store for them. If you add all this up you have the strange claim that for almost three years German trains, operating on a continental scale in densely civilized regions of Europe, were regularly and systematically moving millions of Jews to their deaths, and nobody noticed except for a few of our Jewish leaders who were making public "extermination" claims.

On closer examination even those few Jewish leaders were not acting as though it was happening. Ordinary communications between the occupied and neutral countries were open, and they were in contact with the Jews whom the Germans were deporting, who thus could not have been in ignorance of "extermination" if those claims had any validity.

This incredible ignorance must also be attributed to Hans Oster's department in German military intelligence, correctly labelled "the veritable general staff of the opposition to Hitler" in a recent review.

What we are offered in evidence was gathered after the war, in trials. The evidence is almost all oral testimony and "confessions". Without the evidence of these trials there would be no significant evidence of "extermination". One must pause and ponder this carefully. Were trials needed to determine that the Battle of Waterloo happened? The bombings of Hamburg, Dresden, Hiroshima and Nagasaki? The slaughter in Cambodia? Yet this three year program, of continental scope, claiming millions of victims, requires trials to argue its reality. I am not arguing that the trials were illegal or unfair; I am arguing that such historical logic as the legend rests on must not be countenanced. Such events cannot happen without generating commensurate and contemporaneous evidence for their reality, just as a great forest fire cannot take place without producing smoke. One may as well believe that New York City was burned down, if confessions to the deed can be produced.

Detailed consideration of the specific evidence put forward in support of the legend has been a focus of the revisionist literature and cannot be undertaken here, but I shall mention one point. The claim of the legend is that there were no technical means provided for the specific task of extermination, and that means originally provided for other purposes did double duty in improvised arrangements. Thus the Jews were allegedly gassed with the pesticide Zyklon, and their corpses disappeared into the crematoria along with the deaths from "ordinary" causes (the ashes or other remains of millions of victims never having been found).

Surely any thoughtful person must be skeptical.

> —Arthur R. Butz is an associate professor
> of electrical engineering.

(end of article) last modification: 5 May 1998.

Back to home page.

Using what Alan November (1998) calls "meta-web information," well-trained students could use several methods to measure the credibility of Butz's information. They could:

- Search the Internet using multisearch engines like Dogpile.com, which would bring up hundreds of references for *Arthur Butz*, including the press release of Northwestern University's president in which he explains the university's position on the professor's Web site.

- Use AltaVista's link command, which allows a user to search the Web for all the sites that are linked to a particular site. Such a search, according to November, would yield 879 links to Butz's page, among them the Online Fascist Resource Page, the White Power Central page, and the Texas Aryan Nationalist Skinheads page. November identifies two primary groups connected to the site: "hate mongers" and "hate monitors."

- Go outside the Web to seek information from real people and alternative sources in order to create a more complete picture and increase the likelihood that their information is, in fact, dependable.

Throughout your online reading, you must return to the essential questions you asked before you began: What am I looking for? What do I plan to do with this material? What are my criteria for reading or using any information?

Classroom Connection: Reading the Vietnam War on the Web

Let me illustrate what all this reading looks like in the classroom with a short narrative of a possible project on the Vietnam War. All the information that follows is authentic except for the *For the Record* Web site, which I created for the purposes of this unit.

I am a high school student assigned to research the Vietnam War over the Internet. Going online to conduct an initial search, I enter *Vietnam War* and get a list of annotated hits that could be from anywhere and of any quality, since I get 68,833 sites listed (see Figure 2–3). I've got to return to my prereading list to remind myself what I'm looking for. From there, I can decide how to narrow this search.

For this discussion, I'll look at the sites listed on the first page. Even looking just there, I see I must be discriminating as I evaluate which, if any, are worth checking out. Each one serves a unique primary purpose, though most clearly offer other value. I might find Edwin Moise's university Web page a useful guide to begin with; after all, he is a professor of history and has spent years preparing this extensive bibliography just for me. Other sites, such as the National Alliance, might put me in contact with people close to the story I want to tell; I figure perhaps I could e-mail some of them with questions, so I mark that site as one to visit. And the *Encyclopedia of the Vietnam War*, while a commercial site designed to sell the encyclopedia, will probably offer me valuable links that the writers themselves used to gather all that information; I make a note to check the local library's collection to see if it includes this encyclopedia for future reference. In all, I visit seven of the ten sites listed on the first page, bookmarking five of them for possible use later on.

My initial e-mails to several Webmasters, some of which are forwarded to actual veterans of the Vietnam War, yield a confusing range of truths that I must weigh against the various other texts I am reading. I must ask myself if one individual's experience or one filmmaker's perspective amounts to credibility or reliability. Yes, one director was in Vietnam as a soldier, so he knows what he experienced; but he was stationed at a relatively calm base near the beginning of the war and so saw little of the subsequent hell that injured so many.

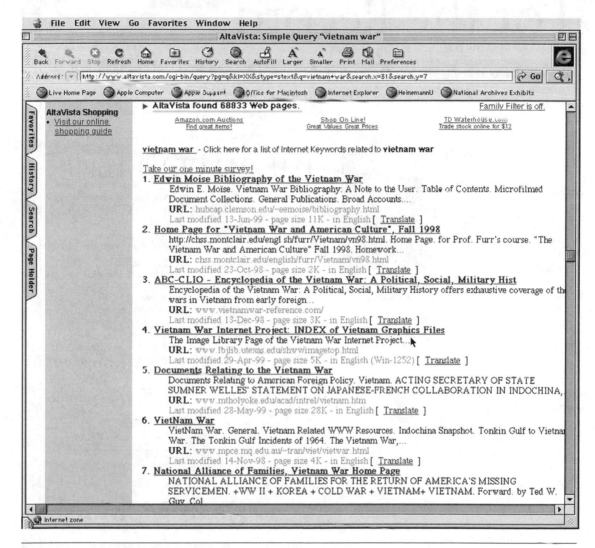

FIGURE 2–3 AltaVista sample search screenshot for proposed Vietnam inquiry. (*Reproduced with the permission of AltaVista. AltaVista and the AltaVista logo are trademarks of AltaVista Company.*)

Because my biggest handicap is my lack of personal knowledge of the event, I decide I need help establishing my criteria for good information. Further searching on the Net brings up *For the Record* (see Figure 2–4), a site that seems to be just what I need. Using the questions provided earlier, I decide the site is credible due to its affiliation, its credentials, and its motivations.

What questions do I have to ask myself to read this site effectively? The Historical Record Foundation sounds impressive, but so does the

For the Record

A Publication of the <u>Historical Record Foundation</u>   Concord, Massachusetts   Visitors: 547,249

Daily Quote
"Anybody can make history. Only a great man can write it." Oscar Wilde

October 7, 1999	October 7, 1899	October 7th in History

The <u>Historical Record Foundation</u>, founded in 1965 by Harvard Professor <u>Jeffrey Goldstein</u>, is committed to preserving and correcting the historical record in order that people will not forget the past nor repeat its mistakes. Drawing from <u>an international panel of historical experts</u>, the HRF uses its publication, For the Record, to keep people informed of crucial revisions of, omissions from, and additions to the historical record. <u>Learn more about our methodology and criteria.</u>

The Uses of History

- <u>in commercials</u>
- <u>in films</u>
  - <u>Elizabeth</u>
- <u>in speeches</u>
- <u>in art</u>
- <u>in textbooks</u>
- <u>in television</u>
- <u>in the news</u>
- <u>in campaigns</u>
- <u>in exhibits</u>
- <u>in literature</u>

POLLUTION HURTS ALL OF US. GET INVOLVED NOW.

<u>Watch this famous commercial</u> and <u>read Jonah Harman's essay</u> about the depiction of Native American history in contemporary culture.

For the Record

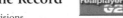

- Revisions
- Corrections
- Additions
- Omissions
- New Inquiries

What Do *You* Think?

Patty Hearst should be pardoned and her affiliation with the SLA expunged from her records.

Yes ◯   No ◯

Featured Links

- <u>Center for Historical Accuracy</u>
- <u>Center for Historical Truth</u>
- <u>Ask the Historian</u>
  - <u>Who is "the Historian"?</u>

Submit

THE PAMPHLETEER

"I know no way of judging the future but by the past."
Patrick Henry

American novelist Tim O'Brien has devoted himself to chronicling the experience and meaning of the war in Vietnam, but are Mr. O'Brien's observations accurate or are they elegant truths limited to the narrow confines of his own experience? O'Brien shed some light on this question while speaking at a convention of English teachers on the notion of truth in fiction. He was part of a panel of writers included novelists Julie Alvarez and Bharati Mukherjee who have been the subject of this column on several occasions for the same reasons we discuss Mr. O'Brien's work today. In his novel *In the Lake of the Woods*, O'Brien turns his attention to the alleged massacre at Mai Lai, where some suggest that American soldiers participated in the slaughter of civilians. O'Brien makes his first assault on the historical record by including fictionalized "footnotes"

> "What I just told you never happened, but it is true."
>
> —Tim O'Brien

<u>read the rest of the story</u> ➤ ➤ ➤

American Memory
Historical Collections for the National Digital Library

Have you encountered questionable "truths" in the news, a politician's speech, or your child's textbook? Send them in with all the appropriate information (source, context, names, etc.) and we will look into it for you

---

FIGURE 2–4 Sample Web Page *For the Record*. I designed this page to include a variety of features kids need to know and be able to interpret. This is not a real Web page nor is it a real organization.

Institute for Historical Review, a group that publishes revisionist history that alleges, for example, that the Holocaust was a hoax. Thus, I need to ask such questions as:

- What is the foundation's stated objective?
- Who funds the foundation?
- What did Goldstein, the Harvard professor, represent?
- How does the foundation determine whose idea of "the record" is correct (i.e., what are its sources and methodologies)?
- What else does it publish, promote, and provide?
- Are its links connected to respected authorities or agencies in the field of history?
- What does the format—layout, appearance, voice—of the home page tell me about the foundation's credibility?
- How complete are its efforts to monitor and rectify the historical record?
- What does the URL tell me about the Web site and its affiliations?
- How many people have visited this site and what might that tell readers about the perception of this site in the eyes of its visitors?
- What other services or products does the foundation offer through its site?
- What is its apparent objective according to the offerings and the overall content?
- How current is the information?
- Is there any evidence of bias—stated or implied—in the site's content or organization?
- If there is bias, is there a means of contributing an opposing view to provide a more balanced perspective to the site?
- Why does the foundation provide the information "Who is 'the Historian'?" and what does this tell readers about the site's authors?
- What is the implication of the Wilde epigraph?
- Does the location of the organization in Concord, Massachusetts, carry any possible meaning in this context that supports or detracts from the credibility of the Historical Record Foundation?
- In short, is this a serious, reliable, and credible Web site that merits attention and provides information useful for a project on Vietnam?

The necessity of all of these steps and the potential seriousness of the content of Web sites should sound an alarm for us all. The excitement of the Internet, of the world at your fingertips, must be allowed to pass so that it can be replaced by a sense of urgency: students need to read the Web critically, and not just when they are looking at Web sites but also when they read e-mail, chat rooms, listservs, and newsgroups.

Standards Connections

Requiring that our students read the Internet critically fits within the reading standards that most states have adopted. For instance, the California Language Arts Standards for seventh grade provide a particularly succinct description of what students should know and be able to do when reading critically:

STRUCTURAL FEATURES OF INFORMATIONAL MATERIALS

2.1. understand and analyze the differences among various categories of informational materials (e.g., textbooks, newspapers, instructional manuals, signs) in terms of their structure and purpose

2.2. locate information using a variety of consumer, workplace, and public documents

2.3. analyze text that uses cause and effect patterns

COMPREHENSION AND ANALYSIS OF GRADE-LEVEL-APPROPRIATE TEXT

2.4. identify and trace the development of an author's argument, point of view, or perspective in text

2.5. understand and explain the use of a simple mechanical device by following technical directions

EXPOSITORY CRITIQUE

2.6. assess the adequacy, accuracy, and appropriateness of the author's evidence to support claims and assertions, noting instances of bias and stereotyping

So teaching our students to read the Internet critically helps them reach the standards set by state boards. Additionally, however, we realize that this critical Internet reading is something our students need to master as they move into an ever more digital, online age where truth can be created and manipulated with the stroke of a key or the click of a mouse.

Closing Thoughts

The Internet is still so recent and dynamic that everyone mistakes it for something new. Surely it is a remarkable tool that for all its power remains in its infancy. But we should not mistake the form for the function, the means for the message. As far back as the 1800s, more than 75 million catalogs were mailed throughout the United States to people who waited all year long for the latest Montgomery Ward or Sears and Roebuck catalog. People learned about the world through these pages, which were packed with ads, information, and images, all inspiring desire and wonder in those homesteaders who depended on the catalogs for so many goods. As historian Daniel Boorstin notes in *The Americans: The Democratic Experience* (1973), "Montgomery Ward's business depended on the confidence of a buyer in a seller whom he had never seen." Most of the elements incorporated into effective Web pages were also present in those catalog pages. In fact, the catalogs were considered so encyclopedic, much as the Internet is today, that they were often used as the primary textbook in some rural schools, according to Boorstin:

> Just as, three centuries before, New England schoolchildren had learned the path to salvation along with their ABC's and had learned how to read at the same time they learned the tenets of their community, so farm children now learned from the [Sears and Roebuck catalog]. In rural schoolhouses, children were drilled in reading and spelling from the catalogue. They practiced arithmetic by filling out orders and adding up items. They tried their hand at drawing by copying the catalogue models, and acquired geography by studying the postal-zone maps. In schoolrooms that had no other encyclopedia, a Ward's or Sears' catalogue handily served the purpose; it was illustrated, it told what something was made of and what it was good for, how long it would last, and even what it cost. Many a mother in a household with few children's books pacified her child with the pictures from the catalogue. When the new book arrived, the pictures were indelibly fixed in the memory of girls who cut them up for paper dolls.

In some ways, our society grows more similar to the frontier all the time as each person, like those homesteaders, has his or her own little place on the vast plain of the Internet, where, to survive and prosper, he or she must develop the same skepticism and craft, shrewd intelligence and bartering skills that helped those early pioneers. Perhaps the one difference between those homesteaders and today's digital pioneers is the amount and quality of time they spend reading. Internet reading is not inherently reflective; it's hard to think too much about where you are going when you are driving a hundred miles an hour as many do on the Internet. To be truly effective readers, in any domain, of any text, we must pull off the road occasionally to evaluate where we are and where we are going so we can not only appreciate the journey but know how to repeat it in the future.

Further Studies

Alexander, Janet E., and Marsha Ann Tate. 1999. *Web Wisdom: How to Evaluate and Create Information Quality on the Web.* Mahway, NJ: Lawrence Erlbaum.

Kennedy, Angus J. 2000. *The Rough Guide to the Internet.* New York: Rough Guides.

3

Reading Textbooks

There is no theme to this pudding.
—Winston Churchill

Love goes toward love as schoolboys from their books;
But love from love, towards school with heavy looks.
—William Shakespeare, from *Romeo and Juliet*

It was the third week of my junior year in high school, in Mrs. Koe's American history class, and things were getting serious. That's right, I had not yet covered my textbook. I probably hadn't read it either, but that's a different story, or at least a different chapter. Everyone had his or her book covered now except me. Mrs. Koe moved toward me with a large red marker in her hand, talking through the microphone attached to her throat. We had to listen to her swallow in stereo, listen to her tell us about history while also hearing her throat gurgling the water she constantly made me fetch for her. Everyone watched her as she moved toward me with that pen in her hand. I sat in the front right corner, near the door for the quickest possible exit. Suddenly she was upon me, uncapping the pen and drawing a red circle the size of the Japanese flag on my forehead while I and the class looked on in disbelief. "Now you will go home tonight, Mr. Burke, and when you brush your teeth, you will see that red circle and say, 'Oh, that's right, I have to cover my textbook for Mrs. Koe!' " Not since Mr. Kane had made Kim Simmons take out her gum, stick it in her own hair, then cut it out had I been so stunned by a teacher's exercise of power! We expected that of Mr. Kane, though: he was a teacher and a pig farmer. But Mrs. Koe was serious business; to her, the textbook was sacred.

Eventually I covered my book—who knew what her next strategy was going to be!—but the book never felt sacred to me. This is perhaps best illustrated by my answer to a short-answer question later in the year that asked us to identify the first man to walk on the moon. I proudly answered that it was Colonel Steve Austin (from the popular television show *The Six Million Dollar Man*), knowing, I should add, that it was not the right answer. The obvious point and a real dilemma for both teachers and students is that textbooks are rarely engaging reading experiences. Nor are they always used by teachers as effective teaching tools through which students can learn what we want them to know about a subject. Of course, many teachers do make great use of them. Verne Cleary, a respected history teacher in the school where I began teaching, describes how he uses textbooks:

Social studies teachers need to place the textbook in the context of larger learning objectives. You touch on this as well. But, teachers need examples/models for how to NOT make the textbook the center of instruction. Way too many history teachers let the textbook drive the class. For example, I teach with central questions that I pose for students in a unit of study (such as "Was World War I a just war?"). This question is posed on the first day of the unit and it guides our inquiry every day. At the end of the unit, students write an essay or create a project (such as a newspaper, metaphor, or brochure) that argues this question using evidence from activities and the textbook. So, when students read the textbook, they're reading with the purpose of looking for evidence to answer the central unit question. They're looking to see how a new event they're reading about fits into the big picture. How does it connect to the unit question? This provides a clear structure for them to remember and process events and people. Also, I create Reading Guides for the textbook rather than simply assign questions in the back of the book. The Reading Guides direct them to read with the provocative unit question in mind. In this way, the textbook serves as an important resource but it is never the center of instruction and it does not drive the content. I do that. I, as the teacher, must guide the inquiry. (1999)

See Chapter 5, "Reading Literature," for a more detailed discussion of the curriculum-as-conversation principles outlined in Verne's comments.

NOTE

This chapter looks at how we can better use these books in the classroom by considering the following:

- What the books consist of (e.g., elements, features, devices)
- How the books can be used as learning tools
- How the books are designed
- How students need to be able to read to use them well and make sense
  of their content

The Challenges of Textbooks

In many respects, today's textbooks, regardless of the subject area they
cover, resemble the World Wide Web and call on readers to use many of
the same strategies discussed in Chapter 2. How are textbooks similar to
the Internet and why must we draw on these same strategies?

- Both offer a vast range of texts in different media (words, genre,
  images, writing style, eras, sources).
- Textbook publishers, eager to anticipate the future trends, increasingly
  provide digital and online resources and links to supplement their
  textbooks, thereby minimizing the difference between the two as they
  come to form one complex, interactive text.
- Textbooks resemble one twelve hundred-page-long hit list of documents and details about, for example, American history. It's as if each
  chapter or subheading were a hotlink in an AltaVista search in which
  the search engine was asked to find everything it could about American history. It then becomes the teacher's job to help students learn to
  sift through the mountains of information from various sources, to
  assess what is not there as well as the quality of what *is* there, and to
  determine how the information and material relates to their purpose.

This last point regarding purpose is crucial and we shall return to it
later. Throughout the book, I emphasize the importance of making the
student occupy the role of scientist or historian (among others) in order to
help her develop her thinking within that domain. Textbooks, if used as
one resource to which the student-expert (in science, history, health) can
turn, offer a useful tool for learning. Several metaphors come to mind to
describe the textbook: conversation, reference library, guest lecturer, bible,
road map. To the extent that readers—and this is obviously true with any
text they are reading—must interact with the book, *use* it, as opposed to
routinely reading it and answering assigned questions, they will read it
better, more actively, and thus continue to strengthen their abilities as
readers. Consider, for example, the learning involved in creating a student
historian's guidebook, as described in *Beyond the Textbook: Teaching History
Using Documents and Primary Sources* (Kobrin 1996): "Much depends on
what the teacher decides to emphasize and on what puzzles or interests

the kids. The bulk of the student historian's text would consist of material usually found in the teacher's edition of a traditional textbook but also helpful to students." Here are the proposed contents of such a guidebook, the working title of which is *It's My Country, Too*:

- Several versions of possible periodization schemes for U.S. history, each with its own justification
- Sample student theme essays with marginal notes critiquing strengths and suggesting improvements
- Guidelines for creating historical maps
- Examples of historical maps with notes about why, for whom, and how these particular maps are useful
- Examples of themes that transcend chronological periods
- Core content examples cross-listed by chronological period and topic
- Student historian practice projects that raise specific process problems (for example, working with primary sources that contain dramatic internal contradictions or include complex values issues)
- Test items for the core content examples
- A bibliography of interesting, diverse, and accessible films, filmstrips, videos, software programs, CD-ROMs, and lesser known sources (for example, architectural drawings, demographic tables, pictorial histories of people at work, youth archives)
- Lists of resource organizations
- Stories by fictional students about having the power of the historian in their own hands

A quick look at Prentice Hall's U.S. history textbook *America: Pathways to the Present* (Cayton et al. 2000) suggests the authors used the previous list as their own guideline. In other words, the latest round of textbooks includes many of these features, but students often need serious help in navigating their way through these five-pound textual labyrinths, especially at the outset. One useful alternative might be to have students create their own guidebook using the one in the textbook as an exemplar but not a template; in other words, they would not be allowed to use any of the same categories, themes, or organizational structures as the textbook.

Schools looking for powerful and appropriate ways to incorporate technology into the curriculum might also provide students with opportunities to create their own online, digital textbook that both students and teachers could update as they move through the year. Consider the example from the National Archives Constitution Community, which was created to help students study constitutional issues and meet national academic standards while also learning how to read primary source documents as they engage in authentic and substantial conversations (see Figure 3–1).

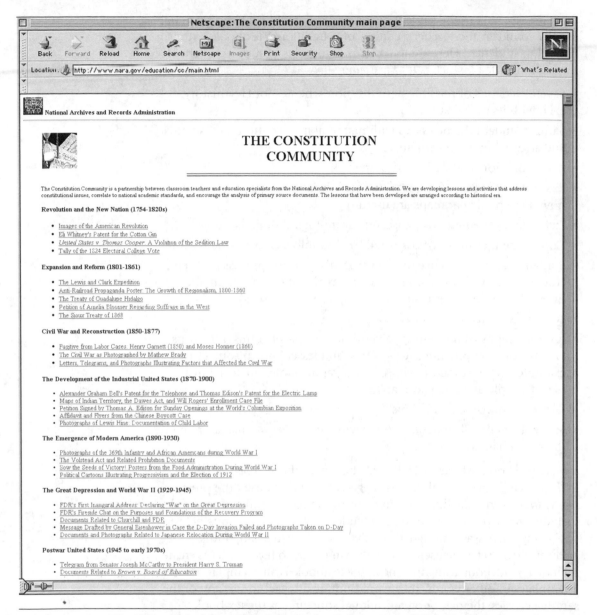

FIGURE 3–1 The National Archives' "The Constitutional Community" Web Site Main Page. See my own digital anthology, *The Weekly Reader*, at <www.englishcompanion.com>.

Responding to Gilbert Sewell's (2000) remarks that older textbooks were better written and more demanding, Clyde Winters argues,

Contemporary teachers recognize the limitations of the history text. As a result, they encourage their students to participate in engaged learning activities in which they produce their own knowledge. In many classrooms around America, students work in cooperative groups and use print media and technology to study aspects of American and world history in detail, and then present the fruits of their research to their peers. Teachers want their students to learn history intimately, and not just from a history text. (2000)

Science teachers, as well as others who use textbooks, no doubt feel the same, especially when they look at the superficial treatment they are too often forced to give to substantial material.

NOTE

Check out more of the National Archives Web site at <www.nara .gov.> In addition to resources and activities, it regularly assembles quality online exhibits of National Archives material. See Figure 3–1.

There is one other approach that will develop the critical reading skills needed to read textbooks successfully. Inhabiting the role of evaluator, students can read the text not for content alone but to evaluate the presentation of that content. Placed in the role of reviewer or evaluator of a textbook he is using to study a subject, the student must suddenly ask such as questions as:

- What questions is the book *not* asking or answering?
- What evidence do the authors provide to illustrate and support their observations?
- How balanced is the authors' view in light of current understanding of this subject?
- Are ideas, events, or people represented in appropriate and accurate ways throughout the book?
- How might this book best be used in light of its content, form, and function?

A high school student demonstrated the power of such evaluative reading when, in response to her state legislator's essay contest, she proposed a bill that would require all textbooks older than ten years to be replaced. An article about the student, Kristin Schleicher, describes her argument:

"Last year, I pored over a tattered chemistry textbook that had been first used in 1979 . . . I knew that my textbook could not possibly contain a discussion of any new breakthroughs that had occurred in the field in the last 20 years," wrote Schleicher in her essay.

"What student can get excited about learning from a dingy manuscript with ripped pages, meaningless 'current' statistics and indecipherable scribbles left in the margin?" she said.

Since 1979, at least 10 more elements have been discovered, said Tina Stanford, a chemistry teacher at Acalanes High School in Lafayette. Chemistry textbooks of the last decade are more kid-friendly, she said, with better graphics to explain concepts involving particles too small for the eye to see. And, she said, they have more practical information on how chemistry relates to the real world. (Bell 1999, A12)

Such critical reading is precisely the sort of reading students must be taught and given an opportunity to practice when reading textbooks, for students encounter within these books not only errors, as Karen Schleicher illustrates in her essay, but bias and, increasingly, commercial content that they must be able to recognize and scrutinize with a media consumer's critical eye. Sadly, these same obsolete textbooks often include better, more challenging writing, which, in the opinion of some, builds better readers:

Many history textbooks seem to reflect lowered sights for general education, coupled with the conviction—widely held among editors and educators—that a snappy, scattered format with few words and many classroom activities will alleviate student boredom with history and reading and writing . . . Pictures are not always worth a thousand words. Precision of thought depends on clear, fluent language. Effective learning demands that students have the ability to collaborate with text and be able to grasp through language (comprehend) why an individual, event, or institution is notable. Graphics can enrich text, but only if they complement or extend concepts and episodes that are centered in the text. Maps, tables, graphs, and lists especially can help to illuminate historical subjects. But many illustrations and sidebars serve no such instructional purposes. (Sewell 2000, 52)

The problem of textbook quality has reached a state of crisis, giving corporations the feeling that the classroom and thus students' captive attention is up for sale, or so the following article suggests:

Mathematics: Applications and Connections, a textbook used by many California sixth graders, begins its discussion of the coordinate system with an advertisement for Walt Disney. "Have you ever wanted to be the star of a movie? If you visit Walt Disney-MGM Studios Theme Park, you could become one." In the margin of the same page is a photo of Sleeping Beauty's castle. Under the caption "Teen Scene" appears the following: "Disney-MGM Studios has an Indiana Jones Epic Stunt Spectacular where scenes from action-packed Indiana Jones movies are recreated live. If you attend this event, you may be chosen as an 'extra' for an exciting chase scene." That is just one of thousands of examples of brand names, sports teams, movies and commercial logos scattered through many of the math textbooks approved by the state for use in kindergarten through grade 12. (1999)

Harper's Magazine took Glencoe-McGraw-Hill to task for the same issue in a small article titled, "How Many Licks in a Tootsie Pop?" (1999). The article included several examples of word problems from *Mathematics: Applications and Connections,* which uses "real-world examples [because they are] effective in engaging students' interest and enhancing the learning process." *Harper's* went on to point out that McGraw-Hill had no financial interest in any of the products mentioned in the word problems. Here are a few examples:

- The bestselling packaged cookie in the world is the Oreo cookie. The diameter of an Oreo cookie is 1.75 inches. Express the diameter of an Oreo cookie as a fraction.
- Kellogg's introduced Cocoa Frosted Flakes in 1997. The package is a rectangular prism 12 inches high, 8 inches wide, and 3 inches deep. How many square inches did the label designer have to cover on the package?
- According to the results of a test conducted by *Zillions* magazine, 12 out of 17 kids prefer the Sony PlayStation to Sega Saturn. Suppose there are 3,400 kids in your community. Predict how many will prefer the PlayStation.

Again we see the trend of dissolving boundaries: if textbooks seem more and more to resemble the Internet, so, too, do the textbooks also come to resemble advertisements, yet one more type of text we must watch for and know how to read so that we may move through the world confident of our inability to be persuaded unknowingly. This raises one final incarnation we must be aware of: the textbook as test-prep manual. It seems almost inevitable that as states align themselves with standards and schools feel increasing pressure to prepare their students for such subject-specific tests as the SAT II, the books will come to mirror those tests in form and function.

For more on reading such tests, see Chapter 4, "Reading Tests."

NOTE

Thus, the teacher becomes the primary defense against commercialism, anti-intellectualism as manifested through standardized test preparation, and outdated materials. What students read ends up being as important as how or why the students read a certain text. Students creating the textbook guidebook described earlier, or students such as Kristin Schleicher, become the readers we want all our students to be through a balanced but critical use of textbooks in the class. Figure 3–2 shows a page I created to illustrate different features and functions that can make textbook pages so confusing and difficult.

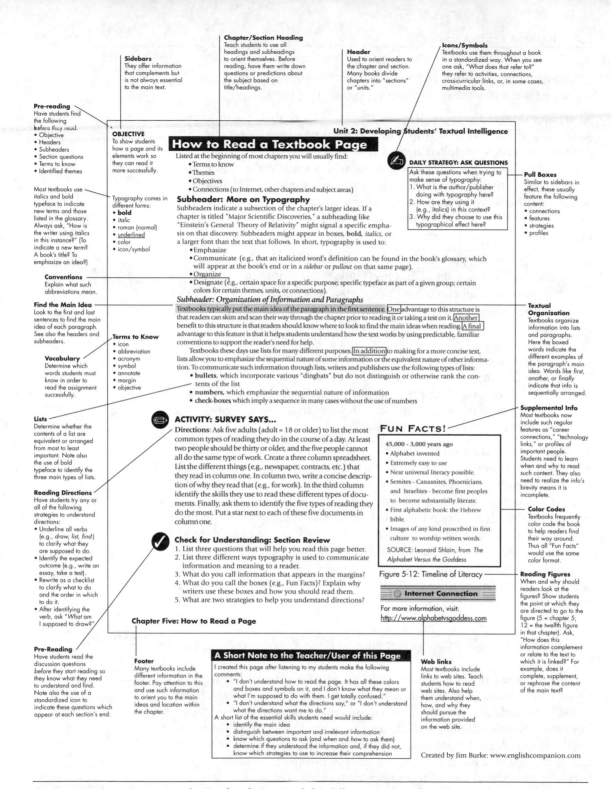

How to Read a Textbook Page

Listed at the beginning of most chapters you will usually find:

- Terms to know
- Themes
- Objectives
- Connections (to Internet, other chapters and subject areas)

Subheader: More on Typography

Subheaders indicate a subsection of the chapter's larger ideas. If a chapter is titled "Major Scientific Discoveries," a subheading like "Einstein's General Theory of Relativity" might signal a specific emphasis on that discovery. Subheaders might appear in boxes, **bold**, *italics*, or a larger font than the text that follows. In short, typography is used to:

- Emphasize
- Communicate (e.g., that an italicized word's definition can be found in the book's glossary, which will appear at the book's end or in a *sidebar* or *pullout* on that same page).
- Organize
- Designate (e.g., certain space for a specific purpose; specific typeface as part of a given group; certain colors for certain themes, units, or connections).

Subheader: Organization of Information and Paragraphs

Textbooks typically put the main idea of the paragraph in the first sentence. One advantage to this structure is that readers can skim and scan their way through the chapter prior to reading it or taking a test on it. Another benefit to this structure is that readers should know where to look to find the main ideas when reading. A final advantage to this feature is that it helps students understand how the text works by using predictable, familiar conventions to support the reader's need for help.

Textbooks these days use lists for many different purposes. In addition to making for a more concise text, lists allow you to emphasize the sequential nature of some information or the equivalent nature of other information. To communicate such information through lists, writers and publishers use the following types of lists:

- **bullets**, which incorporate various "dingbats" but do not distinguish or otherwise rank the contents of the list
- **numbers**, which emphasize the sequential nature of information
- **check-boxes** which imply a sequence in many cases without the use of numbers

ACTIVITY: SURVEY SAYS...

Directions: Ask five adults (adult = 18 or older) to list the most common types of reading they do in the course of a day. At least two people should be thirty or older, and the five people cannot all do the same type of work. Create a three column spreadsheet. List the different things (e.g., newspaper, contracts, etc.) that they read in column one. In column two, write a concise description of why they read that (e.g., for work). In the third column identify the skills they use to read these different types of documents. Finally, ask them to identify the five types of reading they do the most. Put a star next to each of these five documents in column one.

Check for Understanding: Section Review

1. List three questions that will help you read this page better.
2. List three different ways typography is used to communicate information and meaning to a reader.
3. What do you call information that appears in the margins?
4. What do you call the boxes (e.g., Fun Facts)? Explain why writers use these boxes and how you should read them.
5. What are two strategies to help you understand directions?

Chapter Five: How to Read a Page

OBJECTIVE

To show students how a page and its elements work so they can read it more successfully.

Typography comes in different forms:
- **bold**
- *italic*
- roman (normal)
- underlined
- color
- icon/symbol

DAILY STRATEGY: ASK QUESTIONS

Ask these questions when trying to make sense of typography:
1. What is the author/publisher doing with typography here?
2. How are they using it (e.g., italics) in this context?
3. Why did they choose to use this typographical effect here?

FUN FACTS!

45,000 - 3,000 years ago
- Alphabet invented
- Extremely easy to use
- Near universal literacy possible.
- Semites - Canaanites, Phoenicians, and Israelites - become first peoples to become substantially literate.
- First alphabetic book: the Hebrew bible.
- Images of any kind proscribed in first culture to worship written words.

SOURCE: Leonard Shlain, from *The Alphabet Versus the Goddess*

Figure 5-12: Timeline of Literacy

Internet Connection

For more information, visit:
http://www.alphabetvsgoddess.com

Margin annotations

Sidebars
They offer information that complements but is not always essential to the main text.

Chapter/Section Heading
Teach students to use all headings and subheadings to orient themselves. Before reading, have them write down questions or predictions about the subject based on title/headings.

Header
Used to orient readers to the chapter and section. Many books divide chapters into "sections" or "units."

Icons/Symbols
Textbooks use them throughout a book in a standardized way. When you see one ask, "What does that refer to?" they refer to activities, connections, cross-curricular links, or, in some cases, multimedia tools.

Pre-reading
Have students find the following before they read.
- Objective
- Headers
- Subheaders
- Section questions
- Terms to know
- Identified themes

Most textbooks use italics and bold typeface to indicate new terms and those listed in the glossary. Always ask, "How is the writer using italics in this instance?" (To indicate a new term? A book's title? To emphasize an idea?)

Conventions
Explain what such abbreviations mean.

Find the Main Idea
Look to the first and last sentences to find the main idea of each paragraph. See also the headers and subheaders.

Vocabulary
Determine which words students must know in order to read the assignment successfully.

Terms to Know
- icon
- abbreviation
- acronym
- symbol
- annotate
- margin
- objective

Lists
Determine whether the contents of a list are equivalent or arranged from most to least important. Note also the use of bold typeface to identify the three main types of lists.

Reading Directions
Have students try any or all of the following strategies to understand directions:
- Underline all verbs (e.g., draw, list, find) to clarify what they are supposed to do.
- Identify the expected outcome (e.g., write an essay, take a test).
- Rewrite as a checklist to clarify what to do and the order in which to do it.
- After identifying the verb, ask "What am I supposed to draw?"

Pre-Reading
Have students read the discussion questions before they start reading so they know what they need to understand and find. Note also the use of a standardized icon to indicate these questions which appear at each section's end.

Pull Boxes
Similar to sidebars in effect, these usually feature the following content:
- connections
- features
- strategies
- profiles

Textual Organization
Textbooks organize information into lists and paragraphs. Here the boxed words indicate the different examples of the paragraph's main idea. Words like first, another, or finally indicate that info is sequentially arranged.

Supplemental Info
Most textbooks now include such regular features as "career connections," "technology links," or profiles of important people. Students need to learn when and why to read such content. They also need to realize the info's brevity means it is incomplete.

Color Codes
Textbooks frequently color code the book to help readers find their way around. Thus all "Fun Facts" would use the same color format.

Reading Figures
When and why should readers look at the figures? Show students the point at which they are directed to go to the figure (5 = chapter 5; 12 = the twelfth figure in that chapter). Ask, "How does this information complement or relate to the text to which it is linked?" For example, does it complete, supplement, or rephrase the content of the main text?

Footer
Many textbooks include different information in the footer. Pay attention to this and use such information to orient you to the main ideas and location within the chapter.

A Short Note to the Teacher/User of this Page

I created this page after listening to my students make the following comments:
- "I don't understand how to read the page. It has all these colors and boxes and symbols on it, and I don't know what they mean or what I'm supposed to do with them. I get totally confused."
- "I don't understand what the directions say," or "I don't understand what the directions want me to do."

A short list of the essential skills students need would include:
- identify the main idea
- distinguish between important and irrelevant information
- know which questions to ask (and when and how to ask them)
- determine if they understood the information and, if they did not, know what strategies to use to increase their comprehension

Web links
Most textbooks include links to web sites. Teach students how to read web sites. Also help them understand when, how, and why they should pursue the information provided on the web site.

Created by Jim Burke: www.englishcompanion.com

FIGURE 3–2 How to Read a Textbook. I created this "illuminated text" to illustrate how much is going on within a typical textbook page.

Elements of the Text

On some pages of the newest textbooks, there are so many elements, features, and devices that they resemble collages more than pages from a book. (See the sample textbook page I created in Figure 3–2.) And each element matters. Color, illustrations, and other images, not to mention the multimedia supplements, cost too much to be added for fun: they form a matrix of meaning for readers. Colors and symbols can provide thematic connections to other chapters or ideas throughout the book. Maps and other visual explanations can serve several purposes, allowing the teacher to teach map reading in the context of helping the students see patterns within the Civil War, for example. The elements of many texts are arranged in different ways to allow teachers to use the books in various ways; tables of contents reveal different thematic and chronological arrangements, all of which are built on a foundation of smaller skills units and textual connections that strive to unify the textbook. A quick survey of Prentice Hall's *America: Pathways to the Present* (Cayton et al. 2000) quickly establishes just how much is contained between these two covers. This five-pound, twelve hundred-page textbook includes the following elements:

- Allusions
- Appendices
- Art
- Author information (affiliation, credentials, other publications)
- Bibliography
- Biographies
- Cartoons
- Chapters
- Charts
- Cover
- Depth of coverage of a subject
- Design of the pages and overall book
- Editorial perspective
- Essays
- Foreword
- Glossaries (English and Spanish)
- Graphs
- Headings (for units, chapters, sections, and subsections of chapters)
- Helpful features (e.g., "Key Points")
- "How to Use This Book"

- Illustrations
- Index
- Introduction
- Journals
- Laws and commentaries
- Letters
- Literature
- Maps
- Navigational information (e.g., words, symbols, sidebars)
- News articles
- Organizational design with respect to subject and coverage of people, places, times, events, eras, trends, processes, and procedures
- Photographs
- Post-chapter/post-unit questions, activities
- Pre-chapter overviews
- Profiles
- Pullout boxes
- Questions (review, practice, comprehension, discussion)
- Sections/units
- Sidebars
- Speeches
- Summaries
- Table of contents
- Tables
- Time lines
- Title
- Typographical features
- URLs

We also find such features as "Artifacts" (literary and geographic); "Timelines"; "Skills for Life" (which lists dozens of distinct skills students are expected to use in the course of the class or in life beyond school); "Concepts"; "Biographies"; "Turning Points"; and "My Brush with History," in which eyewitnesses describe what they saw and experienced at key historical events. Additional features include the publisher's alliance with and inclusion of articles from the venerable *American Heritage* magazine in the book and on its regularly updated Web site.

The important observation here is that the publisher and the author make choices as to content, form, style, and perspective. They decide in committees—textbooks are developed, not written in the traditional sense of the word—what should be in and what should be out, what gets emphasis, what gets coverage. *Brill's Content* looked at textbooks and asked:

> So how does McGraw-Hill determine what fifth-graders ought to know about U.S. history? State educational review boards wield enormous power over textbook publishers' final product. "We rely on the states to tell us what they want in their books," says [Tom] Condon, editorial director of the social studies department at McGraw-Hill School Division. While the president's impeachment made the cut for McGraw-Hill's newest social studies book, only "possible illegal actions" are mentioned—neither Monica Lewinsky nor Kenneth Starr are mentioned by name. (Yellin 2000, 23)

Frances FitzGerald, in *America Revised: History Schoolbooks in the Twentieth Century* (1980), writes:

> To the uninitiated, the very thought of what goes on in a textbook house must inspire a good deal of vertigo. Way up in some office building sit people—ordinary mortals with red and blue pencils—deciding all those issues of American history, not to mention those of literature and biology. What shall we think of the Vietnam War? Of the American Revolution? What is the nature of American society and what are its values? The responsibility of these people seems awesome, for, as is not true of trade publishers, the audiences for their products are huge, impressionable, and captive. Children have to read textbooks; they usually have to read all of each textbook and are rarely asked to criticize it for style or point of view. A textbook is there, much like Mt. Everest awaiting George Mallory, and it leaves no alternative. The textbook editors, therefore, must appear to be the arbiters of American values, and the publishing companies the Ministries of Truth for children.

Thus, our students must be attentive to the elements of these different texts and even more attentive to the choices made in the creation of the book. For a textbook, in addition to being a historical document reflecting the views of the era in which it was made, is also a collection of many other documents—essays, editorials, speeches—each one of them making its own demands on the reader. Returning for a moment to the skills listed under "Skills for Life" in *America: Pathways to the Present*, I find the following different types of reading or thinking skills, all of which are described as necessary to read this book and its different documents successfully:

- Analyzing advertisements
- Analyzing political speeches
- Analyzing presidential records

- Analyzing tombstones
- Checking consistency
- Demonstrating reasoned judgment
- Determining relevance
- Distinguishing fact from opinion
- Distinguishing false from accurate images
- Drawing conclusions
- Evaluating magazine advertisements
- Examining photographs
- Exploring oral history
- Expressing problems clearly
- Formulating questions
- How maps show change over time
- Identifying alternatives
- Identifying assumptions
- Identifying central issues
- Interpreting an economic activity map
- Making comparisons
- Predicting consequences (Cayton et al. 2000)
- Reading a political cartoon
- Reading tables and analyzing statistics
- Recognizing bias
- Recognizing cause and effect
- Recognizing ideologies
- Using cross-sectional maps
- Using letters as primary sources
- Using population density maps
- Using time lines
- Using a time zone map

Questions to Ask

- What events, ideas, people, or perspectives might the authors have left out to avoid controversy?
- What are/were the political and social climates in which this textbook was created and how, if at all, might they have shaped the content, the form, and the function of this book?
- What is the perspective of the author/publisher of this text and how does that shape my perceived meaning?

- What is the relationship between what students read in the textbook and what they hear or learn in class through simulations, discussions, lectures?
- What is the important idea or information in this particular text or assigned reading?
- How do I determine whether an idea is important?
- By what criteria are people, events, places, and so on chosen by the authors or publishers (e.g., for the sake of coverage? importance? test preparation? high interest?)?
- What do students need to know and be able to do to read this book, this chapter, or this specific excerpt successfully?
- Do they know how this text works (e.g., what a word in bold typeface implies)?
- What role (reference, sacred text, supplement to other texts) does the textbook play in the classroom?
- What would ___(the Japanese)___ say about the textbook's description of ___(Hiroshima)___ ?
- What does the textbook *not* include—information, perspectives, events, people, places—that it should? And why do I think the authors left it out?
- How thorough is the book in its coverage of the subject? For example, one textbook I looked at offered as its "biography" of General Douglas MacArthur only three paragraphs.
- Is the book's vision coherent and consistent throughout the book?
- What is my role or relationship with this textbook as reflected by the book itself and the support materials addressed to me? Is it a "teacher-proof" text or one that expects or at least allows me to use the book to support constructivist, inquiry-based instruction?
- What is the reading level of the textbook and the reading ability of the students using it? What are the implications for me if my students' reading abilities do not match the demands of the text?
- Are the book's conclusions or observations still true? For example, a history textbook might offer a description of Secretary of State Robert MacNamara based on his actions and ideas in 1967, many of which he himself has responded to or even debunked in his subsequent memoir about the Vietnam War.
- Is the author of the textbook or a given passage from within that text-book a credible voice in light of what we know now? For example, the history teacher with whom I collaborate uses an out-of-print but excellent textbook called *Tradition and Change*, which consists of case studies and primary source documents. When he has students read about South Africa, he immediately addresses the need for more current

information by bringing in *Time* articles and having the students interview South Africans via various resources available through the Web.

- What other materials or resources might I use to supplement this textbook on this particular issue or subject?
- What question am I, is this textbook, or is my class trying to answer and how is the book being used to help answer it?

Classroom Connection

NOTE

Consider digging through the book room or your department office to find previously used textbooks for your subject. Have students read these and compare the treatment of certain ideas or subjects across the books and years, drawing conclusions and supporting these with examples from the books. Try to find time also to talk about the evolving look and design of textbooks. Look also at quality and the difficulty of the writing.

Just as literary critic Stanley Fish asked in his provocative book *Is There a Text in This Class?* (1982), I sometimes wonder, when I see these massive textbooks for science, mathematics, literature, and history, if the publishers think there is a teacher for this class. Most books now come with abundant support materials that include the publisher's Web site, CD-ROMs (which contain everything from printable graphic organizers to premade tests), transparencies, audiocassettes, video recordings, and additional readings. As I write this, one of the major publishers has just released a line of textbooks complete with tests, all of which are available online for students to take and which the publisher's software will grade, returning the completed scores to the teacher by day's end. Thus, I wonder where we, as teachers, fit into the mix. I ask myself and my subject matter what our role is or should be in the classroom, especially as it relates to the textbook.

NOTE

In *In the Age of the Smart Machine*, Shoshona Zuboff (1989) offers a fascinating study of workers who find themselves increasingly displaced by machines able to do their work and the existential crisis this causes in them. See also Ray Kurzweil's *The Age of Spiritual Machines: When Computers Exceed Human Intelligence* (1999) in which he argues that nearly all education will take place through machines by the year 2009.

Surely we ask our students to read to learn, but we also face the reality that they need to learn to read certain features or types of text. This view of teacher as guide or facilitator is supported by various studies that Lapp, Flood, and Farnan (1996) discuss in their book *Content Area Reading and Learning: Instructional Strategies*: "If there is one area in great need of improvement in the education of future content area teachers, it is in encouraging them to be as innovative and active as guides to textbook reading as they are in other components of instruction. It is the teacher, not the textbook, who is responsible for guiding the process of learning, even of learning from the text" (31).

Several questions help us focus our attention on the role of the textbook and the teacher in the classroom:

- What are we supposed to do?
- Why are we supposed to do it?
- How can we accomplish this end best?
- When is it appropriate to do this work?

It is the first question that is most pressing. The answer is clear: help students learn when and how to use a range of strategies to read the different types of text they encounter within the textbook. Olson and Gee (as referenced in Lapp, Flood, and Farnan 1996) identify six primary strategies we all recognize are useful. We should teach the students how to:

- Preview vocabulary and other concepts
- Use manipulatives (e.g., maps, pictures)
- Retell what they read
- Summarize what they read
- Visualize what they read
- Brainstorm notions related to a topic

These and many other strategies are discussed in my book *Reading Reminders: Tools, Tips, and Techniques* (2000), which serves as a companion to this book.

NOTE

A few other approaches are worth mentioning, as each offers help in a different way that might be of use to certain students. Have students:

- *Read the headings and subheadings as questions:* If the section is titled, "Smoking: The History of a Habit," the student asks himself why people have smoked across time and why the reasons might have changed.
- *Ask the essential questions:* While reading, the student asks herself, the author, or those discussed in the textbook the same questions all reporters and writers use: why, how, who, what, when, and the one that will push her to a deeper level of reading—so what?

- *Read the paragraph and its parts:* Textbook prose makes up in organization what it lacks in style. Each paragraph is rigidly organized in a hierarchical structure, with the topic sentence at or near the beginning (or at the end) of the paragraph. The topic sentence is followed by supporting examples and details used to illustrate the idea being described. Show students how the paragraphs work—that is, put up examples to discuss and deconstruct on the overhead—so they can see how to read through a chapter by skimming for initial details at the topic-sentence level.

- *Study the graphic organizers:* Different organizers help students read more closely, but their effectiveness depends on the type of text and the reason students are reading it. See the comparison Web site for printable versions.

- *Take notes:* Several systems are commonly used, but I favor the Cornell system, which allows for different uses. The student can create, for example, a three-column Cornell page that allows him to keep his notes from the textbook and the class discussion on the same page, with a third column for key connections between them or other such notes.

WEB SITE

You can find many different "Tools for Thought" designed to help students read more critically and take better notes on my Web site at <www.englishcompanion>.

- *Make annotations:* Few people have their own textbooks to mark up, so there are two other ways to help students read closely: Post-it Notes and photocopied passages. Post-its are more useful as a personal annotation strategy for students; actually annotating a photocopied page and then anchoring the class or group discussion in that selection of the text is, however, very useful and educative. It allows you and the students to examine design elements (of the page, its paragraphs, the argument being put forward), identify and discuss main ideas, or conduct a stylistic analysis of a literary work or primary source document.

- *Create outlines:* Students can be taught to outline for various purposes and in different ways. I don't advocate overfocusing on the actual format—"Sara! This should be (1) *not* (a)!"—but instead emphasize the use of such structure in their thinking. Some may find it more useful to make outlines while they read, while others benefit from making the outlines after they read in order to see the relationships between all the different parts. No doubt there are other ways, too; all are valid so long as the outline helps them impose order on the text they are trying to read.

Strategies are crucial if students are to read a textbook effectively, but they are only part of the puzzle. Once students know *how* to read the text at hand, there remains the daunting question of *why* they are reading it in the first place. Arthur Applebee (1996) writes in *Curriculum as Conversation* that "our traditions of teaching and learning must be transformed so that students can learn to enter into the ongoing conversations that incorporate our past and shape our future." A range of studies (Applebee 1996; Lapp, Flood, and Farnan 1996) support the use of textbooks as tools for active learning as opposed to teaching (i.e., passive learning via reading and answering questions about that reading). Such instruction demonstrates the power of curriculum as conversation that Applebee discusses, using the textbook and other supplementary materials to help students in their role as scientists, mathematicians, historians, or authors to answer the questions the course is asking.

> **NOTE**
>
> **V**isit <http://cela.albany.edu/reports.htm> to read more of Applebee's work and to explore the rich resources available through the center for English Learning and Achievements site.

What does such active teaching and learning look like in the classroom? Here are a few examples:

- *Simulation:* In Frank Firpo's freshman World Civilization class, students are assigned roles based on readings from their textbook, which contains a rich supply of primary source documents. The simulation, which reenacts the Chinese Cultural Revolution, requires students to use the textbook to carry out their own assigned role but to study the documents relating to others' roles, too. The text is the primary source for all information needed to drive the simulation, and their performance in the simulation acts as a performance-based evaluation of their reading. Meanwhile, they are reading Amy Tan's novel *The Kitchen God's Wife,* along with assorted poems and nonfiction works, in their English class, thereby creating a rich intertextual weave between types of text, a range of ideas, and two curricular domains.

- *Write your own textbook:* Some years ago I read an article that suggested the best way to defeat the Cliffs Notes problem was to have students create their own. Instead of breaking down a novel into its components and having each student write up one chapter, divide, conquer, and master the textbook by having students become experts in sections that they must write for and present to the class.

> **NOTE**
>
> **S**ee my own digital textbook *The Weekly Reader* online at <www. englishcompanion.com>.

- *Create your own guidebook:* This is similar to the previous assignment except that the students are creating their own teacher's guide to supplement and support the text. This keeps them anchored in the text itself but provides a critical perspective from which to view and interact with the text.

- *Publish a review:* This idea comes from the prestigious student publication *The Concord Review* (<http://www.tcr.org>), which features scholarly articles about a wide range of historical subjects. It is the only quarterly journal in the world that publishes the academic work of secondary students. Certainly in this era of online publishing, others can break new ground with student writing that simultaneously challenges students to read more closely those subjects about which they are writing.

- *Design a project:* Students in my junior English class participate in the American Studies Project each year, using ScottForesman's interdisciplinary textbook *An American Studies Album* (1995). They use the book as a sourcebook for ideas, examples, and guidance. As part of this unit I show them how to *use* (as opposed to *read*) a book when doing such investigations, then support these reading skills by having them read several self-selected documents from the book. This project, which asks them to come up with an essential conversation about our country and its culture, incorporates a range of types of text but anchors itself in the textbook as a tool to guide them and a common reference point from which we can operate as a class of thirty-five different people going in as many different directions.

WEB SITE

See the book's companion Web site for samples of such assignments as the American Studies Project.

Such approaches help us see what Applebee (1996) means by "curriculum as conversation":

> If curriculum is approached in terms of the significant conversations into which students are to enter, on the other hand, the emphasis from the beginning will be on knowledge-in-action. This in turn will lead to assessments that place their emphasis on students' developing abilities to enter into such conversations. Only at this point, with new approaches to curriculum driving new emphases in assessment, will we have created a unified system of curriculum and instruction, working together to help students enter into the rich traditions of knowledge-in-action that should be available to them as members of our diverse world.

I am able to best understand my own role in the classroom if I think of myself as a designer and director of essential conversations the books helps us have. The textbook, in such a class, is merely one among many tools at my disposal and, through our different uses of the book, I hope students learn to see it the same way. I like to envision the students coming to their biology textbook able to read it as a scientist would, bringing scrutiny and skepticism to both the textbook itself and the subject they are studying. Through such profound textual encounters, which strive to develop reading capacity and intrinsic engagement with the material, we can help students design or compile the text by which they themselves will continue to make sense of the world long after they have left our classes.

NOTE

Standards Connection: Since this chapter focuses on textbooks but not a specific subject, I thought it most appropriate to provide a synopsis of reading standards from all curricular areas. These standards are included in Appendix D. For more information on standards, visit the Mid-Continent Regional Education Laboratory at <www.mcrel.org>.

Closing Thoughts

Any class, by asking the student to inhabit for a time the mind and habits of a practitioner in that field, can succeed only if we develop in students the stamina to work through the inevitable complexities of any subject—ideas and people that can never, ever be reduced to three simple paragraphs. It is this simplification of our world, its reduction down to the smallest bits that must be "covered," that threatens students' reading of our subject areas. The pretense of clarity offered by such synopses robs our students of the chance to experience the very mystery that drew us into the study of our subject in the first place. Textbooks are about answers, whereas learning is at least as much about the questions we can never completely answer.

This is why we must constantly bring into the classroom our own passion for our subject, incorporating into such discussions references to the powerful writing that excites us as well as the opportunity for students to read it. No one ever, to paraphrase Thoreau, dated the change in his life from that day when he first read a textbook, but many a person can point to the day she read a Loren Eisely essay or a Stephen Gould book, heard a Feynman lecture, or even read Thoreau himself. No standard ten-pound history or science textbook can ever achieve the warmth, the voice, the power of James Burke in his book *Connections* (1995), which expands Applebee's ideas to something like civilization as conversation:

> Ordinary people have often made the difference. A self-educated Scottish mechanic once made a minor adjustment to a steam pump and triggered the whole Industrial Revolution. A nineteenth-century weatherman developed a cloud-making device

that just happened to reveal to Ernest Rutherford, a physicist he knew, that the atom could be split. Thanks to a guy working on hydraulic pressure in Italian Renaissance water gardens we have the combustion engine . . . This is because there's no grand design to the way history goes. The process does not fall neatly into categories such as those we are taught in school.

If Mrs. Koe, my beloved high school history teacher, could have brought such a sense of mystery and such powerful questions into our midst, I would have worn that red flag on my forehead as a sign of pride and membership in her class. Such dynamic inquiries as I have discussed in this chapter are based on the fact that we learn through our experiences and encounters with strong ideas—real ideas—not through books themselves. In *Complexity: The Emerging Science at the Edge of Order and Science*, M. Mitchell Waldrop (1992) writes of how he spent time in the community of scientists and thinkers from other domains in Santa Fe and found that what they all share in common is a problem—or a series of problems—with which they are entirely engaged, a problem that will help them better understand their place in the universe. Exposing themselves to the complexity of the real world, learning how to navigate their way through it in their quest to make sense of the world, only inspires and further engages them. How much better to imagine our students plugging into the great conversations of our disciplines, the ones that keep us coming back every day in hopes of infecting our students with the same fascination we continue to find nestled within the mystery and complexity that is our world, ourselves. As Kristen Schleicher wrote in her prize-winning essay about her obsolete chemistry book, "The students of today build the future of tomorrow—surely they ought to learn what tomorrow might have in store."

Further Studies

Kobrin, David. 1996. *Beyond the Textbook: Teaching History Using Documents and Primary Sources*. Portsmouth, NH: Heineman.

Kress, Gunther, and Theo van Leeuwen. 1998. *Reading Images: The Grammar of Visual Design*. London: Routledge.

National Archives and Record Administration and National Council of Social Studies. 1989. *Teaching with Documents: Using Primary Sources from the National Archives*. Washington, D.C.: National Archives and Record Administration and National Council of Social Studies.

Reading a Test

Two of my most stressful testing experiences have occurred in the Department of Motor Vehicles. The first, when I was sixteen, happened while I was doing the actual driving portion of the test: I almost got us in a wreck. Out of the corner of my eye I saw the evaluator's hand checking boxes as fast as he could. "Is there any reason to continue to test?" I asked. "Not really, son," he answered, and so I began the long drive back to the DMV.

The second incident happened when I took the written portion of the test. I had just returned home after serving in the Peace Corps in Tunisia for two years. I had not driven for two years, but somehow managed to make my way to the DMV. Forty miles per hour had never felt so fast. I breezed through the paper test confidently, handing it to the nice man at the window when I was done.

"You missed seven answers, son. You can only miss five," he explained, watching me. I was visibly disappointed; to not be able to drive was like not being admitted back into my own country. I felt like customs was telling me to go back to the desert and saddle up my camel. Then he asked me a question I could not believe.

"If I asked you what the right answer for number 3 was [and here he read the question], what would you say?" He gave me a sheepish look.

"B?" I offered.

"Good!" he said, then winked. "What about number 10, what would you say if you could answer that again?"

"C?" I guessed, looking at him with wonder.

"Excuse me?" he said, casting a wary eye.

"A?" I tried.

"Excellent, Mr. Burke! You passed your test. Now go have a nice day."

Introduction to Testing: Please Use a Number Two Pencil

NOTE

Skimming through the test would give you all the information you need to answer question 1 successfully.

Instead of describing the different types of tests students must be able to read and take successfully, I will give you examples of each type and include in the test itself useful information. The answers for the test follow.

1. Circle the most commonly taught types of tests listed below:

   a. Multiple-choice

   b. Short-answer (aka fill-in)

   c. True/false

   d. Matching

   e. Essay

   f. All of the above

2. Which of the following best describes the Advanced Placement exam:

   a. Norm-referenced

   b. Criterion-referenced

   c. Performance-based

   d. Standards-based

   e. All of the above

3. Match the following items in the left column with those that appear in the right column:

   a. Performance-based   1. SAT

   b. Criterion-referenced   2. AP exam

   c. Norm-referenced   3. Driver's test

   d. Standardized   4. Exhibition of learning

4. True/False: Circle T (True) or F (False) for each of the following statements:

   a. T   F   The purpose of norm-referenced tests is to differentiate between individuals.

   b. T   F   A student score of 630 on the SAT is the same as a score of 590 on the same test.

   c. T   F   Miranda's first-grade reading score placed her in the fifty-fourth percentile. In second grade, she also scored in the fifty-fourth percentile, despite intense efforts to improve her reading. Her reading skills as measured by the test have not improved at all between first and second grade.

   d. T   F   The goal of a norm-referenced test is to make it impossible for everyone to pass.

   e. T   F   The DMV driving test is a perfect example of a criterion-referenced test.

   f. T   F   Norm-referenced tests are designed so that 50 percent of the national sample of test takers score below the midpoint, which is defined as grade level.

5. Essay: Write a short essay in which you explain the meaning and discuss the implications of the following statement as it relates to educational testing: "A pig won't get fatter just because you weigh it more often."

6. Short-Answer: Essay tests are considered the most cognitively challenging tests because _____.

7. Short-Answer: Culture and experience can dramatically affect students' performance on standardized tests because _____.

NOTE

The answers to the test questions are as follows:

1. f
2. a
3. a–4; b–3; c–1; d–2
4. T, T, F, T, T, T
5. No specific answer
6. They ask students to synthesize an array of information and, through their writing, construct meaning and demonstrate understanding.
7. They provide background knowledge and skills that help students succeed on such tests.

The Politics of Testing

This chapter is not specifically about standardized testing, though the current focus on such high-stakes tests is partly responsible for the inclusion of this chapter. In California, as I write this chapter, principals of some schools are told if their scores do not go up by year's end they will lose their jobs or their schools will be reconstituted. The freshmen in my classes this year will be the first generation that must pass the new California High School Exit Exam (HSEE) by 2004 to graduate from high school. Such high-stakes tests grow more common each year. This is not a book about the politics of testing, so such issues of equity, bias, or justice will only receive superficial treatment here. I will, however, take this brief moment to emphasize that standardized, norm-referenced tests typically favor:

- Children who speak Standard English, while undermining the success of students with linguistic differences, especially English-language learners

- Children from upper- and middle-class socioeconomic households due, in part, to greater access to opportunities to learn what they must to succeed on such tests

- Children with conventional thinking patterns, not those who are more reflective or creative in their thinking

- Quick thinkers who are able to process loads of information, all of it in print, under the pressure of time and the threat of serious consequences

NOTE

For more information on the politics of testing, visit <www.fairtest.org> Also go to <www.reading.org> to read the International Reading Association's "High-Stakes Assessments in Reading: A Position Statement on the International Reading Association." Finally, read Alfie Kohn's book *The Case Against Standardized Testing* (2000).

Moreover, in the increasingly competitive climate such standardized tests foster, students now find other decisions being made based on their performance on these and other tests. Tests are being used more and more to:

- Sort students into different programs and placements

- Determine which students will and won't be accepted into schools and programs, since lower scores might damage a school's reputation

- Evaluate students', teachers', schools', and programs' performances as measured by pre- and post-scores

One direct and tragic consequence of this expanded emphasis on testing is the narrowing of the curriculum, a trend that also means diminished learning for too many kids who need a rich curriculum as badly as they need improved skills. There are many other consequences to such testing, but another one that merits mention is the extent to which such a test-driven curriculum undermines the role and the integrity of teachers and the curricula of meaning they strive to teach their students.

Testing Knowledge: Background and Considerations

Even as I wrote the previous sample questions, I realized how complicated the language of tests is. Every misstep could confuse a student and thus lower his score, which proves the point this chapter tries to make: students cannot score well on the many tests they take if they do not know how to read these types of texts. Calkins et al. (1998) write, "just as teachers needed to become familiar with the format of the tests their students were taking, so, too, the children needed to get to know the tests very well in order to avoid certain pitfalls." Am I saying we should shelve the curriculum of meaning in exchange for the SAT test booklet or the state test? No! But students' lives and our own professional practices are increasingly judged according to these scores. By ignoring tests, we endanger our students who must be able to take these tests to get jobs, go to college, or even graduate from high school.

The purpose of this chapter is to raise our awareness about the elements of such evaluative texts. By teaching students how to read the design and the language of tests, we can help them master this particular genre. One of the first obstacles to any discussion of tests is the vocabulary of testing, so let me take a minute to define some core terms. These definitions all come from *A Teacher's Guide to Standardized Reading Tests: Knowledge Is Power* (Calkins et al. 1998):

- *Bias:* A lack of objectivity, fairness, or impartiality on the part of the assessment instrument that leads to misinterpretation of student performance or knowledge.

- *Criterion-referenced test:* Test that provides information about test takers' performance relative to a set of criteria. Test items are selected and scored to demonstrate test takers' proficiencies in relation to the criteria.

- *Norming group:* A sample of test takers who represent those for whom a test is constructed. The sample should represent the different geographic, socioeconomic, racial/ethnic, and linguistic backgrounds of the test taker population in the nation.

- *Norm-referenced test:* Test that provides information about how test takers' performance compares to the performance of a representative national sample of the test takers. Test items are selected and scored to demonstrate test takers' proficiencies in relation to each other.

- *Percentile:* A test taker's standing in relation to others. For example, if a test taker scored 5 points out of 10 and 50 percent of those who took the test achieved above that score, the test taker would be in the 50th percentile.

- *Performance assessment:* A way for students to demonstrate what they know and can do by applying their knowledge and skills in tasks that require them to construct their own responses, create their own products, or perform demonstrations such as writing essays, completing science experiments, solving mathematical problems, and so on.

- *Standardized test:* A set of predetermined questions and/or tasks administered in a uniform manner to all who take it.

Another vocabulary issue, however, involves those words specific to each subject area—for example, *sum, tone, force, civil*—that students must know if they are to succeed on the test. The implications of this are obvious: we must be sure to use the language of our discipline—to teach students the vocabulary of that discipline—if our students are to learn those words and be able to understand their use on a test. A student who does not know the phrase *organizational structure* has no hope of answering a question on the language arts portion of the state exam that asks him to identify the best description for the organizational structure used in the essay.

Readers of tests must do the same things readers of other types of texts do if they are to understand what a test says or asks. They must:

- Ask questions of themselves, the teacher, and the text(s) they are being tested on, then use the answers to these questions to help them identify the important information and the correct answer.

- Marshall their energy and focus their attention on the text despite the fact that it may not be engaging to them.

- Prepare to read it by asking themselves what they need to know and be able to do to read this text successfully.

- Prioritize how to read it by determining what is most important.

- Read the language of the test questions and answers for denotative and connotative meanings, just as they would a poem, attending to the subtle nuances of grammar and semantics that can alter the meaning of the question or the answer.

- Skim and scan to find information they can use to answer the current question or other questions they encounter along the way.

- Use a variety of strategies to help them discern not only what the text is about but what the correct answer is.

Of course, there are important differences between reading tests and reading all the other types of text discussed throughout this book. Namely, the others do not generally cause stress or threaten the reader with possible consequences such as not graduating from high school or continuing to the next grade level.

Before the Test

It is not the purpose of this book to discuss in detail those study skills that can help improve test performance, but the following tips offer a useful guide to teachers, who can pass them on to students through discussions, assignments, and written reminders on the classroom walls. I offer them here as prereading activities.

> **S**tudents and teachers preparing for standardized tests can often find sample questions and other resources online, usually provided by the test publisher or the state department of education.

NOTE

- *Ask what will be on the test.* Though this is a simple and obvious question, many students take a passive stance, assuming the teacher won't give any information about this. If the teacher won't offer any help, students should seek out other students who may have had that teacher. They are gathering background knowledge that they can use to help them read with greater insight and power.

- *Draft sample questions.* While studying, students should write up their own test questions about the material they think—or know—will be on the exam. Students should pay close attention to the phrasing they use and what information they choose as most important. This is what reading specialists call making predictions and speculating about the text ahead; this strategy activates students' schema about how a test works and how they must think when taking it. After each test is over, students should make some notes about the types of questions on it and where the teacher found the information (e.g., subheaders, study questions at the end of chapters) and evaluate where their questions went wrong. This quick assessment of their predictions and the teacher's tests will help them do better next time. Teachers committed to helping students improve their reading (and performance) on tests might make room before the test for students to use their practice questions to facilitate a discussion. This would have the added advantage of allowing the teacher to evaluate students' knowledge prior to the exam.

- *Identify the words to know.* Even if the test itself won't have vocabulary words on it, the questions will include terms students need to know if they are to read and answer them successfully. Students should review their notes and identify those terms most likely to be on the test, then be sure they know the terms and how they might be used on the test. Other places to find such words are in margins, in bold-faced text throughout the chapter, and in chapter overview sections.

- *Review past tests.* If students have taken other tests with this teacher, they can review their past tests to see which questions they missed. They should look for a pattern to their mistakes: Is there something specific they can point to that explains their errors? Do they notice a pattern to the types of questions the teacher asks or the way the questions are phrased? For example, are the questions always drawn from chapter subheadings, end-of-chapter study questions, or bold-faced words? When thinking of the test they will take, students should brainstorm all the possible ways a particular question could be phrased, write these out, and, after examining the key words and possible confusions, rehearse their responses to the questions. They might also consider meeting with other classmates to pool their questions and discuss possible answers.

- *Use all available resources.* Students should ask the teacher or their classmates whether there are study guides, past tests, or online resources that might help them prepare for this test. They can consult their study group, classmates, and, of course, their teacher about content they cannot figure out themselves but know will be on the test.

- *Relax and be ready.* Few factors undermine test performance more than stress, which is often the consequence of either not being prepared or not getting enough sleep. Most teenagers these days are sleep deprived and few consider the importance of eating well before a big test.

Teachers can also help students by providing them with an environment conducive to success. Emotionally, they need to feel secure, relaxed, and supported when taking any kind of test. Physically, they need to be warm, have a comfortable and appropriate seating arrangement, and be well fed, rested, and free of any unnecessary distractions. Intellectually, they must be prepared and know how the test works. Materially, they need access to any supplies necessary for success on the test (pencils, calculators, dictionaries, rulers). Finally, they need to believe the test matters; this means teachers must not speak against the test, use it as an occasion to share their political views on standardized testing, or scare the students by talking about consequences of not doing well.

NOTE

What can you do while students take the test? Opinions differ, but some teachers write up reminders of the amount of time left and some remind students of strategies they have practiced and things to look out for. This is particularly appropriate if the teacher views the current test as an authentic assessment of students' testing skills. Other reminders include telling them to check their answer sheets for any unanswered questions, revisit the directions, and review their answers, especially those they marked as difficult and intended to return to if they had extra time.

Elements of a Test

Before we look at what to do during a test, let's take a minute to look at the form and the function of a test and how the effective reader must read these elements. A test is composed of some or all of the following elements, each of which serves a purpose and can, if misread, alter the perceived meaning of the question and thus cost the reader.

- Answers
- Answer sheet
- Content
- Directions
- Formatting
- Notes
- Passages
- Purpose
- Questions
- Rules
- Samples
- Sections
- Sequencing
- Symbols
- Test booklet
- Typography

Each of these elements can influence how the reader approaches or interprets the text. The student who thinks the directions are meaningless misses their second purpose: to orient the test taker regarding a particular set of questions. Such inattentive reading costs students information that, while not crucial, can prove useful. Related to this problem is the students' knowledge of how a particular test will be scored. On standardized reading tests, for example, students must realize that every answer translates into a score; in other words, though there may be one most-right answer, every other answer is ranked to reveal the degree of reading comprehension the student has reached. Therefore, strategies such as elimination are essential in such circumstances. Still other students get lost in the directions themselves as they encounter words that seem to exist only on tests and thus stand between the reader and her success on the test. Consider the following words, developed by Sharon Cook (1999), which are likely to appear on or relate to the content of an objective language arts test. I have organized them into four groups here.

ACTIONS
- Compare/contrast
- Classified/classification
- Conclude
- Determine
- Draw conclusions
- Identify
- Interpret
- Outline
- Predicting outcomes
- Proofread
- Strategy
- Summarize
- Support (facts to support a conclusion)

ASPECTS
- Accurate
- Assumes
- Author's purpose/attitude
- Combined
- Consist mostly of . . .
- Correct
- Described
- Discrete questions (versus a series of linked questions)
- Events
- Except
- Main idea
- Mistake
- Multiple meaning
- Occur
- Organization(al)
- Passage
- Pattern

- Prior knowledge
- Purpose
- Refers (to)/referred (to)
- Section
- Sentence structure
- Sequence
- Topic sentence
- Underlined

TYPES
- Article
- Chart
- Dialogue
- Essay
- Fiction
- Notice (as in advertisement)
- Paragraph

CONTENT
- Capitalization
- Conflict
- Literary device
- Mood
- Opinion
- Phrase
- Plot
- Prefix
- Punctuation
- Quotation marks
- Setting
- Suffix
- Theme
- Title
- Viewpoint
- Word usage

Such a list only touches the surface of the demands on a reader of a test. Not only must the reader make sense of the way words are used—denotative versus connotative meanings that bring the tricky ambiguities into the test—but he must note the type of words used. Consider how the following types of words function within a test to clarify or confuse the reader:

- *Ambiguous words:* The selective use of ambiguous words in tests trips up many students. Ambiguity is often caused as much by the words used as by those left out. A good example of such ambiguity is the following sample question from the beginning of the chapter: "A student score of 630 on the SAT is the same as a score of 590 on the same test." This sentence is true, but you can get it right only if you know that the scores are considered the same because they both appear in the same statistical band and thus show no statistically significant difference. Asking students how it could be true would generate an educative discussion about reading appropriate to a math class at any level.

- *Antecedent words:* Looking at the antecedents and articles can often yield useful information. If the question says, "This procedure requires that you use *an . . . ,*" the answer will begin with a vowel. Other grammatical clues include looking for subject-verb agreement, a tip especially helpful on fill-in tests.

- *Directive words:* These words are especially important on an essay exam because they provide specific directions. The rubric for a particular test might say, for example, "Extent to which the writer accurately *defines* the problem." If students *evaluated* the problem, they might be off topic and thus get penalized. Directive words include *define, compare, contrast, explain, describe, evaluate, list, identify, summarize, interpret, differentiate, review, outline, prove, analyze.*

- *Procedural words:* These words might appear in the directions or the teacher's discussion of the test. They include words like *rubric* and *standard, DBQ* and *procedure.*

- *Quantitative words:* These include *always, most, never, equal, sometimes, usually, almost, often, all, none.* In *How to Study in College,* Walter Pauk (1997) organizes these qualifiers into what he calls "families" that form a continuum Pauk argues is useful for true/false and multiple-choice questions:

  - All, most, some, none (no)
  - Always, usually, sometimes, never
  - Good, bad
  - Great, much, little, no
  - Is, is not
  - More, equal, less

- *Technical words:* These are specific subject matter words students must know to read the test successfully. They may be words like *adjective* and *linear equation, acceleration* and *trend*. Note the range of possible uses for the last two words; students need to know what *acceleration* means in a physics class and also in a health class.

Aside from the language used in the tests, which provides one of the most serious challenges to readers of tests, tests come in all sizes and shapes. These characteristics—such as the length of the test, the number of questions, and the types of questions—pose serious threats to the untrained reader, who may not know how to pace himself or where to direct his attention. Standardized reading tests, for example, include a range of types of questions on them, each with its own demands on the reader and none of which makes inherent sense to most readers under the pressure of the clock. For example:

- Short passages without any larger context, followed by short questions about the passage
- Longer passages, sometimes complete, followed by questions about the passage
- Passages of varying length, followed by a random combination of multiple-choice and fill-in questions

These questions might ask the reader to examine the passage for information about grammar and syntax as well as style and character development. Some questions might focus on basic details such as the name of a person, while the next one tries to integrate analytical thinking that demands the student return to the text for further reading. On the California High School Exit Exam, for example, students will need to read each passage as many as three times: once to answer questions about language usage and word meaning; a second time to answer comprehension questions; and, for many, a third time to help them respond to the writing prompt that is based on the reading passage.

The final elements worth discussing are those conventions or rules that govern how we take the test and thus how we can read it. Usually these conventions are spelled out in the directions, but not always. These might include whether or not a dictionary is permitted or the student can make notes on the test itself to help her train her attention on the key words or specific details. These and the other elements discussed previously pose less of a threat to the reader who is able to put on his test-taking persona. Just as I have discussed aesthetic and narrative thinking in other chapters, so there is what might be called testing intelligence, a way of thinking that involves reading the test closely using your own knowledge but also incorporating your knowledge about the people who made the test and the others who required it, all of which goes into helping you read the test more successfully. This is hardly different from the way one has to read Dickens: he wrote under certain conditions, with certain

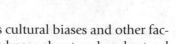

assumptions in mind, influenced by various cultural biases and other factors, and we can read his novels better if we know about and understand them. As Robert Scholes writes, "Where there are texts, of course, there are rules governing text production and interpretation" (1982).

Reading and Taking the Test

Remind students to use the following strategies while taking the test.

- *Skim and scan.* Depending on how much time students have for the test, they should flip through to get a sense of the terrain: number and type of questions, what's easy, what's hard. This will orient them and allow them to prioritize their time and attention.

- *Do the easy questions first.* As with pick-up sticks, students get just as much credit for the easy ones as the hard ones. After skimming through the test, students should knock out the ones they know so they have the time they need to read the others more closely. This will also activate students' background knowledge, thus making it more likely they can figure out the harder questions.

- *Read all the possible answers first before choosing one.* Test makers depend on inattentive readers to make mistakes that conscientious readers will not. Even if students see the answer they know is right, they should remind themselves to read through all answers to make sure there is no surprise hiding in the other options (e.g., "All of the above").

- *Eliminate the wrong answers.* If they don't see the obvious answer, students can work backward by ruling out those that cannot be right.

- *Paraphrase the question.* Students can put questions in their own words to help them better understand what the questions are asking.

- *Watch out for traps.* Some tests use the word *not* to trip students up; they need to learn to stop and ask themselves what the question is really asking. They should be wary of choosing answers that include information from the passage, especially on standardized tests. Instead, they should look for questions that answer the question. Calkins et al. (1998) illustrate this trick by describing a boy who chose the first answer he read about something that happened in the story without considering if it was, as the question asked, the last event in the story.

- *Try to answer the question before looking at the answers.* Paired with the previous strategy, this method gets students primed to know the answer when they see it; if they have already determined the answer in their heads, they know what to look for when they check the possible answers.

- *Read recursively.* Good readers frequently and habitually circle back around to check what they are reading and thinking against what they have already read to see that they agree. This habit also keeps them attentive to what they are supposed to be doing. On an essay test, for example, after reading and underlining the key words in the directions, students should pause periodically to reread the directions. This will help them measure the extent to which they are answering the question; it might also provide useful information to spark new ideas for their essays.

- *Read the test answers out loud in your head.* This sounds like a contradiction, but if students are taking a test that demands they find errors (e.g., a standardized exam that asks them to correct sentences), this technique can really help students. Developing and listening to the different voices we use when we read can dramatically improve students' ability to read any type of text in any situation.

- *Read the answer sheet.* Students need to make sure they know how it works. A group of students in my honors English class neglected to do this and they scored a –2.6 on the reading test. We calculated this to mean they were reading at the level of a fetus in its second month. They ignored a crucial direction on the answer sheet and consequently, all their answers were out of sequence.

- *Answer in the order that works best for you.* Students should work through the test in the order that makes most sense to them and will help them read it best. If reading the multiple-choice and fill-in questions will help remind them of all they should address in their essay, so be it. One important point, however: they must use some sort of system to indicate which questions they still have to answer and be sure to erase any such marks before turning in the test.

After the Test

Students are so glad the test is over that they often forget to reflect on what the experience can teach them. Taking the test is only one part of the useful, intelligent assessment process; reflecting on their performance and discussing which parts of the test gave them trouble and how they overcame those difficulties are other valid teaching moments. Of course, what happens after a test depends also on what type of test it was and what it was assessing.

Regardless of the type of test, however, there are a few things students and teachers should consider doing:

- *Get as much information as possible about students' performance.* For both teachers and students, information about how students did—where they performed well, where they did not—is crucial to their success in the future. Think of the major league athlete: whether he strikes out or hits a home run, his first thought is (or should be) "What happened?" followed by "How can I do that (or avoid doing that) again next time?"

- *Identify the problems they had and determine the causes.* Students should sit down right after completing any test (or even a quiz) and figure out where they had trouble and how they worked through that difficulty. If you have time and it is appropriate, encourage your students to discuss the strategies they used to take the test. Solicit examples of types of questions that stumped people and compare how they and others solved those problems and overcame their confusion. You might even have them put up sample questions on an overhead and do a think-aloud about how they solved it. Such assessment discussions provide insight into the reading process in general and test-taking strategies in particular.

- *Allow students to discuss how they felt about the test.* Kids who hate tests and those who don't do well on tests need to be able to express their feelings, but they also need to hear and be reminded that there are others who really like taking tests, who respond to the challenge. The students who dislike tests must realize they are, in certain ways, in competition with these others, if not now, then years later when they are one of a hundred applicants for a position.

Questions to Ask

Many of the following questions are metacognitive questions that ask readers to evaluate why they know what they know. Such habits of mind help readers generalize their reading skills to other texts, including other types of tests in other classes. In this way, such questions and the habit of asking them when they read help readers develop their test-taking capacity and competence. They know they need to ask questions when they read and, through discussion and practice, learn which ones to ask when reading a particular text.

- Why is that the best answer?
- Why did I not choose that answer?
- How did I arrive at this answer?
- Is this answer based on my experience and opinion, or is it based on information found in the text on which I'm being tested?
- Where else can I look for this information (e.g., another section of the test?)
- What does that word mean in this context?
- What does the rubric or other scoring guide suggest I need to understand or look for in this question?
- What is the most important thing to attend to (prioritize)?
- What is this actually trying to test?
- Is it better to guess or to leave it blank?

Classroom Connection

Many of the following strategies are already a part of your curriculum. We have students read for meaning, find supporting details, annotate texts, and summarize what they read all the time. I'm asking you to extend that range of techniques to include the reading of tests as one more type of text. The following list of types of questions, while overlapping in places, provides a set of cognitive abilities we all agree our students need to possess if they are to be powerful readers:

- *Analytical* (Explain the causes of World War II as they relate to America's decision to enter the war.)
- *Authorial intention* (What was the writer trying to say about early America through his depiction of people in this story?)
- *Categorical* (Which of the following genres best describes this passage?)
- *Cause and effect* (Identify the main causes of the Great Depression.)
- *Comparative* (*X* and *Y* are similar in that they both . . .)
- *Connotative* (What does the word *essence* mean based on the author's use of it in the previous sentence?)
- *Definition* (Which of the following best defines the word *antiquated*?)
- *Evaluative* (Why is *A* the best solution for *B*?)
- *Identification* (Identify all of the verbs in the following passage.)
- *Inferential* (Based on his actions, how does this character feel about his father?)
- *Perspective* (How does the writer feel about this subject?)
- *Purpose* (Which of the following best describes the author's purpose: to inform, to persuade, to entertain, or to explain?)
- *Sequential/logical* (What is the proper sequence for the following images?)
- *Speculative* (If you read on, which of the following outcomes would you expect?)
- *Synthesis* (After reading this story, what do you think would be the best title and why?)

Standards Connection

The following standards for assessment of reading have more to do with how we assess than how kids read. But they are a useful gauge of how far we sometimes are from the real objective: using effective assessment to improve student performance. Consider these assessment standards:

- The interests of the student are paramount in assessment.
- The primary purpose of assessment is to improve teaching and learning.

- Assessment must reflect and allow for critical inquiry into curriculum and instruction.
- Assessments must recognize and reflect the intellectually and socially complex nature of reading and writing and the important roles of school, home, and society in literacy development.
- Assessment must be fair and equitable.
- The consequences of an assessment procedure are the first, and most important, consideration in establishing the validity of the assessment.
- The teacher is the most important agent of assessment.
- The assessment process should involve multiple perspectives and sources of data.
- Assessment must be based in the school community.
- All members of the educational community—students, parents, teachers, administrators, policy makers, and the public—must have a voice in the development, interpretation, and reporting of assessment.
- Parents must be involved as active, essential participants in the assessment process. (from *Standards for the Assessment of Reading and Writing*, NCTE/IRA 1994)

Because these are not always achievable, we might look at the cross-curricular standards for further insight into the reading standards for this type of reading. Drawing from a range of standards, we might assume the following apply to the reading of tests:

- Students read to determine the validity of information.
- Students evaluate a variety of types of information before determining what is true or correct.
- Students explain their choices, drawing support for their thinking from inside the text.
- Students use a variety of strategies, including contextual clues, to help them understand the passages on the test.

Closing Thoughts

The man at the DMV brought to my test a humanity and sympathy we do not associate with testing. Moreover, he renegotiated the power between us by using it to help me, not hurt me. This is rare. I worry, as I close this chapter, that some will vehemently resist the idea of teaching kids how to read a test. They will resist it not because they think tests should not be given such a prominent place in the class, but precisely because tests have such a huge place in their class and serve a very specific purpose: to weed out, to scatter everyone along that elegant and immoral slope we call the bell curve. These teachers see tests as a means of exercising their power over students instead of developing in students the capacity to overpower the tests.

Tests are here to stay, though we can hope they will become more fair and more useful to all students. By developing and practicing their annotation skills, improving their reading pace and stamina (through constant reading of a variety of types of text), and learning to pace and focus themselves during such serious reading encounters, our students simply become better readers. These same skills, so necessary in all areas of reading, prove very useful when students take tests also, it so happens.

On a deeper, more personal level, I must affirm the value of knowing how to take tests well, though again that does not imply that we should turn our classes into test-prep sessions. My father dropped out of high school and got a job with the Office of State Printing, where, through a series of tests available to everyone, he climbed the ladder of success. Finally, the only position above his was one appointed by the governor. In the meantime, my father provided for his family with increasing ease and greater comfort thanks to his capacity to take tests. This is what the real world is like for many people; if our students are not ultimately able to master these tests down the line, can we say we ourselves passed the test as teachers? Please limit your response to this question to no more than five hundred words. When you are done, you may close your booklet and turn in your pencil.

Further Studies

Berger, Larry, Michael Colton, Joe Jewell, Manek Mistry, and Paul Rossi. 2000. *Up Your Score: The Underground Guide to the SAT.* New York, NY: Workman.

Calkins, Lucy, Kate Montgomery, and Donna Santman, with Beverly Falk. 1998. *A Teacher's Guide to Standardized Reading Tests: Knowledge Is Power.* Portsmouth, NH: Heinemann.

Falk, Beverly. 2000. *The Heart of the Matter: Using Standards and Assessment to Learn.* Portsmouth, NH: Heinemann.

5

Reading
Literature

*Why was it, I wondered, that I was most passionate talking
about books I had loved? . . . Those books honored me; those
books changed me. Alone, the greatest writers would sit with me
and, in their own voices, tell me everything there was to know
about the world.*

—Pat Conroy, from *The Prince of Tides*

*"And what are you reading, Miss—?" "Oh! It is only a novel!"
replies the young lady, while she lays down her book with
affected indifference, or momentary shame. "It is only Cecilia,
or Camilla, or Belinda"; or, in short, only some work in which
the greatest powers of the mind are displayed, in which the most
thorough knowledge of human nature, the happiest delineation
of its varieties, the liveliest effusions of wit and humour, are
conveyed to the world in the best-chosen language. Now, had
the same young lady been engaged with a volume of* The
Spectator, *instead of such a work, how proudly would she have
produced the book, and told its name; though the chances must
be against her being occupied by any part of that voluminous
publication, of which either the matter or manner would not
disgust a young person of taste: the substance of its papers so
often consisting in the statement of improbable circumstances,
unnatural characters, and topics of conversation which no
longer concern anyone living; and their language, too,
frequently so coarse as to give no very favourable idea
of the age that could endure it.*

—Jane Austen, from *Northanger Abbey*

When I began writing this book questions like these followed me around:

- What does literature do for readers or require of them that other types of texts do not?
- What *is* literature in an era of increasingly blended texts (i.e., texts that incorporate multiple genres and media)?
- Is film *really* literature, and does it have a valid place in our curriculum?
- How best to describe an English teacher's job: To transmit the culture through a canon of texts? To teach kids a set of skills? To develop students' literary tastes?

Such questions and many others that continue to occur to me stem from the questions Robert Scholes asked in his article "Does English Matter?" in which he wrote:

> A discipline called English must help [students] prepare for unknown conditions. The best preparation we can give our students will be the highest level of competence as readers and writers, producers and consumers of the various texts they will encounter. (1998a)

Further on, Scholes asserts that "the future will belong to English departments wise enough to embrace rhetoric and the media themselves and to find ways of connecting these contemporary texts to their more traditional concerns." Scholes dismisses the long-standing tradition of literature as the sacred text, advocating instead for a canon of textual skills that will prepare students to be "textual animals," able to read anything that comes along.

Arthur Applebee asks us to consider the primary challenge to our field: what is the purpose of English and the teaching of literature in our society at this point? Applebee lobbies for "curriculum as conversation," for "the knowledge-in-action that is learned through participation in living traditions of knowing and doing" (1996). Such conversations as those discussed in Applebee's book and throughout this chapter result in the kind of learning Judith Langer (1999) found in classrooms that shared the following six features of effective instruction:

- Students learn skills and knowledge in multiple lesson types.
- Teachers integrate test preparation into instruction.
- Teachers make connections across instruction, curriculum, and life.
- Students learn strategies for doing the work.
- Students are expected to be generative thinkers.
- Classrooms foster cognitive collaboration.

I trust the collective wisdom of these three leaders within the profession, especially when placed alongside my experience in the classroom teaching kids of all ages and abilities. Theirs are the observations culled from a lifetime of doing and reflecting on the hard work of teaching. Others' observations only confirm the directions in which the world and our work are going and must continue to go. Marshall Gregory (1997), who like Scholes found himself meditating on what he knew after a lifetime of teaching English, concluded that English makes six contributions to student development:

1. The **literary content** of English contributes to students' intellectual development by giving them the ways and means of delving into the importance of story, and, through story, of having vicarious experiences of the human condition far vaster than any of them could ever acquire on the basis of luck and first-hand encounters.

2. **Cognitive skills** that support the critical reading of texts, the precise use of language, and the creation of sound arguments are not the exclusive property of the discipline of English, of course, but arguably such cognitive skills as analyzing, synthesizing, speaking, listening, writing, reading, evaluating, and appreciating are more consistently and comprehensively addressed by disciplinary studies in English than anywhere else.

3. **Aesthetic sensitivity** trains us to recognize and respond to art's dimension of mystery. By "dimension of mystery" I am referring to neither transcendence nor religion, but to the suggestiveness, emotiveness, and inexhaustible power that language can acquire when it is used as art.

4. **Intra- and intercultural awareness** is developed and enriched by studies in English which, thanks again to postmodernists, are no longer devoted so singlemindedly to the classics of Western literature as they once were. Interdisciplinary and nonwestern studies have made English a powerful discipline of cultural awareness.

5. **Ethical sensitivity** consists of two abilities. One is the ability to regulate conduct according to some principle of *the right thing*, however that may be construed by the individual. The other is the ability to *deliberate* about moral and ethical issues both in one's own head and in dialogue with other people.

6. **Existential maturity** refers to mature views about the human condition. I cannot fully define "maturity" because I am still learning what it consists of. But I do know what maturity is not. It is not self-centeredness, it is not unkindness, it is not pettiness, it is not petulance, it is not callousness to the suffering of others, it is not backbiting or violent competitiveness, it is not mean-spiritedness, it is not dogmatism or fanaticism, it is not a lack of self-control, it is not the inability ever to be detached or ironic, it is not the refusal to engage in give-and-take learning from others, and it is not the assumption that what we personally desire and value is what everyone else desires and values.

My point throughout this book, inspired by others' ideas, is that literature is, like all other texts, evolving in both its form and its function, and how and why we read it are negotiations students must learn to handle on their own as they not only participate in but create the essential conversations that lead to the development of their textual intelligence. Such textual intelligence must take into account not only a writer's use of metaphor and language but an artist's or a filmmaker's use of images. Mitchell Stephens, commenting on our societal resistance to reflection, wrote, "the increasing reliance on *images*, which began with photography and accelerated with film, certainly seems to have contributed to a decreasing concern with our inner lives and an increasing concern with *image*—with style, possessions and public relations, with surfaces and appearances, with what Coke commercials are selling" (1998). Kafka would no doubt prescribe a heavy dose of literature to cure this emptiness, arguing that we should "read only the kind of books that wound and stab us. We need books that affect us like a disaster, that grieve us deeply, like the death of someone we loved more than ourselves, like being banished into forests far from everyone . . . A book must be the axe for the frozen sea inside us" (1904).

Literature must then be used as a potentially subversive force, one that invites serious encounters with the people we are and think we want to be, with the people we know and those we do not. "Classroom texts should pose intellectual challenges to young readers," writes Carol Jago in *With Rigor for All: Teaching the Classics to Contemporary Students* (2000). Jago goes on to say "these texts should be books that will make students stronger readers—and stronger people." Such encounters with what Jago calls "enduring stories" challenge students to "critically revaluate [their] own assumptions and preoccupations" (Rosenblatt 1996).

An author challenges us through stories that may, to return to the theme of this book, appear on paper or on a screen, in a poem or in a film, both of which treat literary themes within the context of the essential conversations we all need to have. Louise Rosenblatt writes that "literature treats the whole range of choices and aspirations and values out of which the individual must weave his own personal philosophy. The literary works that students are urged to read offer not only 'literary' values . . . but also some approach to life, some image of people working out a common fate or some assertion that certain kinds of experiences, certain modes of feeling, are valuable" (1996).

But which texts to read? How to read them—and *why*? I believe we must ask a different question, one that makes room for excellence and choice, many voices and the few, such as Shakespeare, who merit a permanent place in whatever curricular conversations we have. That question is not which texts should students read but which conversations should they have and which texts, which voices will best support those essential conversations. Such conversations ultimately incorporate discussions of how stories work, why writers make the choices they do when it comes to narrative design, character development, plot, and so on. But these questions—and their answers—are useless if the student is not participating in the conversation, the one going on with the author and the characters, the past and the present, the students themselves and the classmates around them. And how will the students participate, what will the conversation be made of? Stories. As essayist Roger Rosenblatt wrote:

> Everything we do is a story: History, poetry, painting, sports, science, gossip, ourselves, of course. And it is a story told again and again. We tell the same stories over and over, of our strivings for heroism, for honor, for profit, for social progress, and understanding and sympathy and power—most of all, for love. In one way or another, every story is a love story. Boy meets girl. Boy meets boy. Boy and girl seek bliss.
>
> We yearn—how we yearn—for improvement. That's what evolution is all about—refinement, improvement. And evolution itself is a doozie of a story: Little animals beget bigger animals until one emerges with something to say. What do you have to tell me? What do I have to tell you? We stare at each other over the air of the years, and reach to tell the story of a lifetime.
>
> We did this thousands of years ago, and, with luck, we will do so thousands of years hence, millennium after millennium, once upon a time. (1999)

William Faulkner (1950) echoes Rosenblatt in his Nobel speech, saying the writer has "no room in his workshop for anything but the old verities and truths of the heart, the old universal truths lacking which any story is ephemeral and doomed—love and honor and pity and pride and compassion and sacrifice."

The rest of this chapter looks at why we tell these stories, how they are made, and how they work their magic, providing us the means with which to understand ourselves as characters in the story we call our life, and, if we learn enough, giving us the power to change, to revise our story in hopes of a better ending.

Types of Literature

We use the word *literature* recklessly. We are just as likely to call voting materials literature—saying, "No, I'm sorry, haven't decided who to vote for yet; I haven't read the literature yet"—as we are to call a poem literature. I have made a point of referring to the different types of readings as "texts" throughout this book. As Robert Scholes explains, "Our English word comes from the Latin verb *texere*, which meant specifically 'to weave,' and, by extension, 'to join or fit together anything; to plait, braid, interweave, interlace; to construct, make, fabricate, build.' From *texere* also comes *textum*, 'that which is woven, a web . . . ' " (1998). This sense of craft, of literature as something made, is further discussed in Edward Hirsch's *How to Read a Poem* (*and Fall in Love with Poetry*): "Poiesis means 'making' and, as the ancient Greeks recognized, the poet is first and foremost a maker . . . The word *poem* became English in the sixteenth century and it has been with us ever since to designate a form of fabrication, a type of composition, a made thing" (1999). Sometimes, to return to the earlier focus on literature as a conversation, we discuss how stories work within the larger and ongoing conversation about language and its effect on people, the way language—words and images—can be used to explain and persuade.

The point is that there are, in fact, different types of literature, each with its own forms and functions, purpose and place, and each one is made to suit the needs of the situation. Narrative design, Madison Smartt Bell (1998) argues, is "of first and final importance in any work of fiction," though I would not limit it to fiction, especially in light of the modern trend to apply novelistic techniques to nonfiction stories as in books like *Angela's Ashes* and *The Perfect Storm*.

These are, then, the texts I will classify as literature for the purposes of our discussion in this book:

- Epics
- Essays
- Fables
- Film
- Folktales
- Legends
- Myths
- Novels
- Plays (including monologues and other dramatic forms)
- Poetry
- Short fiction
- Speeches

This list invites us to return to the question of what kids read, how they read it, and why. The *California Language Arts Content Standards*, for example, requires students to "read and respond to historically or culturally significant works of literature that reflect and enhance their studies of history and social science" (California Department of Education 1999). While students need to read demanding texts to improve their reading abilities, it is not for this reason alone that we ask kids to read. We must build their capacities as readers even as we use these same books to support meaningful conversations that develop their capacities—for empathy, for insight, for reflection—as people. As Carol Jago wrote, "Today, as in 1901, to 'open their eyes to clearer vision and nourish and inspire their souls' is an enormous task. [We] need the work of giants in hand to help [us]" (2000).

NOTE

Visit the Pacesetter English Web site for a more thoroughly developed curricular model based on these ideas. Go to <www.collegeboard.com/pacesetter>.

What students read should not be limited to a single text. Rather, each text should be as a strand in some larger weave, contributing a unique voice or perspective to the larger narrative of the class. Such textual cross-fertilization should not be limited to perspective or culture, either; poetry, drama, film, nonfiction, and many other types of texts must be part of the weave.

In short, we should allow author, character, and students to talk to one another; we should help students transcend the boundaries imposed by the page or the screen. Consider the following sample sequence from my sophomore class, which was reading *All Quiet on the Western Front*:

NOVEL
- *All Quiet on the Western Front*, by Erich Marie Remarque

POEMS
- "Dulce et Decorum Est," by Winfred Owen
- "Facing It," by Yusef Komunyakaa
- "Five Ways to Kill a Man," by Edwin Brock

DIARIES
- From *Eye Witness to History*, edited by John Carey

LETTERS
- Excerpts from documentary *Civil War*
- Excerpts from documentary *Letters from Vietnam*
- Excerpts from *Letters of a Nation*, edited by Andrew Carroll

SPEECHES
- Franklin Delano Roosevelt's "We Have Nothing to Fear" speech and "Four Freedoms" speech

WEB SITE

To hear Roosevelt give the "Four Freedoms" speech and see the four paintings Normal Rockwell was inspired to paint, go to the companion Web site.

WEB SITES

- <www.ww1.org>
- <www.favoritepoem.org>
- <nara.gov>
- <www.loc.gov>

VIDEO (EXCERPTS)
- *Thin Red Line*
- Favoritepoem.org site for brief streaming video documentaries about Wilfred Owens's poem "Dulce et Decorum Est" and Yusef Komunyakaa's "Facing It"
- *Gallipoli*
- *Letters from Vietnam*

IMAGES
- "Art of Persuasion," online exhibit at the National Archives
- Vietnam Veterans Memorial
- Miscellaneous art inspired by the war

SHORT FICTION
- "How to Tell a True War Story," by Tim O'Brien
- "The Sniper," by Liam O'Flaherty

INFORMATION
- Collection of statistics on World War I from <www.ww1.org>
- Maps and other visual explanations (e.g., troop movements)

Here you see a sequence that integrates a range of texts, many of them literary, all of them combined to support a variety of conversations over the course of the unit. Such a sequence illustrates a course "in which all the units . . . connect to one another and reinforce one another, with the constant goal being greater awareness of language and greater textual power for the student" (Scholes 1998). As the sequence itself shows, the course becomes the text I am working to create, and the measure of my success is the extent to which these different texts sustain and extend our conversation about not just war but human nature. Such a sequence, made as it is of so many voices and texts, each one demanding different reading and writing skills, helps students develop the textual intelligence they need for the world in which they live and for which they must prepare.

Elements of Literature

Each type of text discussed throughout this book consists of different elements, each of which serves a purpose unique to that type or medium. Literature is no different, consisting of words, devices, structures, and so on, all of which conspire to inform, persuade, and entertain the reader. Explaining how poet Seamus Heaney's poems achieve their power, Helen Vendler writes, "Readers are persuaded into the poem by words, by syntax, by structures, as well as by themes and symbols" (2000). Whether we are talking about how words are arranged within the space of a poem or why a story begins in the middle of the war instead of with the event that caused the war, we are always asking, in essence, such questions as these:

- What is this story made of?
- How does this text work?
- How does this text and its author want me to read it?
- How is this text related to those we have read before—and those to come?
- How do these elements interact to create in the reader an experience of certain emotions or truths?
- Why did this author choose this genre, this form, and how does that contribute to the final impact of the literary text?

While it makes sense to distinguish between the elements of different types of literature and the respective genres within those categories, I prefer to emphasize the similarities instead of the differences. Poems, for example, have narrators, as do novels and some plays. Imagery, too, is essential to all literary forms; without it, we could not see the story unfolding within the dance of words on the page. Tone and style, two crucial elements to any literary work, are present not only through words but through the colors, the images, or even the sounds used in any multimedia text, such as a film, that might be treated as literature in certain contexts.

Elements, however, only matter to the extent that they help readers better understand a story and the techniques the author uses to affect the reader. In *Narrative Design* (1998), Madison Smartt Bell says the "elemental ingredients of fiction may be grouped in one or another of four major categories: plot, character, tone, and form." He then goes on to provide the following concise definitions of each:

- *Plot* is what happens in a narrative.
- *Character* is who it happens to (or who makes it happen).
- *Tone* is what it sounds like.
- *Form* is the pattern of its assembly, its arrangement, its structure, and its design.

These essential elements are as familiar as the idea that a story consists of, as Aristotle said in his *Poetics*, a beginning, a middle, and an end. But literature, regardless of genre or medium, includes other elements that merit the attention of both student and teacher as they can determine not only how literature is read (or taught) but what a particular story means. Consider the element of context, for example. The author's cultural and historical contexts, including the biases and events that may have inspired the text, are as important to consider as the modern context in which the story is read. Do you read Flannery O'Connor as a Southern writer, a female author, or a master of the short story form? Or perhaps students read her story "A Good Man Is Hard to Find" as part of a thematic unit on justice. My point is that the context in which a story is created and, perhaps more important, the one in which it is offered to students function as elements that shape what the story means. See Figure 5–1 for a diagram of the ways context and other elements interact to form complex relationships between a text, students, and teacher.

Visit the *DoubleTake Magazine* Web site (<http://www.double takemagazine.org/teachersguide/subject/index.html>) to see some excellent intertextual units organized around different themes. O'Connor's stories are featured in several of the units. Other such sites are featured on this book's companion Web site.

WEB SITE

It's fine, fascinating even, to read William Golding's *Lord of the Flies* as a study of human nature or "man's essential illness," as Golding refers to it. But part of the conversation should include a discussion of the other ways in which the book could be read. Recasting it to consider what girls would do in such a situation allows for a valid and important conversation about gender and how it affects the characters' behavior and our reading of the text. The book invites discussion about government and holds up well as a case study of Maslow's hierarchy of human needs or Kohlberg's moral reasoning. The story invites obvious comparisons to modern-day gangs, also, and in this respect could be linked to *Romeo and Juliet* to see what the two stories have to say about conflict within the self and society at large. The book also offers a rich course in the study of the writer's craft, in the use of not only symbols but ambiguity, imagery, and language.

You will find many different assignments related to these ideas on the companion Web site.

WEB SITE

My own inclination is not to create such a predetermined frame for the study of a particular text, whether it be a novel or a poem, a film or a

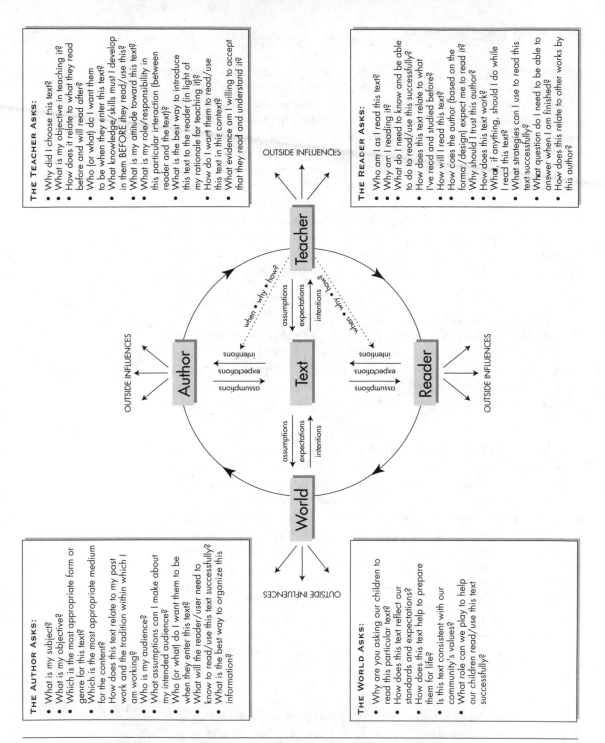

FIGURE 5–1 Diagram of the Relationship Between the Reader, Text, Teacher, and Author. This visual explanation does not imply that the text, which is placed in the middle, is more important than the student. It is, however, the focus of the interaction, which is influenced by these different factors.

narrative essay. Instead, I prefer to ask myself and my students, "So what does this text want us to talk about?" This question, and others like "What do you notice when you read it?" makes room for all the different possibilities, validating the discussion of ethics as much as the conversation about craft and design when reading such a complex book as *Lord of the Flies* or Toni Morrison's *Beloved*. The conversation should, in short, keep readers from reducing a complex literary text down to its essential elements, allowing them to develop and enhance their textual intelligence to discuss how the different elements conspire to allow such outcomes, invite such discussions, create such effects in the reader.

Consider this response, written by Jennifer Lescher about Jimmy Santiago Baca's poem "Fall." A quick reading might suggest this poem is about how hard life can be. Jennifer, however, through discussion with Baca (through the poem), her classmates, and herself, achieved more:

> This poem's first three lines threw me off because I didn't fully understand them. However I proceeded to read on and I found that it was a poem I could easily comprehend. I believe this poem is about someone who has traveled back to their childhood place and by doing this the person has seen how much they have changed through their lifetime. "My heart was *once a lover's swing*," shows how the author is telling the reader that he's changed a lot. When I read the first stanza for the first time I had come to the conclusion that it was full of happy thoughts. When I read it once more I saw how it was bittersweet. He's talking about how when he was young he was fresh and new, and that represents happiness to the reader. The bitter part of this stanza is simply that this is all a memory. Its wording like, "When I *could* touch the stars and believed in myself" shows how the author can no longer achieve these things. As I read the second stanza I noticed a large change in thought and writing. The stanza is dark and very gloomy. It's as if the author is looking around at his old setting where he was once young and he is now identifying the change that has taken place inside of him that was caused by the wear and tear of reality and the real world. "Along the way grief broke me, my faith became hardened dirt," is a line that represents how the author's life took a quick turn and now he can't go back because he's broken. I can some what identify with this poem because when I was in the seventh grade I moved from my childhood small town that I was very attached to and loved very much. I go back there a lot and visit with the people whom I left behind and when I'm there I feel very strange because it's as if I'm also visiting me when I was different and young and I can feel the change that has made itself comfortable inside my soul.

Jen's attention to elements like imagery and language—for example, metaphor and tone—deepen her reading and allow her to enter into a valuable conversation about her own past as well as Baca's poem. The poem itself was used to support a larger discussion we were having about memory while reading Homer's *Odyssey* and Bharati Mukherjee's novel *Jasmine*. To support and extend our own conversation about memory, and about how to read critically and write about literature, I put Jen's response on the overhead and used it to facilitate a class discussion during which others then read their responses and responded to what Jennifer wrote.

Earlier on, in preparation for reading Homer's *Odyssey*, we discussed how stories work and how they are used. Such conversations are important, for they allow students to develop their capacity as readers but also extend their understanding of what it is we teach. I use such occasions—create them, in fact—to discuss how stories are used to persuade, inspire, and explain ideas and events, past and present, to others. Studying leaders from throughout history, Howard Gardner (1996) concluded that the most powerful, most effective leaders shared an ability to use stories to garner support for ideas or effect change within the society. He identified different types of stories, among them stories of:

- The group
- Identity
- The life cycle
- The self
- Struggling with one another
- Values and meaning

WEB SITE

You will find additional resources on the companion Web site to help you teach narrative design.

Gardner also found that effective leaders, using their textual intelligence, told these stories in different ways, using different media so as to achieve the ideal effect on their audience. Writing about stories of identity, for instance, Gardner says "it is *stories of identity*—narratives that help individuals think about and feel who they are, where they come from, and where they are headed—that constitute the single most powerful weapon in the leader's literary arsenal." Gardner continues his analysis of stories and their elements, showing how such leaders will use the basic elements of narrative—conflict, problems, themes—to persuade people to make the leader's story come true by becoming characters in it.

In this age of multimedia, an era full of chaos that is often reflected in fragmented, nonlinear narratives, we must expand our conception of the elements of literature, taking into consideration the traditional elements but also the tradition itself, that being in some cases an element against which the writer is arguing or with which she is playing. In Figure 5–2, I have assembled a list of different elements that can and often do influence the meaning of literary texts and the effect those texts have on us when we read them.

DESIGN

- absences/omissions
- audience (intended, actual, original)
- beginning
- cause
- choices
  - arrangement
  - style
  - words
- completion: excerpted or abridged?
- emphasis
- exposition
- genre
- integration/blending of genres or forms
- length
- logic
- middle
- movement
- narrative frame
- organization (linear, episodic, etc.)
- patterns (heroic cycle)
- problem
- repetition
  - structural
  - syntactical
  - thematics
  - verbal
- shape
- space
- suspense
- tension
- time (management)

LANGUAGE

- alliteration
- ambiguity
- color
- fragments
- imagery
- metaphors
- punctuation
- rhythm
- sentence structures
- sound
- style
- syntax
- tense
- translation (from language, form, genre, medium)
- voice
- words

FEATURES

- action
- allusions
- argument
- character
- climax
- complicating action
- conflict
  - cultural
  - existential
  - external
  - internal
- end
- epigraph
- facts

- intent
- medium
- meter
- names
  - characters
  - objects
  - places
- narrator
  - who is it?
  - why him or her?
  - what is his or her motivation?
  - is he or she reliable?
- pacing
- point of view
- plot
- resolution
- revelation/epiphany/ changes
- reversal (of fortune)
- setting: time and place
- themes
- title
- tone

DEVICES

- allegory
- authorial intrusions
- dialect
- dialogue
  - internal
  - vernacular
  - with others
  - with self
- epilogue
- flashbacks

- foreshadow
- interlocutor
- irony
- mystery
- narrative
- prologue
- stories
- symbols
- typography
- volta (surprise)

MISCELLANEOUS

- assumptions
- bias
- context
- culture
  - author's
  - character's
  - reader's
  - society's
- influences (of other authors, works)
- off stage (awareness of)
- purpose: author's, reader's, teacher's
- reader's experiences
- tradition (you work within and against it)

FIGURE 5–2   Elements of a Literary Text. Literary texts are made of many different elements, as this list shows.

NOTE

Visit the Center for Digital Storytelling online at <http://www
.storycenter.org/> to learn more about the way narrative and multimedia are being integrated into interactive texts.

When illuminating a literary text then, we must ask ourselves—and
teach our students to ask—not only what literature does that the other
types of text do not, or what it does better, but also why the author
expresses this idea in a poem or a short story, why fiction instead of nonfiction. We must learn to ask why the author uses elements like time and
point of view as he does, why first and not third person, why present
instead of past tense, why he emphasizes this character's perspective
instead of another's.

Standards Connection

Standards in the area of reading literature refer not only to how students
read but what they read, to how well they read but also why they read.
States are lining up around the country to tell teachers and their students
what students must know and be able to do in this area. The California
High School Exit Exam, anchored in the state English language arts content standards, requires students to demonstrate their ability to read
both literary and informational texts, both of which are equally represented on the actual exam. That means that the exam will concentrate
half its attention on the content of this chapter and half on that of all the
other chapters combined.

When it comes to reading literature, however, especially challenging, important literature, I agree with Carol Jago, author of *Beyond
Standards* (2001), when she writes, "The kind of work I want from my
students goes beyond any list of standards, skills to be mastered, or
even books to be read. It has to do with habits of mind, thoughtful-
ness, personal integrity toward intellectual pursuits that I find hard to
prescribe." Like Carol Jago, I try to develop these hard-to-prescribe
qualities in all my students. This book is also about the evolving standards of our modern world, standards of what we must all know and
be able to do as readers and creators of myriad types of texts. Robert
Scholes cochairs the Pacesetter English Project, which was given the
task of creating a rigorous, stimulating course of study for high school
seniors. In his article "Does English Matter?" (1998a), Scholes argues
not for a canon of texts or even skills, but rather a set of standards that
ensure that all students learn:

> a canon of methods . . . in the form of intellectual tools that
> they can use effectively. The aim should be to open up possibili-
> ties, to empower. In practice this means a reorientation of

courses around the work of students, with a better balance between textual consumption and production. It is not what is covered that counts but what is learned. It is not what students have been told that matters but what they remember and what they do.

Such a canon of methods will, I believe, prepare my students to succeed on any state test, but I must also keep track of the specific standards outlined in *The California Language Arts Content Standards for California Public Schools* (California Department of Education 1999). I include here a sampling of those standards, taken from the grades 9–10 standards for reading literature:

LITERARY RESPONSE AND ANALYSIS: Students read and respond to historically or culturally significant works of American, British, and world literature and provide evidence of comprehension by conducting in-depth analyses of recurrent patterns and themes. The quality and complexity of the materials to be read are illustrated in the California Reading List.

STRUCTURAL FEATURES OF LITERATURE

3.1 articulate the relationship between expressed purposes and characteristics of different forms of dramatic literature (comedy, tragedy, drama, dramatic monologue)

3.2 compare and contrast the presentation of a similar theme or topic across genres to explain how the selection of genre shapes the theme or topic

NARRATIVE ANALYSIS OF GRADE LEVEL APPROPRIATE TEXT

3.3 analyze interactions between main and subordinate characters in literary text (e.g., internal and external conflicts, motivations, relationships, and influences) and how they affect the plot

3.4 determine a character's traits from what he/she says about himself/herself (e.g., dramatic monologues, soliloquies)

3.5 compare works that express a universal theme, providing evidence to support their ideas (e.g., Russel Baker's *Growing Up* and Ed McClanahan's *The Natural Man*)

3.6 analyze and trace an author's development of time and sequence, including the use of complex literary devices such as foreshadowing and flashbacks

3.7 recognize and understand the significance of a wide range of literary elements and techniques, including figurative language, imagery, allegory, and symbolism; and explain their appeal

3.8   interpret and evaluate the impact of ambiguities, subtleties, contradictions, ironies and incongruities in text

3.9   explain how voice, persona, and narrator affect tone, characterization, plot, and credibility

3.10 identify and describe the function of dialogue, scene design, soliloquies and asides and character foils in dramatic literature

LITERARY CRITICISM

3.11 evaluate the aesthetic qualities (the melodies of literary language; the power and effectiveness of an author's stylistic choices) and how an author's choice of words and imagery creates tone and mood, and advances the work's theme, using the terminology of literary criticism (Aesthetic Approach)

3.12 analyze how a work of literature is related to the themes and issues of its historical period (Historical Approach)

A set of standards taken from an alternative perspective are shown in Figure 5–3.

Classroom Connection: A Portfolio of Possibilities

Again, the ultimate question: what does all this look like in the classroom? The following samples of assignments and student work exemplify the type of work this chapter describes. These different productions also remind us that having textual intelligence means being able to both read *and* produce different types of text, that we should use different types of texts that force students to ask how they should read a given text in a specific situation.

WEB SITE

These and other assignments as well as student exemplars can be found on the companion Web site.

Form and Function

Discussions about form require students, whenever possible, to play with and try their hand at such forms. Just as students who make a decent Web page suddenly understand how easy it is for anyone to appear legitimate, so too will emulating a literary form help them understand how it is made, how it works, and what function it serves. The following examples, all taken from different types of poems, show how much fun kids can have but also what serious work they can accomplish through such exercises. Here is sophomore Lyra Hanes' ode based on

The Traits of an Effective Reader Reading a Literary Text Scoring Guide

DEVELOPING INTERPRETATIONS

- Identify problems, gaps, ambiguities, conflicts, symbols, and/or metaphors in the text
- Analyze the text to pose explanations that bridge gaps, clarify ambiguity, and resolve textual problems
- Using the context to connect analytical explanations to a "bigger picture"

5 The advanced response interprets to analyze and think critically about informational texts.
☐ Directly answers the question by employing problem-solving techniques using specific evidence, clues, and "on target" information
☐ Examples, quotes, and events are cited from the text and connected strongly to the analysis
☐ Responds beyond the question to engage the bigger picture by creating framework of historical significance, cultural importance, or universal theme

3 Interprets to expand the text, but still developing connections to a larger world view.
☐ Uses some language that indicates an initial layer of interpretation and understanding
☐ A safe response citing very obvious examples. Connections between the examples and the analysis are not always evident
☐ Does not move beyond the question—engaging the "bigger picture" is still a developing skill

1 The emerging response sees interpretation as "talking about a book." Reading and interpreting are still separate processes. Little evidence exists that the student understands the concept of interpretation.
☐ Does not adequately address the question
☐ Does not cite examples, quotes, or evidence from the text to use as a basis of interpretation
☐ Sometimes restates the question words

INTEGRATING FOR SYNTHESIS

- Put information in order to explain the text's process or chronology
- Compare and contrast characters, story lines, events, and primary and secondary sources in order to make defensible judgments and interpretations
- Recognize and describe cause-and-effect relations
- Integrate personal experience, background knowledge, and/or content knowledge with the text to create a "synthesis" of text plus knowledge

5 The advanced response integrates textual material and other types of knowledge to create synthesis of ideas.
☐ Directly, specifically, and concretely performs the synthesis application directed by the question by using synthesis language
☐ Uses well-chosen examples that have a strong parallel development if the question demands it
☐ Responds beyond the question, integrating several layers of knowledge into a harmonious whole

3 The developing response integrates textual material with other types of knowledge to create a surface-level synthesis.
☐ Uses some synthesis language to reflect a basic understanding of the skills of integrating for synthesis
☐ Uses general and "safe" examples
☐ The layers and types of knowledge in the response are not always well integrated

1 The emerging response employs some skills of synthesizing, but a fully developed integration is still emerging.
☐ Does not perform the synthesis application directed by the question
☐ Does not accurately use synthesis language
☐ Does not integrate sources, texts, and understandings to a measurable degree

CRITIQUING FOR EVALUATION

- Experiment with ideas in the text
- Express opinions about the text
- Raise questions about the text
- Make good judgments about the text by using a synthesis of material derived from multiple sources
- Challenge the ideas of the author by noting bias, distortion, and/or lack of coherence
- Contrast the accuracy of textual information with other sources and form solid, defensible critiques

5 The advanced response evaluates to assert a strong voice in the text.
☐ Directly and thoughtfully answers the question, using evaluation terminology effectively and precisely to indicate the reader's critique of the text
☐ The examples are well developed, placed in context, and connected well to other ideas
☐ Responds beyond the parameters of the question to critically engage the text and its ideas in a solid, defensible judgment

3 The developing response hesitates to evaluate thoroughly; it still plays it somewhat "safe."
☐ Generally answers the evaluation question, but hesitant to critically engage with the text
☐ Selects safe and obvious examples that are connected to other ideas in fairly limited ways
☐ Does not yet move beyond the question to venture into the larger world of critical discourse

1 The emerging response is just beginning to explore a critical stance to the text.
☐ Uses evaluation terminology sporadically or not at all
☐ The examples are incomplete or sketchily described, and not connected to other ideas or issues
☐ The response is incomplete or restates the question words

FIGURE 5–3 Northwestern Regional Educational Lab Scoring Guide for Literary Texts. © The Northwestern Regional Educational Laboratory, Portland, OR. *Reprinted by permission in* Illuminating Texts *by Jim Burke.* (Figure continued on next page.)

The Traits of an Effective Reader Reading an Literary Text Scoring Guide

DECODING CONVENTIONS

- Decode the writing *conventions* of grammar, punctuation, word recognition, and sentence structure
- Recognize the organizational *conventions* of the author, the title, the characters, the theme, the conflict, and the resolution of stories and plays
- Identify the genre *conventions* (poetry, drama, fiction) of the types of modes (narrative, autobiographical, persuasive, ironic) appropriate to each literary genre, the distinctions between genres, the expectations the readers have for genres

5 The advanced response uses conventions information to form a confident "thinking frame" of a text.

- ☐ Directly answers the question using text structure language in specific and precise ways
- ☐ Selects well-chosen and well-supported examples to illustrate understanding of conventions
- ☐ Responds "beyond" the question by enlarging the initial thinking frame

3 The developing response uses conventions information to form an initial "thinking frame" of the text.

- ☐ Uses some basic text structure language to indicate general understandings
- ☐ Selects "safe" and obvious examples to illustrate understanding of the conventions
- ☐ The response is fairly safe and stays definitely within the confines of the question

1 The emerging response is beginning to decode conventions and the challenge of decoding gets in the way of a "thinking frame" for the text.

- ☐ Does not adequately answer the question but may use some text structure language
- ☐ Focuses on more general information rather than providing examples from the text
- ☐ The response can be characterized as sketchy and incomplete

ESTABLISHING COMPREHENSION

- Use strategies to "squeeze" meaning out of the text
- Identify the plot, the major (round) characters and minor (flat) characters, the "turning moments," and main themes of the text
- Distinguish between significant and supporting details and events for plot, characters, main ideas, and main themes
- Summarize and paraphrase with purpose to move toward making inferences and interpretations

5 The advanced response demonstrates a purposeful, expansive, and knowledge-able comprehension of the text.

- ☐ Directly answers the question using comprehension terms to indicate precise understandings
- ☐ Selects well-chosen examples to illustrate in-depth comprehension. Examples are well developed using clear, specific language and terms
- ☐ Responds "beyond" the question by increasing comprehension of the text into inferential and interpretative levels

3 The developing response demonstrates an adequate comprehension of the text. Purposeful comprehension is still evolving.

- ☐ Uses some comprehension terms to indicate general understandings
- ☐ Selects "safe" and obvious examples to illustrate literal comprehension
- ☐ Does not venture information beyond the initial question

1 The emerging response is searching to establish a basic comprehension of the text.

- ☐ Does not provide examples for evidence but sometimes restates the question
- ☐ Little evidence that a basic comprehension of the text has been achieved
- ☐ The response can be characterized as sketchy and incomplete

REALIZING CONTEXT

- Identify the time period and its accompanying social realities in the text
- Identify the setting of the text and its relationship to social factors
- Identify the vocabulary reflective of the context
- Recognize the writing mode, tone, and voice of the author or source selected with respect to the context
- Recognize the cultural aspects of the text

5 The advanced response realizes context and sees inferential meanings and intended purposes, both implicit and explicit.

- ☐ Directly and specifically answers the question to demonstrate understanding of inferential meaning
- ☐ Selects well-chosen examples to illustrate understandings of contextual issues
- ☐ Goes beyond the question's limits and extends into in-depth understandings of contextual relationships

3 The developing response realizes the context of the text to some degree and recognizes obvious types of inference. The idea of contextual relationships between many factors and issues is still in development.

- ☐ Uses some context terminology to show a basic level of understanding
- ☐ Selects "safe" and obvious examples that stay close to the surface of the text
- ☐ Stays within the safe confines of the question

1 The emerging response guesses at context, but has difficulty accessing inferential knowledge.

- ☐ Does not use examples from the text to illustrate inferential understandings
- ☐ Not enough evidence to demonstrate an understanding of contextual layers of the text
- ☐ Demonstrates little effectiveness at "reading between the lines"

FIGURE 5–3 Continued

May be copied for classroom use. Jim Burke. 2001. Illuminating Texts. Portsmouth, NH: Heinemann.

different odes by Pablo Neruda we were reading while we read *Macbeth* (who could no longer sleep):

ODE TO SLEEP

—Lyra Hanes

Sleep
Oh my sleep.
It takes me to a place
Where I bathe in daisy water,
Because violets sting.
Grassy eyes that stare me
Down, doubt me, make me feel
Like a weed.
A place where your citrus smile
Meant to make me feel like dirt.
And willow-flow ways can steal
Him away in a whirl of petals
And a ghost of vanilla.
I sigh a teakettle sigh and drop
My head into my lily hands.
Poppies can make me high enough
To pick
Sweet apples
On ivy-hope vines.
Then in that single instant
Between sleep and awake
It's gone.
Sleep . . .
Oh, my sleep.

Junior Maritza Sanchez wrote the following poem in her junior class, which was studying Whitman's poems as part of a unit on the American voice. This young woman, born in Columbia, hears America every bit as well as Whitman did:

I HEAR AMERICA SINGING

—Maritza Sanchez

I hear America sing,
I hear fifteen and sixteen year olds driving unmercifully through the
    streets,
I hear hip-hop, dance, salsa, rock, R&B, and even country music.
I hear the infinite dialing, and dialing . . . and the ring . . . ring . . .
    ring . . . ring . . .
Right before the cool, hip message comes on.

I hear *NSYNC, Britney Spears, LL Cool J, even Eminem on the
    radio and everywhere,
I hear them later from the lips of six thru sixty year olds
I hear it all, I listen carefully, try to pay attention, but wait!
Hold on, . . . I hear my pager, my cell phone, and I've *got* to check my
    e-mail.
I hear America sing.

I hear the complaints of young and old about how life this and life
    that
I hear us bitch about our "society" when WE are it.
I hear the never changing, "Kids these days!" and then a long deep
    sigh
I hear the cry of the young and old,
I hear the cry for independence, for freedom, for life turn into
A cry for luxury, jealousy, war, "everyman for themselves!!" it says.
I hear America sing.

I hear Spanglish, Italiaglish, Frenglish, and so on,
I hear how no one likes them but they all can't help using them.
I hear kids laugh at silly cartoons, new ones and ancient ones,
I hear kids swear even before they can understand what it means.
I hear people swear as if it was nothing . . . I mean, it really *is* noth-
    ing, right?
I hear cars honking 'cause everyone is in a hurry to get somewhere . . .
But then once you get there, what?
I hear America sing.

I hear people cry because they feel misunderstood
But do *they* understand?
I hear disrespect in the voice of teens and kids,
But why not? Are *we* respected?
Are *we* understood?
Who cares! Right?
I hear people judge and misjudge others 'cause they don't quite
    match their Sketchers shoes with *those* pants . . ."What were they
    thinking?!"
I hear people mock each other 'cause of the lack of name brands in
    their wardrobe
I hear silly remarks about others' hair behind their backs
But to their face there's the always lasting smile and the "That's sooo
    cool!" comment that we could swear we mean.
I hear America sing.

I heard it yesterday,
I hear it today,
And I'll hear it tomorrow and always,

We will keep on singing . . . but do we act on it?
Are we proactive or just reactive?
I hear America sing.

One of my favorite poems to use for modeling is Wallace Stevens'
"13 Ways of Looking at a Blackbird." It allows us to look at a story, a
book, or an idea from any number of different perspectives; it also provides a very useful entrée into a conversation about the ideas or the texts
at hand. Here is Kenya Baines' "13 Ways of Looking at War," a poem
written in response to Remarque's *All Quiet on the Western Front*, which
my sophomore class was reading:

13 WAYS OF LOOKING AT WAR

—Kenya Baines

1.
Along the war front,
The only thing moving
Was the eye of the bullet.

2.
I was of three minds,
Like a soldier
In which there are three consciousnesses.

3.
A soldier cries in the morning winds.
It is a small part of the day.

4.
A man and a soldier
Are one.
A man and a soldier and war
Are one.

5.
I do not know which to hate more,
The horror of war
Or the horror of man
A man dying
Or just after.

6.
Death filled the long war front
With horrible sorrow
The shadow of agony
Crossed it to and fro.
The mood

Traced in the shadow
An incomprehensible cause.

7.
O rough men of war
Why do you imagine happy times?
Do you not see how war
Walks on the dreams
Of the men about you?

8.
I know many superiors
And lucid, constant routines
But I know too
That war is involved
In what I know.

9.
When the war calmed down,
It marked the edge
Of one of many circles.

10.
At the sight of war
Destroying young men,
Even the strongest men
Would cry out sharply.

11.
It rages through the land
In a dark coach.
Once, a fear overcame the people
In that it took
The shadow of its children
   Away
For war.

12.
The front is moving.
The war must be spreading.

13.
It was evening all afternoon.
It was dark
And it would remain dark.
A war waits
In the shadows.

The America Project

The following assignment, the America Project, asks students to reflect on some aspect of their own society after reading Bharati Mukherjee's novel *Jasmine*, in which the author constantly examines what America is, what it means. Here is the assignment:

> **V**isit the companion Web site for examples of student work done on this assignment.

WEB SITE

INTRODUCTION

Throughout *Jasmine*, Bharati Mukherjee examines the different Americas in which people live. Some of these Americas are cultural, others are regional, some are generational; still other differences result from race, wealth, and gender. Other distinctions are evident throughout the story as people move between identities, roles, values, and problems. This project's primary objective is to examine some aspect of our culture from multiple perspectives and, by studying it, arrive at some new insight into such questions as:

- Who is American?
- What does it mean to be American?
- What does America mean or represent?

   In the course of your investigation, you will also be working on the following skills:

- Developing useful, insightful questions about complicated subjects.
- Searching for, organizing, and interpreting different types of information that represent a range of perspectives.
- Making connections between ideas and expressing your ideas through words and images using the most effective media and formats.
- Presenting your findings through images and words (written and spoken).

Finally, you must look at your subject from three perspectives. Here are some examples:

- *America:* What it means to someone from India, someone born in Burlingame, California, and a homeless person; what it means to a ninety-year-old, a forty-five-year-old, and a fifteen-year-old.
- *Art:* Three different artists' perceptions of America (e.g., Andy Warhol, Walker Evans, and Wayne Thiebeau).
- *Film:* Three works from one director on the same theme (e.g., John Waters' series of teen films); films about war from three different

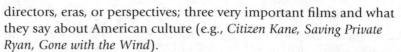

directors, eras, or perspectives; three very important films and what they say about American culture (e.g., *Citizen Kane, Saving Private Ryan, Gone with the Wind*).

- *Music:* Rock, rap, blues; past, present, future; three musical artists' views of America (e.g., Bruce Springsteen, Tupak, Bob Dylan)
- *Poetry:* Using the book *Americans' Favorite Poems* (I have three copies of it) and its companion Web site (<www.favoritepoem.org>), read a sequence of poems that provide three different views about America. (Note: reading three poems would not be adequate.)

POSSIBILITIES
- Art (<http://www.time.com/time/time100/artists/index.html>)
- Culture (The following Web sites all contain excellent content.)
  - *American Memory*
    <http://memory.loc.gov/ammem/amhome.html>
  - *Lost & Found Stories*
    <www.npr.org/programs/lnfsound/stories/index.html>
  - National Archives exhibits
    <http://www.nara.gov/exhall/exhibits.html>
- DoubleTake (<www.doubletakemagazine.org/teachersguide/activities/index.html>)
- Film
- Ideas (<http://www.time.com/time/time100/scientist/index.html>)
- Image: __(#)__ ways of looking at America
- Leaders (<http://www.time.com/time/time100/leaders/index.html>)
- Music (see Rock and Roll Hall of Fame at <www.rockhall.com>)
- Poetry (<favoritepoems.org>; <www.poetry.org>; <www.poems.org>)
- Religion
- Values (What does America believe in?)
- Wars (see Stephen Ambrose's *Americans at War*)

REQUIREMENTS
- Reading
  - Bibliography of what you read, watched, and listened to (including Web sites, articles, books, films, and so on) during the course of your project. Must be properly formatted (see *Writer's Inc.* for guidance in this area).
- Writing
  - Three-page typed reflection on what you found out about your subject, the answers to your question(s).
  - Examples from and discussion of all three domains in your paper.

- *Alternative:* A series of poems written about your subject with a one-page analysis of what your poems say about the subject, complete with quotes from your own poems to support your ideas.
- *Alternative:* A video or another multimedia production that includes a one-page analysis of what your production says about the subject (i.e., discusses what you were trying to accomplish through your video, what it says about America).
- *Alternative:* A musical performance, either of original or carefully selected American music, that includes a one-page analysis of your selections and how they relate to your subject.
- *Alternative:* An original work of art (or a multimedia presentation of art collected online and organized into a show organized around an idea) with a one-page typed analysis of or introduction to the show.
- Speaking
  - Be prepared to present on Tuesday and Wednesday, November 21 and 22, 2000.
- Thinking
  - Think in Threes graphic organizer
  - Evidence of planning, thinking, working
  - A list of the questions you asked to help you and those questions you were trying to answer through your research

ASSESSMENT
Your work will be evaluated according to the:

- Degree of creativity, originality, and intellectual risk
- Quality of your:
  - Production
  - Presentation
  - Thinking
  - Work (all projects are to be done individually, though PAIRS may lobby me for special consideration)
  - Writing

Character Study

Since kids are busy shaping and making sense of their own character, others' character intrigues them, providing useful opportunities to try on other selves within the safety of fiction. Here is a sequence from my sophomores' study of *Macbeth*; this particular student made one of the most dramatic turnarounds I've ever witnessed in a student: he literally decided, after nearly failing for a time, to do his work to the best of his ability every day—and then did just that.

The first step called for students to come up with adjectives to describe a particular character, in this case Macbeth. David Lopez wrote:

RELENTLESS

Definition: unyielding, unrelenting; steady and persistent.
Synonyms: grim, inexorable, stern, unforgiving.
Antonyms: forgiving, appeasable, exoreable.
Explanation: Shown by Macbeth doing anything and everything he needs to do in order to become king. Originated from his own, as well as Lady Macbeth's desire for power and money.

The next step asked them to come up with five adjectives for their own character, a means of making a connection between their reading and their own lives and selves. David wrote:

RELENTLESS

(same definitions, synonyms, antonyms)
Shown by my relentless pursuit of achieving amateur wrestling greatness. Originated from my '99–00 wrestling season with coach Spataro who taught me to be relentless in pursuit of my goals.

The next two steps called for them to write two one-page papers elaborating on one of the adjectives describing themselves and Macbeth. Here is what David wrote about Macbeth:

The main thing that Macbeth wants in this story is to become king of Scotland. I think Macbeth wants this because of the power, money, and noteriety that comes with the throne. From what I've read so far, Macbeth is willing to do almost anything to get the throne, including kill. One problem that this creates for Macbeth is that he could get caught for the murder, have his crown stripped from him, and get arrested. I don't know how he will cover it up, but I know Macbeth will stop at nothing to do so. The consequence of Macbeth's desire to become king is that he is now a murderer. He let temptation get the best of him, and he took another human life. This desire tells us that Macbeth won't settle for anything short of the best. For example, he wouldn't settle for being "Thane of Cawdor," he needed to be king. King, and nothing less. Macbeth is an extremely selfish and greedy individual.

The final stage, using Weldon Kees' poem "Aspects of Robinson" as a model, asks them to write a poem about their character, further elaborating on their character. Here is David's poem about Macbeth:

ASPECTS OF MACBETH

Macbeth sitting on his new throne
Flossing his new crown

Paranoid that someone suspects him
Talked into it by Lady Macbeth
Fearing he will get caught.

Macbeth
walking back from his meeting
With the witches
Contemplating the fact
Of their predictions
Thinking it could be true
Pondering how to make it so
Ambitious to take the throne.

Macbeth, bloody daggers in hand
Thinking about what he has done
Filled with joy yet with fear
Fear of the truth
Fearing people will find out the truth.

Macbeth unable to sleep
Full of guilt
Fearing persecution
Paranoia taking him over
Fearing he will get caught.

Another important conversation, a vital part of character study, is how we and characters change over time. Freshmen in my class read both the *Odyssey* and Bharati Mukherjee's novel *Jasmine* while studying India in their social studies class. One conversation we had focused on how, why, and the importance of the ways in which Jasmine changes by the end of the story. Sarah Coit wrote:

The Jasmine at the end of the book is not the same character as the Jasmine in the beginning of the book. Much like the feudal Jyoti is different from Jasmine, Jasmine's experiences and learning have changed her, expelling new characters along the way. Each character has adapted to her situation in life. Jyoti, for example, was able to fit in with the traditional India, while Jasmine was the modern Indian. Jazzy and Jace, two other incarnations, are the Americans, and finally Jane the true American, the true individual.

When Jasmine first arrives in America, her main goal is to burn herself and complete her mission in life. A new character emerges after Jasmine is raped, a character with new desires, new wants and a new mission. Jasmine, for the first time in her life, wants happiness. Jasmine is determined to outsmart her fate as a sad widow. She finds her escape from fate in America.

Jasmine is a loyal woman. She has been loyal all her life to other people. Loyalty brought Jasmine to America and loyalty has kept Jasmine with Bud. Jasmine has never been loyal to herself but her new desire for happiness creates a new loyalty to herself. Jasmine must decide what she is willing to give up to find happiness. Jasmine can leave Bud because she will always have a part of him with her when the baby is born. Jasmine is able to give up everything because she is not really giving these different selves up because they created her. The people in Jasmine's life created Jane, Jane whose mission in life is to find happiness.

Understanding Character Through Occupation

In *The English Teacher's Companion* (1999) I argued for the importance of occupation in learning, saying:

Effective education involves occupation. Construction—of a class, of knowledge, of relationships, of meaning, of a story— implies occupation in both senses of the word: to work and to inhabit. Defining the word *occupation*, you find such dictionary explanations as "to hold or possess," "to engage, employ" (*American Heritage* 3rd edition); reflecting for a moment on contemporary usage, we hear students speak of being "into" something or dismiss something because they are "not into it."

Everything teachers do prepares—or should prepare—students for the work their life will ask of them. In today's world this means, for example, teaching them to read a variety of texts such as they will encounter as employees, parents, homeowners, or citizens. Former Secretary of Labor Lynn Martin wrote, "More than half of our young people leave school without the knowledge or foundation required to find and hold a good job" (U.S. Department of Labor 1991). Whether or not these statistics are true, we do need to prepare our students to do what the world will ask of them when they graduate.

We also speak, however, of inhabiting—through art and stories—an imaginative space. We think in terms of getting kids to imagine themselves occupying certain jobs, but also envisioning themselves inside sentences where they roll up their sleeves and look closer at meaning, nuance, character, style. Indeed, *inhibit* and *inhabit* derive from the same Indo-European root which suggests that through inhabiting different roles—writer, speaker, reader, performer—students will lose their inhibitions. Students in my freshman class, for example, put William Golding on trial each year, charging him with libel against humanity. Some of them take on the role of characters from the book while others adopt roles such as lawyers and expert witnesses who are called to testify (in character) in the trial. Students undergo a remarkable transformation as they inhabit these roles, their costumes forcing them to think and act in ways that help them to understand the book better and to discover new aspects of themselves.

These occupations of character require students to read the work of and become one from a list of many writers, thinkers, and characters. Here is freshman Kate Tiedeman's witness statement, written and subsequently performed from the perspective of the historian Hannah Arendt:

My name is Hannah Arendt. I am an author, historian, and a political philosopher. I have taught at Princeton, Berkeley, the University of Chicago, Columbia, and Northwestern. I have also written numerous books, such as *The Origins of Totalitarianism*, and one of my most controversial works *Eichmann in Jerusalem: A Report on the Banality of Evil*. I am also internationally recognized as the best known American political theorist of my generation.

In my book *Eichmann in Jerusalem* I discuss a thought that Eichmann was more banal and bureaucratic rather than radically evil. This continues to be one of my themes throughout several of my books, as well as my belief that we fulfill society's expectations of us.

In my books I address the fact that we are society's creatures and we are shaped by society. Eichmann, for example, was not so much the evil Jew hater, to me he seemed to be more like a feeble spirited clown, with no power to distinguish between good and evil. He was a void filled by a society's expectations of him, and even to the end he was happy that he had remained so faithful to Hitler. I also maintain that when we are without a sense of belonging or if we feel that we have no real place in society, as the boys on Golding's island felt, we are more susceptible to follow and feed power to a leader of some sort. We are led towards totalitarianism and we follow evil, such as Jack Merridew in *Lord of the Flies*, and we follow this evil without questioning this person's actual authority or the origin of their supposed evil. We follow blindly. The boys on Golding's island provide the perfect example of this. They weren't unified and none of them felt like they belonged, so when Jack led the revolt they followed willingly, and highlighted this by killing to ensure their power. I also think that this type of imperialism, or any kind of imperialism, is insane and has nothing to do with the normal human condition. But also, even with these issues there can be no simple explanation of behavior, even in light of what has happened before. Some events can cause a predisposition for people to behave in certain ways, or make it easier for them to do so.

I believe that we are creatures of culture, and we are shaped by it, but this sort of imperialism, represented in *Lord of the Flies*, is not the human condition.

Closing Thoughts

If we do not provide our students opportunities to occupy their minds as well as their hearts, they will cut and paste our curriculum from Web sites, they will watch the books we want to them to read, and they will miss the meaning we hope they will make. They will feel as Kevin does in the letter that follows.

Every year, students in my colleague Diane McClain's American literature class send out letters to other juniors across America, asking them what "American Literature" means at their school. Through these letters, Diane invites her students and those classes to which her students write to participate in a substantial conversation about this country and its culture. While not representative of most responses, Kevin's letter challenges us all to make sure our students, in addition to learning the intellectual skills they need to have, have regular opportunities to converse with:

- Their teacher
- The author through the text
- Themselves through discussions and written reflections
- The literary tradition within or against which the author is working
- Their classmates
- The world outside of school, the one for which they are preparing, the one which will eventually become their responsibility

Here is Kevin's response letter:

> My name is Kevin Mayes, and I am a junior at Lakeside High School. To let you know a little about myself as well, I am captain of the varsity tennis team. I love hardcore and techno music, and I have a 4.0 GPA, even though I don't try very hard and I would much rather do anything than homework. I also want to go to film school in California. I love movies more than anything else in life. The American Literature class at Interlake is only one semester long, so I've only been in the class since January. I will do my best to help you on your project, but I'm afraid Interlake isn't exactly a shining example for academics most of the time.

My class didn't even start reading a book until we were more than a month into the semester. For that first month all we read were these snippets out of this *Elements of Literature* book. They were very boring and I didn't get any feel for American Literature whatsoever. We are still discussing the one and only book we have read in the last four months—*Ethan Frome*. Although this book was written in America, it is written from a time period in the early 1900s when drab and life-like was the new popular style of writing. The really sad thing is that the only reason *Ethan Frome* was chosen was because it was the only book my teacher had enough copies of to distribute to all students, not because of its educational value or being any better than other American literature. I wanted to read *Slaughterhouse Five* or *On the Road* by Jack Kerouak, but I got stuck with good old *Ethan Frome*. We just finished watching the movie in class today but it sucked way harder than the book ever did. Don't get me wrong, I'm not saying the book was bad, it just was written for people in a time period when everything was so much more restricted and forbidden than it is now.

I'm sorry that I can't be more help than I am, although it's not really my fault. I don't mind reading that much (although I would prefer movies), I just haven't been given the chance in the class I'm in. I wish I would be assigned to read some book by an American writer that would just blow my mind, but there is slim to no chance of that ever happening. The way things work at Lakeside never changes. It consists of reading mindless dross, discussing that dross, doing a project based on that dross, and then moving on to a whole new mess of dross. I know the only *required* book on the American Lit curriculum is *The Great Gatsby*, which is longer than the last book we read so it may take us an entire semester (dread). If you need anything else feel free to email me.

Sincerely,
Kevin Mayes

I don't want my students saying this about my class, about my teaching, or about their learning and our country's literature. Having used the words, the stories, and the literary forms to help us enter into these essential conversations, I want students like Kevin to see literature as an invitation, to be able to describe their experience with it more like Carol Jago, in *Beyond Standards*, describes one student's experience in the following passage:

Amanda is an avid reader who faced enormous challenges in her sixteen years. She spent time in several foster homes and, though she has now returned to her mother and is living in a relatively stable environment, continues to puzzle over the relationships between adults and their children. She was struggling to find an author she cared enough about to research, so I suggested that instead she focus on books about youngsters who were forced by the absence of their parents to take responsibility for their own lives while still very young.

Within the next month Amanda read *Dangerous Angels* by Francesca Lia Block, *Girl* by Blake Nelson, *The Tribes of Palos Verdes* by Joy Nicholson, *Hideous Kinky* by Esther Freud, *Anywhere but Here* by Mona Simpson, *Bogeywoman* by Jaimy Gordon, *Stripping and Other Stories* by Pagan Kennedy, *Pamela: A Novel* by Pamela Yu, *Less Than Zero* by Bret Easton Ellis, *The Culture of Complaint* by Robert Hughes, *Tea* by Stacey D'Erasmo, and *A Tribe Apart* by Patricia Hersch. As Amanda told me in an email message while struggling to formulate her thesis, "I know that some of these books are horribly written, Mrs. Jago, but they work for the idea." (2001)

Amanda uses her developing textual intelligence to choose and compare these different stories and types of text. More important, however, is that she is talking to herself, to her own family (through the stories), to the literary tradition of which the different books are a part, and to Mrs. Jago, a teacher Kevin no doubt wishes he had and Amanda is glad she does.

Further Studies

Applebee, Arthur. 1996. *Curriculum as Conversation: Transforming Traditions of Teaching and Learning.* Chicago, IL: University of Chicago.

Jago, Carol. 2000. *With Rigor for All: Teaching the Classics to Contemporary Students.* Portsmouth, NH: Heinemann.

Langer, Judith. 1995. *Envisioning Literature: Literary Understanding and Literature Instruction.* New York: Teachers College Press/International Reading Association.

6

Reading Information

*Simplicity of reading derives from the context of detailed
and complex information properly arranged.*
—Edward Tufte, from *Envisioning Information*

*Printing made us all readers. Xeroxing made us all
publishers. Television made us all viewers.
Digitization makes us all broadcasters.*
—Lawrence Grossman, NBC News president

Defining Information

Consider the trail of information I have generated today and which
might, in some not so distant scenario, be for sale to companies: I sent
a package via FedEx using a corporate account; I rented a car using the
credit card I keep for business; I made phone calls using my family's
phone card; I bought gifts for my children using our family credit card; I
ordered supplies online; I purchased a ticket for a flight I'm about to
take; and, as I sit here in the Boston airport waiting for that flight, I listen to CDs I purchased yesterday with my bank's ATM card. Add to this
the genetic information we now have about my health, which is to say
my future and that of my family. If, as the early Internet gurus claimed,
"information wants to be free," that's a lot of information about me
and what I like, where I go, what I do, what I need—in short, about
who I *am*.

During the same period that I was generating so much useful information about myself, I was reading at least as much. I read fairly confusing street signs, service agreements, contracts, schedules, maps, airport

diagrams, poems (while standing in line), a Web site I printed up the day before, pamphlets for some products I am considering buying, various e-mails I received that morning but did not have time to read, and *USA Today,* a paper consisting of words, images, charts, graphs, advertisements, symbols, and much more.

Much of the reading discussed in this chapter is what Louise Rosenblatt, in *The Reader, the Text, and Poem* (1978) calls "efferent" reading. Rosenblatt defines such reading as being concerned primarily with "what [the reader] will carry away from the reading" (24). She explains:

> I have chosen the term "efferent," derived from the Latin "efferre," "to carry away." This seems to be freer of misleading implications than "instrumental," which would in most instances seem appropriately to contrast "aesthetic" [reading]. Yet instrumental implies a tool-like usefulness that does not fit some kinds of nonaesthetic reading. The mathematician reading his equations, the physicist pondering formulae, may have no practical purpose in mind, yet their attention is focused on the concepts, the solutions, to be "carried away" from their reading.

NOTE

Most states refer to such "efferent" texts as "functional" or "workplace" texts in their standards documents or curriculum frameworks.

The range of texts to which Rosenblatt limits herself pales in comparison to the number and diversity of texts commonly read and written today, largely because of our evolving textual intelligence and improved means of communicating information through technology. Rosenblatt also acknowledges that the same text may be read either efferently or aesthetically, an important point as many find information capable of expressing remarkable beauty if designed thoughtfully. Frank Smith, however, writing in his book *Between Hope and Havoc: Essays into Human Learning and Education* (1995), refutes Rosenblatt's conception of such information and the nature of the reading act itself. His view is that "we acquire information *only* when we are reading for experience . . . To make sense of what we read we have to read for experience—or rather, reading has to *be* an experience . . . We don't live for information, we live for experience. And what we remember is usually in the form of a story, a story of 'what happened' to us or to someone else with whom we can identify, or at least empathize. Any 'facts' (or 'information') that we remember are usually part of those stories."

While I accept Rosenblatt's definition of *efferent* as an idea, and Smith's notion of the role of story, I don't find it as useful as *infotext*, a term coined by Karen Feathers in *Infotext: Reading and Learning* (1993). Feathers offers the following definition:

> Infotexts are the books, textbooks, journals, newspapers, and computer manuals that we read to gather information about particular topics. They may be oral—lectures and speeches—as well as written. The size, shape, appearance and content of info texts may change from year to year, but they remain the same in one important way—they deal with information.

Types of Information

To Feathers' description, I would add the following: *why* and thus *how* we read—or, to use Smith's word, experience—a text determines if it is an infotext. In *The Scribal Society*, Alan Purves (1990) summarizes what he feels are the three major kinds of infotext, each of which is shaped by the author's purpose and the audience's needs:

- *Recorded information:* We find this sort of documentative writing in laundry lists and telephone messages, as well as forms, checks, bills, certificates, and letters confirming conversations. In these kinds of writing, both the information and how it is organized are virtually established before writers ever begin to write. All they have to do is fill in the blanks.

- *Reported information:* The information is known or easily available to the writer, but she has to organize the information herself, and she must select the style and tone in which to write. I call it *reporting* because the writer is a witness to the scenes, events, or ideas; her task is to find an appropriate style of text in which to place this information. Many of the narratives that people put into letters fall into this category, as do descriptions of people, places, or things we observe. So too do minutes of meetings, reports of telephone conversations "for the record," business letters requesting something or explaining why the request cannot be fulfilled, and academic or scholarly articles.

- *Exploratory discourse:* The selection of the information and the form in which it is to be stored [or conveyed] are both chosen by the writer. The writer must invent or generate the ideas, events, and scenes, and must choose the way in which to organize them, as well as the particular style and tone to use . . . [The] choice is based on knowledge of what kind of text conventionally fills what sort of function and on knowledge of what limitations in information, organization, and style and tone accompany that particular kind of text.

More and more, the same information comes to us in a variety of media, each medium chosen for its capacity to persuade, to inform, or to entertain the audience most likely to read it. We don't, for example, read the media, or advertisements, or newspapers: we read the information they contain, information the publishers, writers, and producers package for and convey through the most appropriate medium. As I mentioned earlier, they have a lot of information about what kind of information we want or need, and they have just as much information about how we like to get that information, and how we will or won't use it.

How We Use Information

We must not only know how to read this range of information but also understand how its form, media, and delivery system can affect its meaning or how we should read it. Information, unlike the other types of reading discussed in this book, is something we *use* to help us do things: plan, design, decide, organize. To return to Rosenblatt's definition of *efferent*, information is something we carry away from our transactions with a text and use to make our way through the world. Kids who cannot read a map should not be surprised by their final destination; teachers, too, have a part to play in teaching students how to get from point A to point B so they know not only how to read the map but also how maps and other visual explanations work.

Edward Tufte (1990) elaborates on the role and the use of information in our daily lives in his magnificent book *Envisioning Information*:

> We thrive in information-thick worlds because of our marvelous and everyday capacities to select, edit, single out, structure, highlight, group, pair, merge, harmonize, synthesize, focus, organize, condense, reduce, boil down, choose, categorize, catalog, classify, list, abstract, scan, look into, idealize, isolate, discriminate, distinguish, screen, pigeonhole, pick over, sort, integrate, blend, inspect, filter, lump, skip, smooth, chunk, average, approximate cluster, aggregate, outline, summarize, itemize, review, dip into, flip through, browse, glance into, leaf through, skim, refine, enumerate, glean, synopsize, winnow the wheat from the chaff, and separate the sheep from the goats.

No matter what we ultimately do with or to this information, we will certainly read it. By "reading it," I mean seek to make sense of it within the context in which we encounter it, by looking at the appropriate features that contain or work to shape the meaning of the information. As the authors of *The Social Life of Information* (Brown and Duguid 2000) wrote: "The way a writer and publisher physically present information, relying on resources outside the information itself, conveys to the reader much more than information alone. Context not only gives people what to read, it tells them how to read, where to read, what it means, what it's worth, and why it matters." Again, how we read this information—in a newspaper article, a chart, an image, a Web site, or a story—will depend entirely on *why* we are reading it.

> **F**or further discussion of textbook reading and the quality of the writing, see the Chapter 3, "Reading Textbooks."

NOTE

Communicating Information

Ironically, just at the time when we are asked to read more information than ever before, kids are, according to Sandra Stotsky, author of *Losing Our Language* (1999), being asked to read increasingly simplified texts, especially in the area of science textbooks. Stotsky argues that kids are asked to read texts that are made more simple—by images, graphics, and icons—and that contain less information—information, moreover, that is further simplified due to the less sophisticated vocabulary and sentence structures increasingly used by textbook authors. Some would no doubt disagree with Stotsky, seeing the blending of image and word on the page or the screen as proof of our own evolving textual intelligence, that is, using a range of types, features, and devices to more effectively communicate information to *all* readers, some of whom may need more than words to fully grasp the information, since authors themselves often need more than words to convey their ideas.

Mitchell Stephens, author of *the rise of the image the fall of the word*, adds his own perspective, emphasizing video's capacity to convey information and our evolving ability to handle so much information in such a short time. He points to an ABC television documentary, *In the Name of God*, that examined changes in America's churches. Stephens' real interest is on the opening segment that precedes the actual documentary. During these ninety-six seconds, we see:

> fifty-one different images, most showing separate scenes: churchgoers praying, laughing, weeping and collapsing; a Christian stage show; a congregation joining in aerobics; ministers preaching; ministers using show-business techniques; ministers defending their use of show-business techniques. Intercut are pictures of religious icons, bending and blurring. Three candles are shown blowing out. Additional images are sometimes superimposed. Words from the Bible flash on the screen. Ethereal yet insistent music plays. Cameras dart here and there . . . The piece has almost a ballet like beauty, but it is not particularly profound. It is, after all, only the introduction to an otherwise traditional documentary . . . However, this segment of videotape . . . impart[s] a remarkable amount of information and impressions in that short period of time—to the point

where the more conventionally edited one-hour documentary that follows begins to seem superfluous. (1998)

Understanding Information

Ours is now a world where information comes in different sizes and shapes, colors and media. Information underlies nearly all the other chapters of this book, a point that is reinforced by the growing number of books and state standards for media literacy and information literacy; college programs in information design, information management, and information science; and general use of the terms *infotainment* and *infomercial*. If stories are told and novels written, if arguments are put forth or advanced, information is designed, used, and analyzed. Always the question stands between us and the information: what do "they"—that is, the author, the organization, the corporation, or the government—want us to carry away from the transaction? Rushkoff emphasizes our power as readers of information, saying, "we still have the ability to recognize when we are being influenced and to lessen the effect of these techniques, however they originate. There are ways to deconstruct the subtle messages and cues coming at us from every direction" (2000). Throughout his book *Coercion*, Rushkoff reminds and demonstrates to us how pervasive, dangerous, and powerful—even volatile—information can be. Infomercials and infotainment accost us everywhere, even as we stand pumping our gas before the once-silent gas pump; informants and informers threaten entire organizations and industries such as the tobacco companies with the disclosure of information. As Rushkoff concludes in his book,

> Media literacy is dangerous—not to the individuals who gain it, but to the people and institutions that depend on our *not* having it. Once we master the tools of media literacy, we cannot apply them selectively. If we learn the techniques that an advertiser uses to fool us, we have also learned the tricks that a government uses. If we demystify the role of our hi-tech pundits, we may demystify the role of priests as well. (24)

While the types of information described by Purves and others are at the heart of this chapter—and this book—they take on many forms depending on the author's purpose and the media's constraints. Lewis Lapham (1997) illustrates such constraints perfectly in his introduction to a new edition of Marshall McLuhan's *Understanding the Media* when he writes,

> I had occasion to write a six-hour television history of the twentieth century . . . and was allowed 78 seconds and 43 words in which to explain the origins of World War II and provide the transition between the Munich Conference in September 1939

and Germany's invasion of Poland in September 1939. [I realized] that television is not narrative, that it bears more of a resemblance to symbolist poetry or the pointillist painting of Georges Seurat than it does to anything conceived by a novelist, a historian, an essayist, or even a writer of newspaper editorials.

Under such conditions, we begin to understand why Mitchell Stephens believes that video conveys more information in less time using fewer words and more images. Commenting on Stephens' ideas about video and our increased ability to process so many different types of information simultaneously, James Gleick (1999) argues that we have become more "sophisticated": "We're like fighter pilots doing a panel scan, absorbing data from all our instruments at once ... multitasking ... in real time." Gleick elaborates on this modern ability to digest an array of information in multiple forms that are not evidently related, saying, "We have learned a visual language made up of images and movements instead of words and syllables. It has its own grammar, abbreviations, clichés, lies, puns, and famous quotations." And Leonard Shlain, author of *The Alphabet Versus the Goddess: The Conflict Between Word and Image* (1998), takes it one step further, saying that such visual abilities—our shift from being dependent on *logos* ("the word," in Greek) to *logo* (icon)—are actually, through repeated and increased patterns of use, changing the way our minds and society function as a whole:

> A medium of communication is not merely a passive conduit for the transmission of information but rather an active force in creating new social patterns and new perceptual realities. A person who is literate has a different view than one who receives information exclusively through oral communication. The alphabet, independent of spoken languages, transcribes the information it makes available, has its own intrinsic impacts.

The form (i.e., genre, medium, format) will typically depend on what the author is trying to accomplish. Thus, for example, if the information is designed to show cause and effect, that narrows the available options. A map used to orient mass transit riders will function differently than one created to show the effect of a new transit line to the airport on traffic patterns. Figure 1–3 listed some primary types of text that we use to convey or which contain information. While information then varies from financial to cultural, procedural to historical, such information, consisting of words, images, numbers, or some combination of them all, is arranged in many different forms.

These different types of text, however, represent and convey different types of information, sometimes simultaneously. The Declaration of Independence, for instance, is historical and political, rhetorical and procedural, literary and informational in the type of information it conveys.

Thus, we return again to the author's initial reason for creating the text to help us determine how it should be read; however, we must also ask about the person's or institution's purpose for asking us to read the document today if, as in the case of the Declaration of Independence, we are being asked to read it.

The skills necessary to defend ourselves against such an info barrage are pretty sophisticated, however. We need to be able to ask questions, but they must be the right questions, posed at the right time to the appropriate people. When it comes to infotexts, such textual intelligence requires that we understand something about the following—and many other—domains of knowledge:

- Design
- Grammar
- Logic
- Mathematics (i.e., statistics, percentages, graphs, charts)
- Rhetoric
- Semantics
- Technology
- Typography

In her wonderful book *The Universe in a Teacup: The Mathematics of Truth and Beauty*, K. C. Cole writes about how ill-equipped most of us are to navigate the complicated terrain of information:

> *Newsweek* magazine plunged American women into a state of near panic some years ago when it announced that the chance of a college-educated thirty-five-year-old woman finding a husband was less than her chance of being killed by a terrorist . . . Scientists, statisticians, and policy makers attach numbers to the risk of getting breast cancer or AIDS, to flying and food additives, to getting hit by lightning and falling in the bathtub. Yet despite (or perhaps because of) all the numbers floating around, most people are quite properly confused about risk. I know people who live happily on the San Andreas Fault and yet are afraid to ride the New York subways (and vice versa). I've known smokers who can't stand to be in the same room with a fatty steak, and women afraid of the side effects of birth control pills who have unprotected sex with strangers. (1999)

Cole concludes that how we interpret information about risk, for example, often depends on our ability to interpret carefully crafted language. Ours is a world where information comes at us not only in words but in icons, symbols, logos, images, illustrations, and, of course, numbers. Cole goes on to write:

Looking for truth in numbers presents obstacles far beyond the peculiar nature of the human thinking apparatus we carry around in our heads (and also in the rest of our bodies). There's also the difficulty of getting true information from what some people call the real world. We only glimpse that world through the patterns, or signals, we see in our heads. But those patterns and signals are created, at least in part, outside ourselves: Call them information, messages, signals, relationships, ideas. Whatever you call them . . . understanding anything requires getting a handle on that stuff out there and on the ways in which knowledge about it arrives on our internal radar screens.

NOTE

See Chapters 2 and 7 for further ideas about what is real, what is true.

The Elements of Information

So far we have considered a vast array of texts that are used to narrate, to explain, and to persuade, sometimes simultaneously. The integration of not just words and images but colors and typography is not new, though modern technology has allowed for a much more sophisticated use of these and other elements. The early Sears mail-order catalogs exemplify the intelligent use of many elements that were used to sell but also to establish their credibility—even to educate children—see the extract from Daniel Boorstin's discussion on page 37.

WEB SITE

For an example of such an ad, go to the companion Web site.

Language, as Renee Hobbs reminds us in "Literacy in the Information Age" (1998), is:

only one of a number of symbol systems which humans use to express and share meaning. Changes in communication technologies over the past 100 years have created a cultural environment that has extended and reshaped the role of language and the written word. Language must be appreciated as it exists in relationship to other forms of symbolic expression—including images, sound, music and electronic forms of communication.

If we don't know what infotexts are made of—the features, the devices, and so on—we will not be able to read them well nor defend ourselves against misinformation. Knowledge about how information is used to coerce us to think, feel, or behave in certain ways gives people power over their own minds. Such are the initial findings of a study done at the University of Massachusetts, where researchers examined the effect of different antismoking campaigns on teenagers:

> The ads were designed not to educate teens about the health risks of smoking (they already know that) but instead to show them that there is another group of powerful adults, in addition to their parents and teachers, that is trying to tell teens what to think about tobacco. These ads give kids a look at the cynical manipulation behind the targeting of teens by tobacco marketing campaigns. Kids who saw these ads in Massachusetts were half as likely to smoke as others their age. (Dickinson 2000)

NOTE

For examples of such campaigns, to go <www.thetruth.com>.

Certain elements within a text are more concrete. These might include, for example, color, shape, typography, size, or volume. Color, for example, is constantly used to convey information because color printing is now more affordable and because in such multiple media texts as Web pages, color can add content as well as functional information that tells us how to *use* as well as read the text. Usability and Web design guru Jakob Nielsen (2000) emphasizes the importance of using color (and other features) in predictable ways so readers know what to expect: "Users have grown accustomed to blue being the link color, so they have zero delay in figuring out how to work with a page if it uses blue for unvisited links." Tufte (1997) identifies four primary ways that color is used in information design:

- To label (color as noun)
- To measure (color as quantity)
- To represent or imitate reality (color as representation)
- To enliven or decorate (color as beauty)

It is worth noting that the fourth way of using color does not contain or add information, though to determine that, we must, as readers, first ask the essential questions. Students in my remedial reading classes find the color coding in their textbooks particularly confusing and will, unless taught how to make sense of this information, ignore it at their own academic peril.

Typography also exerts a powerful effect on the reader and affects the impact information does or does not have. The visual elements of any document should accomplish several important ends. They should help the reader by making the information more interesting and clear. Certainly in this era of desktop publishing, we bring to each document a set of expectations that would have been unimaginable even ten years ago. As Robert Bringhurst writes in his classic book *The Elements of Typographic Style* (1996), the proper elements on the page, a balance between typographic and visual information, can achieve "some earned or unearned interest that gives its living energy to the page."

The intelligent use of these different textual elements enables the writer to:

- clarify ideas
- emphasize certain information
- reveal crucial relationships between programs and ideas

Typography contributes significantly to the surgeon general's message that appears on cigarette packages, for example. This familiar bit of health-related information uses a number of well-known typographic devices to undermine the user's ability to take in and be affected by the information contained in the warning:

- The use of ALL CAPS, which makes it very difficult for the reader to distinguish between letters
- The use of a box to surround the words and further intrude on the smoker's visual field, thus making it difficult for the brain to grasp the information
- The use of a sans serif font—that is, a font like Geneva or Helvetica that has no spurs or other decorative features—which research has consistently found makes it difficult for the readers' eyes and slows them down

Such details as these amount to what Tufte (1997) calls *"differences that make a difference."* Other factors, listed in Figure 1–1, also make a difference in meaning and effect depending on how they are used and the context in which they are read.

Other textual features are not so physical, so obvious as those listed in Figure 1–1; instead, they are abstract, embedded, or implied, but they are just as important, if not more so. Examples of such elements include, but are not limited to:

- Accuracy
- Authenticity
- Bias
- Clarity
- Ethics
- Importance
- Objectivity
- Purpose
- Relevance

- Reliability
- Truth
- Validity

Assessing the Quality of Information

All of these features in the previous list boil down to the question of whether or not we can trust the information and its sources. Certain information is obtained by unethical means or, despite its authority, is used to support unethical ends and positions. Other information is corrupted by the author's self-interest or the lack of supporting, credible evidence. Information in a newspaper driven to sell differs from that in a newspaper committed to inform. Indeed, the media in particular finds itself in a market defined by the need to provide news but also to sell more than the dozens or even hundreds of other news sources available; thus what information is offered and whether or not the story is "told slant" are always relevant questions. When organizations and businesses can buy as many as twenty pages in reliable publications like the *New Yorker* and weave into the magazine what looks upon passing glance like part of the magazine, complete with articles by nationally known writers that are subtly marked as "advertisement" across the top, the line between fact and fiction or information and propaganda gets pretty thin. As *Brill's Content* magazine says on its cover, "skepticism is a virtue."

This virtue, which I would call a capacity or even a habit that we all need, becomes more essential all the time as reporters and their sources are increasingly discredited as unreliable or even nonexistent in several cases, even in articles that have won the Pulitzer Prize for reporting. In an article titled "Outbreak of Fiction Is Alarming News," *Washington Post* reporter Howard Kurtz lists several high-profile examples that happened around the same time:

> The *New Republic* fires a hot young writer for fabricating parts of 27 articles. The Boston *Globe* dumps a popular columnist for making up characters, articles, and quotes. CNN and Time come under hostile fire for a questionable report alleging that American troops once used nerve gas in Laos. And, in the latest embarrassment yesterday, the Cincinnati *Enquirer* fires a reporter, apologizes to Chiquita Brands for "deceitful, unethical and unlawful conduct" and agrees to pay the company more than $10 million. (1998, B01)

Additional elements also merit consideration. The first has to do with completeness: is what we read, hear, or see all there was, or was it edited, manipulated, or otherwise changed? A review of a PBS documentary titled *New York: A Documentary Film*, directed by Ric Burns, cited some of the documentary's failures as follows: "This is a history of New

York in which you hear nothing about the painter John Sloan and the Ashcan School or about the New York Armory show of 1913. It is a history of New York in which you hear nothing about organized crime. It is a history of New York in which a great Gotham figure, the flamboyant Mayor Jimmy White, gets referred to and passed over in a nanosecond, and it is a history of New York that does not even comment on the myth of Broadway" (Siegel 2000). Such omissions and misinformation emphasize the danger of that most pernicious element of too many texts today: doublespeak. Siegel accuses Burns' documentary of visual doublespeak, which, according to Fox (1998), is "the use of images that pretend to communicate but really do not; images that make the bad seem good, the negative appear positive; images that shift and avoid responsibility; images used to mislead, deceive, obfuscate the truth."

The pressure for a range of publications across media—what are increasingly called content providers—to establish and promote their integrity has gained some momentum in the period of time that followed the Lewinsky-Clinton hearings, all of which culminated in the immediate distribution of the Starr Report via the Internet. Magazines like *Brill's Content* made such declarations of principle part of their identity. For example, the following mission statement appears in every issue of *Brill's Content*:

WHAT WE STAND FOR

1. Accuracy. *Brill's Content* is about all that purports to be nonfiction. So it should be no surprise that our first principle is that anything that purports to be nonfiction should be true. Which means it should be accurate in fact and in context.

2. Labeling and Sourcing. Similarly, if a publisher is not certain that something is accurate, the publisher should either not publish it, or should make that uncertainty plain by clearly stating the source of his information and its possible limitations and pitfalls. To take another example of making the quality of information clear, we believe that if unnamed sources must be used, they should be labeled in a way that sheds light on the limits and biases of the information they offer.

3. Conflicts of Interest. We believe that the content of anything that sells itself as journalism should be free of any motive other than informing its consumers. In other words, it should not be motivated by the desire to curry favor with an advertiser or to advance a particular political interest.

4. Accountability. We believe that journalists should hold themselves as accountable as any of the subjects they write about. They should be eager to receive complaints about their work, to investigate complaints diligently, and to correct mistakes of fact, context, and fairness prominently and clearly.

Writing for *Brill's Content*, author-designer Edwin Schlossberg asks, in his article "A Question of Trust," "What makes information trustworthy?" (1999, 70). Robert Berring, writing in the *California Monthly*, asks a variation on the same question: "Why do we trust certain sources and not others?" (1998, 15). Schlossberg goes on to emphasize the need for a means of measuring the trustworthiness of information, especially when found on the Internet. He writes, "Contemporary technology challenges us to recognize trustworthiness without the usual name-brand information sources or community standards" (1999, 70). Returning to Berring's article, he discusses the "old model of information authority," which has since been replaced by television and, increasingly, the Internet. He describes how the Starr Report would have been handled in the old days:

> In the old world of paper-based information, the special prosecutor's report would have been treated as a "government document." First, summaries or abstracts would have appeared, as a press release or an executive report. Then the whole report would have been printed and distributed as part of the depository library system. It would have ended up available to anyone who wanted it at a public library—perhaps a year later. It might also have been read into the *Congressional Record*, making it part of another information stream almost as long and winding as a congressional document. A paperback book might appear, as happened with the *Pentagon Papers*.
>
> In the old paradigm of paper publication, the information would have been publicly available, but not instantaneously omnipresent. There would have been filters between the average person and the information. Some of these filters would be human and subjective. Editors may have redacted the report, summarized it, abstracted it. Congressmen who were involved, and perhaps a handful of reporters, would have read the whole thing. When the report reached most citizens it would have come not as raw data, but as information processed through a series of authority filters . . .
>
> The typical literate citizen lived in an established universe of known landmarks. The instantaneous publication of information over the Internet is different. It's causing a kind of Gresham's Law in the media, and debasing everybody. Everyone is now racing to put out the fastest, sauciest story, and reducing information to infotainment. (1999, 15)

Edward Seaton (1999) himself, president of the American Society of Newspaper Editors, urged all newspapers to reflect on their purpose and their responsibility to both their readers and the information their stories carry. In an op-ed piece in the *San Francisco Chronicle*, he wrote, "Publishing our written standards and guidelines for readers will be a

NOTE

This push for immediate access and publication further confirms James Gleick's assertion about "the acceleration of just about everything." The latest example of such a push for access is the immediate release to the public of audiotapes of the Supreme Court hearings regarding the vote recounts in Florida during the 2000 presidential election.

key to improving our credibility. Readers will understand why we do what we do. They will also be able to judge what we publish."

Perhaps sophomore Derek Haskins comes closest to explaining how we need to think about the information we encounter when we read, watch the news, or hear someone speak about an issue. Derek wrote "How to Know a Fact When You See One," in which he explained:

> What is the difference between a fact and opinion? Simple, a fact, according to the dictionary, is something (as an event or an act) that really exists or has occurred. An opinion, according to the dictionary, is a belief based on experience and on seeing certain facts but not amounting to sure knowledge. So how do you tell the difference? For one, if a statement is coming from a biased person it's probable that it's an opinion. For example, the statement, "It is programs like *Doom* that are to blame for the Littleton massacre." If this statement is coming from someone who was a victim of the Littleton massacre, or if it's one of the culprits of the massacre, then it's probably an opinion, or for a culprit, an opinion to help them excuse what they did . . . In conclusion, the way to determine fact from opinion is to determine what is absolute truth and not, but what's absolute truth? Not a clue, I'm just here to determine fact from opinion.

As Derek states, other essential issues when it comes to measuring the quality and integrity of information are the alliances and the possible biases of the source; increasingly, this means who owns the company that reports the story. Major network television shows, for example, will review newly released films in glowing terms, conveniently neglecting to note that their parent company owns the company that made the film. Here is the disclosure statement offered up front by *Brill's Content*, which states its mission is to monitor such breaches of integrity and trust:

DISCLOSURE

Brill Media Holding, L.P., the parent company of this magazine, has recently entered into an agreement in which NBC, CBS, and Primedia (a large magazine company) will participate as limited partners in an Internet business to be run by Brill Media Holdings.

Although the two ventures are separate and these media companies by contract specifically disclaim any involvement in or influence over this magazine, there is nonetheless an indirect connection between the magazine and these companies. Any complaints about perceived bias by the magazine in favor of NBC, CBS, or Primedia should also be directed to Mr. Gartner.

Figure 1–1 demonstrates that features and devices are not decorations but used and designed to achieve certain effects. Regardless of the medium, whether visual or written, performed or designed, each has its own means of using features to:

- Analyze
- Compare
- Contrast
- Deceive
- Differentiate
- Emphasize
- Equate
- Intensify
- Organize
- Persuade
- Reinforce
- Simplify
- Subordinate

One of the most important functions of these different elements is to emphasize certain details, themes, or ideas. Certain information can be emphasized in any or several of the following ways:

- Grammatically/semantically/syntactically
- Linguistically (spoken)
- Physically (gestures)
- Structurally (placement, arrangement, sequence)
- Visually (colors, spatial arrangement)

Intelligent readers must now bring skepticism and scrutiny to bear on every detail of any text they read, which includes everything from the layout of the malls we shop in to the pleas that come from our ministers:

Telemarketers make us afraid to answer the phone in the evening. Salesmen bearing free gifts (with strings attached) make us reluctant to accept presents from our neighbors. Greedy televangelists twisting Bible pitches into sales pitches, and church charity drives employing state-of-the-art fund-raising techniques make us wary of religion. Our president's foreign policy is channeled through spin doctors before it reaches Congress or the people, leading to widespread cynicism about the political process. Our sporting events are so crowded with product promotions that we can't root for a team without cheering a corporate logo. Our movements through department stores are videotaped and analyzed so that shelves and displays can be rearranged to steer us toward an optimum volume of more expensive purchases. Scientists study the influences of colors, sounds, and smells on our likelihood of buying. (Rushkoff 2000)

Because of these omnipresent features designed to trap—as opposed to inform—me, I find it most useful to ask, when reading, whether what *seems* to be a meaningful element—color, weight of lines, arrangement of information—contains meaning, that is, contributes to or somehow changes the meaning of the text I'm trying to read. Returning for a moment to Frank Smith's notion of reading *as* experience, we might sum up this section of the chapter by asking what story the author is trying to tell, and how her use of different features and devices affects that story. Pushing the story analogy a step further, we might ask whether the information we are seeing, reading, hearing, or otherwise experiencing is a reliable narrator of a truth we seek through our reading. In a brief section titled "Unreliable Witness," the authors of *The Social Life of Information* write:

> information has trouble, as we all do, testifying on its own behalf. Its only recourse in the face of doubt is to provide more information . . . People look beyond information to triangulate reliability. People look past what others say, for example, to gauge trustworthiness. Some clues might be formal and institutional: Who does a prospective client work for? What is her credit rating? Others are informal, such as dress, address, and cars . . . Readers look beyond the information in documents. Published documents, for example, often embody the institutional authority of the publisher. The investment in a document's material content is often a good indicator of the investment in its informational content. Physical heft lends institutional weight to what it says. Readers rely on more informal warrants, too. For example, they may examine a report to see whose handwriting appears in the margin, whether the spine is broken, how well the pages are thumbed, where the highlights fall, or whose names are on the routing slip. (Brown and Daguid 2000, 187)

Questions to Ask

All of this talk about truth, deceit, and skepticism leads to the big question: what questions can and should we ask to evaluate the information we read? Here are some to get you and your students started, though when or whether you ask them will depend on the context of what you're reading.

- Does this infotext reveal the truth about its subject or conceal it?
- Is the information current and accurate?
- What are the sources of this information?
- Do the means of conveying this information—words, images, illustrations, multimedia—help clarify and support the data?
- Does the author clearly identify the sources of the information?
- Are those sources valid, reliable, current, and appropriate?
- Am I able to make informed—that is, appropriate, useful, even wise—decisions based on the information provided in this text?
- Can the information in this text be checked against the thing to which it refers—for example, a diagram of an airport or a written description of a building?
- Is the information in this text complete? Original?
- What criteria should I use to evaluate this information?
- How is this information being used?
- Why did the author and/or publisher choose this particular medium for this message?
- What questions do I need to ask in order to read this infotext successfully?
- Was this information purchased? Found? Gathered? Generated?
- In what context was this information created/produced? How might that have created a bias or affected the decisions the author made about what to include and what to omit?
- Who was the original audience for this information?
- Where, how, and from whom did the author get this information?
- Was the information obtained and used in an ethical manner that establishes and maintains its integrity?
- Does the author have any probable bias or self-interest in this subject or people's response to the text that might undermine the textual integrity?
- Does the author provide appropriate means of evaluating the information, for example, by comparing this with other, reliable, established sources in this field?
- Is the author offering this information as fact or opinion, truth or speculation?
- Is this information based on:
  - Experience
  - Observation
  - Interviews with multiple, reliable sources

- What means does the author use to establish the validity, the credibility, the accuracy, and the reliability of the information and its sources?

- Does the author make a good-faith effort at full disclosure by acknowledging biases or other factors that might undermine or color her reporting?

- Is this same information provided in alternative forms and media? If so, what are they and what is the author trying to accomplish through these other media?

- Why am I reading this information?

- Does the author's text use multiple means of helping the reader understand the information? How do these function to clarify?

- What textual features—stylistic, structural, typographical, rhetorical—does the author use to convey, shape, or organize the information?

Such questions, along with the willingness to ask them and the knowledge of how to ask them, are crucial when we are reading information to help us make important decisions. During the time I wrote this chapter, I was shopping for a computer, evaluating presidential candidates, and choosing a school for my son. On a more local level, the mayoral race was reduced to a debate over what is true: Is the city in the red or in the black? Is one candidate abusive of power and women or not? Has the city improved or not? Many of the testimonials on behalf of the candidates came with photographs of the testifier, as well as his or her affiliation and title. Such elements help establish the credibility of people and the information they provide, which is also why such Internet reporters as Matt Drudge face constant challenges to their credibility, since people can post information anonymously through sites like Drudge's.

Standards Connection

We just read about standards that many within the information industries are trying to establish or help us create for ourselves, but what would such info-education look like within our own profession? While Douglass Rushkoff laments the absence of media and information literacy education within public schools, the truth is that many states and professional organizations are beginning to develop and implement such standards.

Running throughout standards are these core skills:

- Analysis
- Evaluation
- Identification
- Interpretation

To these skills, we might add one that Thomas Friedman, author of *The Lexus and the Olive Tree* (2000), calls "information arbitrage." He writes:

> Whether you are selling pork bellies or insights, the key to being a successful [information] arbitrageur is having a wide net of informants and information and then knowing how to synthesize it in a way that will produce profit . . . You have to learn how to arbitrage information from these disparate perspectives and then weave it all together to produce a picture of the world that you would never have if you looked at it from only one perspective . . . In a world where we are all so much more interconnected, the ability to read the connections [is an essential skill].

WEB SITE

For more information about the American Library's information literacy standards, visit <www.ala.org> and this book's companion Web site.

While information and media literacy standards have much in common, the information standards are typically written with research in mind. Media literacy standards apply more to reading—that is, viewing, interpreting, analyzing, evaluating—texts produced in multiple media for a variety of audiences and purposes. The following media standards, which I synthesized from different sources, complement the previous information literacy skills.

MEDIA STANDARDS
- Understands and interprets visual images, messages, and meanings
- Describes how illustrators' choice of style, elements, and media help represent or extend the text's meanings
- Interprets important events and ideas gathered from maps, charts, graphics, video segments, or technology presentations
- Uses media to compare ideas and points of view
- Analyzes and critiques the significance of visual images, messages, and meanings
- Interprets and evaluates the various ways visual image makers such as illustrators, documentary filmmakers, and political cartoonists represent meanings
- Compares and contrasts print, visual, and electronic media, such as film, with written story
- Evaluates the purposes and effects of varying media such as film, print, and technology presentations

- Evaluates how different media forms influence and inform
- Assesses how language, medium, and presentation contribute to the message
- Understands and interprets visual representations
- Describes how meanings are communicated through elements of design, including shape, line, color, and texture
- Analyzes relationships, ideas, and cultures as represented in various media
- Distinguishes the purposes of various media forms such as informative texts, entertaining texts, and advertisements
- Analyzes and critiques the significance of visual representations
- Accesses, analyzes, evaluates, and produces communication in a variety of forms
- Interprets various media forms for a variety of purposes
- Recognizes strategies used by media to inform, persuade, entertain, and transmit culture such as advertising, perpetuation of stereotypes, and use of visual representations, special effects, and language
- Evaluates the persuasive techniques of media messages such as glittering generalities, associations with personalities, logical fallacies, and use of symbols
- Compares and contrasts media with other art forms
- Analyzes techniques used in visual media
- Explores the emotional and intellectual effects of visual media on viewers
- Recognizes how visual and sound techniques, such as special effects, editing, camera angles, reaction shots, sequencing, and music, convey messages in media
- Analyzes strategies used by media to inform, persuade, entertain, and educate
- Analyzes the influence of media on consumers
- Analyzes and evaluates media's efforts to address social and cultural problems

It is worth making one last connection to standards in this area. Figure 6–1 contains the Northwestern Regional Educational Lab's (NWREL) traits of effective readers of informational texts.

NOTE

You can read more about NWREL's work in the area of standards by going to <http://www.nwrel.org/eval/reading/scoring.html>.

The Traits of an Effective Reader Reading an Informational Text Scoring Guide

DEVELOPING INTERPRETATIONS

- Identify problems, gaps, ambiguities, conflicts, and/or disparate points of view in the text
- Analyze the text to pose explanations that bridge gaps, clarify ambiguity, and resolve textual problems
- Using the context to connect analytical explanations to a "bigger picture"

5 The advanced response interprets to analyze and think critically about informational texts.

☐ Directly answers the question by employing problem-solving techniques—using specific evidence, clues, and "on target" information
☐ Examples, quotes, and events are cited from the text and connected strongly to the analysis
☐ Responds beyond the question to engage the bigger picture by creating framework of historical significance, cultural importance, or universal theme

3 Interprets to expand the text, but still developing connections to a larger worldview.

☐ Uses some language that indicates an initial layer of interpretation or understanding
☐ A safe response citing very obvious examples. Connections between the examples and the analysis are not always evident
☐ Does not yet move beyond the question—engaging the "bigger picture" is still a developing skill

1 The emerging response sees interpretation as "talking about a book." Reading and interpreting are still separate processes. Little evidence exists that the student understands the concept of interpretation.

☐ Does not adequately address the question
☐ Does not cite examples, quotes, or evidence from the text to use as a basis of interpretation
☐ Sometimes restates the question words

INTEGRATING FOR SYNTHESIS

- Put information in order to explain the text's process or chronology
- Compare and contrast examples, facts, or events in order to make defensible judgments or interpretations
- Recognize and describe cause-and-effect relations
- Integrate personal experience, background knowledge, and/or content knowledge with the text to create a "synthesis" of text plus knowledge

5 The advanced response integrates textual material and other types of knowledge to create synthesis of ideas.

☐ Directly, specifically, and concretely performs the synthesis application directed by the question by using synthesis language
☐ Uses well-chosen examples that have a strong parallel development if the question demands it
☐ Responds beyond the question, integrating several layers of knowledge into a harmonious whole

3 The developing response integrates textual material with other types of knowledge to create a surface-level synthesis.

☐ Uses some synthesis language to reflect a basic understanding of the skills of integrating for synthesis
☐ Uses general and "safe" examples
☐ The layers and types of knowledge in the response are not always well integrated

1 The emerging response employs some skills of synthesizing, but a fully developed integration is still emerging.

☐ Does not perform the synthesis application directed by the question
☐ Does not accurately use synthesis language
☐ Does not integrate sources, texts, and understandings to a measurable degree

CRITIQUING FOR EVALUATION

- Experiment with ideas in the text
- Express opinions about the text
- Raise questions about the text
- Make good judgments about the text by using a synthesis of material derived from multiple sources
- Challenge the ideas of the author or source by noting bias, distortion, and/or lack of coherence
- Contrast the accuracy of textual information with other sources and form solid, defensible critiques

5 The advanced response evaluates to assert a strong voice in the text.

☐ Directly and thoughtfully answers the question, using evaluation terminology effectively and precisely to indicate the reader's critique of the text
☐ The examples are well developed, placed in context, and connected well to other ideas
☐ Responds beyond the parameters of the question to critically engage the text and its ideas in a solid, defensible judgment

3 The developing response hesitates to evaluate thoroughly; it still plays it somewhat "safe."

☐ Generally answers the evaluation question, but hesitant to critically engage with the text
☐ Selects safe and obvious examples that are connected to other ideas in fairly limited ways
☐ Does not yet move beyond the question to venture into the larger word of critical discourse.

1 The emerging response is just beginning to explore a critical stance to the text.

☐ Uses evaluation terminology sporadically or not at all
☐ The examples are incomplete or sketchily described, and not connected to other ideas or issues
☐ The response is incomplete or restates the question words

FIGURE 6–1 Northwestern Regional Educational Lab Scoring Guide for Informational Texts. © The Northwestern Regional Educational Laboratory, Portland, OR. *Reprinted by permission in* Illuminating Texts *by Jim Burke.*

May be copied for classroom use. Jim Burke. 2001. Illuminating Texts. Portsmouth, NH: Heinemann.

The Traits of an Effective Reader Reading an Informational Text Scoring Guide

DECODING CONVENTIONS

- Decode the writing conventions of grammar, punctuation, word recognition, and sentence structure
- Recognize the organizational conventions of the author or organizational framework and features of the text
- Identify the genre conventions newspaper, magazine, textbooks, brochures, instruction) and the types of modes appropriate to each informational genre (cause-and-effect, comparision, sequential, etc.)

5 The advanced response uses conventions information to form a confident "thinking frame" of a text.

- ☐ Directly answers the question using text structure language in specific and precise ways
- ☐ Selects well-chosen and well-supported examples to illustrate understanding of conventions
- ☐ Responds "beyond" the question by enlarging the initial thinking frame

3 The developing response uses conventions information to form an initial "thinking frame" of the text.

- ☐ Uses some basic text structure language to indicate general understandings
- ☐ Selects "safe" and obvious examples to illustrate understanding of the conventions
- ☐ The response is fairly safe and stays definitely within the confines of the question

1 The emerging response is beginning to decode conventions and the challenge of decoding gets in the way of a "thinking frame" for the text.

- ☐ Does not adequately answer the question but may use some text structure language
- ☐ Focuses on more general information rather than providing examples from the text
- ☐ The response can be characterized as sketchy and incomplete

ESTABLISHING COMPREHENSION

- Identify and explain the vocabulary key to the main text
- Identify the main idea, major and minor examples, facts, expert authority, and turning moments
- Distinguish between significant and supporting details that elaborate the main idea
- Summarize and paraphrase with purpose to move toward making inferences and interpretations

5 The advanced response demonstrates a purposeful, expansive and knowledge-able comprehension of the text.

- ☐ Directly answers the question using comprehension terms to indicate precise understandings
- ☐ Selects well-chosen examples to illustrate in-depth comprehension. Examples are well developed using clear, specific language and terms
- ☐ Responds "beyond" the question by increasing comprehension of the text into inferential and interpretive levels

3 The developing response demonstrates an adequate comprehension of the text. Purposeful comprehension is still evolving.

- ☐ Uses some comprehension terms to indicate general understandings
- ☐ Selects "safe" and obvious examples to illustrate literal comprehension
- ☐ Does not venture information beyond the initial question

1 The emerging response is searching to establish a basic comprehension of the text.

- ☐ Does not provide examples for evidence but sometimes restates the question
- ☐ Little evidence that a basic comprehension of the text has been achieved
- ☐ The response can be characterized as sketchy and incomplete

REALIZING CONTEXT

- Identify the time period and its accompanying social realities in the text
- Recognize the perspective—point of view—of the text and its relationship to social factors
- Identify the vocabulary reflective of the context
- Recognize the writing mode, tone, and voice of the author or source selected with respect to the context
- Recognize the subject matter's context and its applications to many aspects of the text

5 The advanced response realizes context and sees inferential meanings and intended purposes, both implicit and explicit.

- ☐ Directly and specifically answers the question to demonstrate understanding of inferential meaning
- ☐ Selects well-chosen examples to illustrate understandings of contextual issues
- ☐ Goes beyond the question's limits and extends into in-depth understandings of contextual relationships

3 The developing response realizes the context of the text to some degree and recognizes obvious types of inference. The idea of contextual relationships between many factors and issues is still in development.

- ☐ Uses some context terminology to show a basic level of understanding
- ☐ Selects "safe" and obvious examples that stay close to the surface of the text
- ☐ Stays within the safe confines of the question

1 The emerging response guesses at context, but has difficulty accessing inferential knowledge.

- ☐ Does not use examples from the text to illustrate inferential understanding
- ☐ Not enough evidence to demonstrate an understanding of contextual layers of the text
- ☐ Demonstrates little effectiveness at "reading between the lines"

FIGURE 6–1   Continued

Closing Thoughts

We live in a world dulled by the amount of information around us, much of which is irrelevant, useless, or just plain wrong. As citizens, consumers, and human beings, we are challenged to find both method and meaning in the midst of it all. Thus, we will see people using more and more machines or "bots" to do their reading for them. This trend became apparent to me during the writing of my previous book, *I'll Grant You That* (Burke and Prater 2000). One man who worked on the companion CD "read" the entire book manuscript in minutes using the command-F key; he wanted only to find references to the CD-ROM. Every time his search engine ran across another reference, he noted it and told his computer to keep searching. As more texts become available online, such reading of infotexts will become increasingly prevalent. This book itself consists of more than its printed pages; the pages you are reading are but a part of the larger, complete text that includes the companion Web site and, through that, related links to other, further removed texts (poems, images, documents).

We return then to the earlier analogy of the tool belt. Readers must acquire a range of intellectual tools and the talent to know how and when to use them. We need tools—habits, questions—to help us read the Internet and the information we find there; yet we must also realize that the Net itself is a powerful tool we can use to help us read other infotexts. The following example, taken from Tom McDermott's journal as part of my online course, exemplifies this use of the Net and the type of skills needed in this and the coming world:

> School activity speakers [are] preaching their anti and pro something or other messages. Last year we had a guy name Wild Man Misner dazzle our students for a full eighty minutes. No kidding. They sat quiet and still for eighty minutes while this self-professed former Marine recon-type told them tales of bravery and woe. His anti-drug stories captured the kids' imaginations. His size and bearing had nearly all of them under control. They cheered wildly for him when he wound up his presentation. Only one kid was suspicious.
>
> Mike Costa had just finished the book *Stolen Glory*, and some of the things the speaker fed the school smelled sour to him. He used the Freedom of Information Act to check out this guy's war record and discovered that Mr. Misner hadn't done anything he said he'd done to establish his credentials as a reformed tough guy. Except for his record as a drug felon, he was a total fraud. I think we're still negotiating the return of the three thousand dollars we paid the guy to speak.

This incident raises a number of profound questions (not to mention hoots and cheers!). Authority—of people, of institutions, of texts—is no longer taken for granted, nor should it be. Liars and criminals can look professional because they can buy the same slick computers and programs as a corporation can. We must learn to measure the credibility of new information against what we currently know and by the criteria established by reputable agencies and people. The inability to use or read information effectively is too expensive, too dangerous. Edward Tufte (1997) argues that the Challenger space shuttle exploded in part because the scientists could not communicate their information clearly and their audience could not read the information well enough to make the proper decision. Only when physicist Richard Feynman, known for being a gifted teacher, used a glass of ice water to simulate what happened—that is, used a different media to convey what numbers and words could not—did these men understand the principle, sadly, much too late.

The discredited marine and the respected Challenger panel illustrate one of the most important points in this chapter: information does not equal knowledge or wisdom. Brown and Duguid (2000) distinguish between explicit and implicit—what others call explicit and tacit—knowledge. They explain the difference with the following example: "It's possible, for example, to learn about negotiation strategies by reading books about negotiation. But strategy books don't make you into a good negotiator, any more than dictionaries make you into a speaker . . . To become a negotiator requires not only knowledge of strategy, but skill, experience, judgement, discretion" (135). Such experience, such knowledge can be acquired by students only if we provide them with actual and meaningful opportunities to encounter the world and test themselves against it while still under our guidance. This means not only reading information but producing it; not just interpreting and analyzing it but manipulating and testing its veracity against a variety of standards to hone their skills and sensibilities.

Armed with a robust textual intelligence, our students will enter the world knowing how to identify and having the power to recognize and resist the barrage of techniques used to coerce them, confuse them, or otherwise deceive them. This information, these skills, these habits are common to all disciplines. For not only is information coming to us in sophisticated forms with purposes that are not always clear, it is also disappearing, leaving in its wake a trail of flawed, incomplete, and often useless replicas stored on different media. So it is that our nation's own past as contained in its newspapers is vanishing, unable to be reclaimed, its stories unable to be retold, its information reread.

Further Studies

Brown, John Seely, and Paul Douglas. 2000. *The Social Life of Information*. Cambridge: Harvard Business School Press.

Tufte, Edward. 1990. *Envisioning Information*. Cheshire, CT: Graphics.

———. 1997. *Visual Explanations: Images and Quantities, Evidence and Narrative*. Cheshire, CT: Graphics.

7

Reading Images

I think in pictures. Words are like a second language to me.
—Temple Grandin, from *Thinking in Pictures and Other Reports from My Life with Autism*

The camera was his notebook.
—Belinda Rathbone, referring to photographer Walker Evans

My wife and I drove all morning through the French countryside, translating what we saw into certain paintings we pretended to know, guided by signs with symbols we mostly understood. We passed by advertisements we could not read but easily understood, images of modern life juxtaposed against the ancient brick walls of the villages through which we drove. Eventually we were led by the one true landmark out there, one that slowly rose and disappeared and then rose again from the impressionist landscape: Chartres Cathedral and its spire, which stood like a compass pointing toward God's own blue sky.

Umberto Eco (1995) described Chartres Cathedral as the earliest form of television, remarking that the main difference was the quality of the sources from which the artists drew their stories back then. This makes sense to me now after the day we spent in Chartres, following Malcolm Miller around the cathedral as he "read" it for us. Malcolm Miller, who has spent his entire life studying and giving not only remarkable but entertaining interpretive tours of the church, actually describes it as a book he will need his whole life to read properly. Like Eco, Miller regards the cathedral as a multimedia text consisting of engravings, stained-glass windows, paintings, words, images, and the performed texts of sermon and song. And they interact with one another according to their form and function, the very architecture reflecting the principles of universal order that are similarly embodied in stories told through the images that surround visitors to Chartres. (See Figure 7–1.)

Miller escorted us outside to one of the doors and, after warning us not to look up lest we catch a dollop of pigeon guano in the eye, translated the sculptured text of the portal. His ability to read these carved images incorporated all the same skills we typically use to read a poem or an essay, which are based on a knowledge of:

- Design
- Features
- History
- Language
- Original context
- Relationships
- Style
- Symbols

FIGURE 7–1 Sample detail from Chartres Cathedral. *Photograph by Jim Burke.*

One of the most important and often challenging questions about reading images—and many other nonword texts—is "Where do I begin?" When we look at a page of a novel or a poem, we have certain obvious design clues and a common knowledge about how a page is designed to be read (e.g., in English, from top left corner to bottom right corner). These are, at least on the surface, linear texts, though some authors, such as James Burke in *The Knowledge Web: From Electronic Agents to Stonehenge and Back—and Other Journeys Through Knowledge* (1999), have begun to experiment with multiple entry points in a published text, using sidebars to provide readers with options. Images are different. Some, such as the images found in *Photographs That Define Our Times: Time's Great Images of the 20th Century* (Time Publications 1999), speak to us with an immediacy we would rather feel than explain. You do not *read* the image of the hotel employee kneeling before the body of Bobby Kennedy; you experience it, you participate in it. Compare such an image, however, with the opening ninety-six seconds of a one-hour 1995 ABC documentary about American churches, described by Mitchell Stephens (1998) in *the rise of the image the fall of the word* (see page 115).

Surely this visual text requires a level of reading, of active meaning making through construction and inference using a variety of strategies. The power of such images as the Kennedy photo and the ABC video collage must be understood if our students are to be able to defend themselves against the influence images could achieve, and have achieved, for example, through wartime propaganda posters.

WEB SITE

For examples of World War I and World War II propaganda posters, visit the companion Web site.

When Malcolm Miller explains the story being told through images at Chartres Cathedral, he draws on his knowledge of Christianity and art history the same way historians look to their subject to help them make sense of a historical trend or event. So it goes with poems, speeches, even statistical information, all of which, like the Chartres portal, are situated in a time, a tradition, and a technique with features that, if read patiently and intelligently, can help us understand the story the artist wants to tell. Miller narrates the doorway beginning with the first of the four Gospel writers, using such textual details as the way his hands are arranged or how the lamb is curled up at another's feet. He pauses as any reader would to ask questions that help him clarify or support his reading; this thinking aloud helps us learn to read it better by showing us how he thinks as he looks, what he sees when he reads. He asks such questions as:

- What are we looking at?
- Why are we looking at it?
- What questions does it bring to mind?
- Why did the artist make it?
- How did the artist make it?
- Why did the artist place it here, over this door?
- Why did the artist choose stone over paint or stained glass?
- What did it mean to people back when it was originally made?
- Why didn't the artist sign his name to these works of art as today's artists do?

As with Malcolm Miller, cartoonist Scott McCloud reminds us, in his remarkable book *Understanding Comics: The Invisible Art* (1993), that for centuries we used images and words with equal fluency. Whether we used images or words didn't really matter, "so long as it worked," McCloud argues. He goes on to say, through his graphic history of art and cartoons, "words and pictures have *great* powers to tell stories when creators fully exploit them *both*."(152)

See some examples of McCloud's work and further explore his ideas by visiting his Web site at <www.scottmccloud.com>.

NOTE

Visual Literacy: What It Is, What It Looks Like

When I think of this experience of being in the presence of a master reader—the same feeling I get when Helen Vendler explains a poem, David Denby examines a film, Lewis Thomas explicates a cell, or Richard Feynman describes a pattern—I realize that some people think in pictures and that we all understand abstract ideas better when we can see what they look like or mean. As Temple Grandin said in the quote that opens this chapter, "I think in pictures. Words are a second language to me." Not only do people think in different ways, but they use images for different purposes. Physicist Stephen Hawking, for example, had to develop an entire lexicon of shapes and images for himself, a geometric vocabulary through which he could describe the world he spent all his time trying to understand. Van Gogh, in a letter to his brother Theo, wrote of his inability to explain his feelings in words. "Really, we [artists] can speak only through our paintings" (Shlain 1993).

In *Frames of Mind: The Theory of Multiple Intelligences*, Howard Gardner (1983) discusses Van Gogh and other artists at length, describing their particular intelligence as "spatial," which he describes as the capacity to "perceive the visual world accurately, to perform transformations and modifications upon one's initial perceptions, and to be able to re-create aspects of one's visual experience, even in the absence of relevant physical stimuli." Donald Hoffman, author of *Visual Intelligence: How We Create What We See* (1999), offers his own definition: "Vision is not merely a matter of passive perception, it is an intelligent process of active construction. What you see is, invariably, what your visual intelligence constructs." In other words: to see is to read, or, to paraphrase Shakespeare, all the world is a text and we are merely readers of it.

Thus, when we speak of reading images, we should realize they can be used to:

- Describe
- Explain
- Narrate
- Persuade

We encounter images used in these ways all day long. Examples include:

- A series of photographs depicting a scientific process (see textbook pages for a specific example) that explain how this process happens
- The stained glass windows at Chartres (or any such cathedral) used to tell the story of Jesus as it appears in the New Testament
- Photographs of a natural disaster that describe the scale and the nature of the disaster
- Any of the thousands of advertisements we see in the course of a day that use images to persuade us to think or feel certain ways about ourselves and their products

WEB SITE

Visit the companion Web site or <www.adcouncil.org> for several examples of powerful images used to persuade people to think or act differently.

More and more, however, we use images for several different purposes simultaneously. In the case of the Apple Computer "Think Different" ad campaign, the images were recycled for use in an entirely different context, one the subjects may very well have objected to. Further on, I offer a range of possible purposes that include remembering, honoring, persuading, and informing. Consider the image in Figure 7–2. What are some possible titles for this image? What could this image be used to say or do?

FIGURE 7–2   Photo of Vietnam Memorial. *Photograph by Jim Burke.*

Here is what sophomore Alicia Pivarotto wrote after studying this image on a screen in my classroom as part of a unit on *All Quiet on the Western Front*:

THE PICTURE

> I've been there
> To the memorial
> I saw all the names
> It seemed endless
> How many names
> Are on that wall?
> Too many
> It was a smooth granite.
> Dark
> Because that's how you felt
> When you saw it
> The names were carved in
> I ran my fingers over it
> And I thought I heard the
> Screams of the soldiers

And I thought I heard the
Cries of the families
Just from one brush against it.
Was this the wall's real purpose?
For us to feel
Their pain . . .
I felt it
I feel it now
Looking at this picture.

NOTE

See Leonard Shlain's time line of human literacy in Appendix E.

Leonard Shlain, author of *The Alphabet Versus the Goddess: The Conflict Between Word and Image* (1998), provides the following comparison of words and images:

> Images are primarily mental reproductions of the sensual world of vision. Nature and human artifacts both provide the raw material from the outside that the brain replicates in the inner sanctum of consciousness. Because of their close connection to the world of appearances, images approximate reality: they are *concrete*. The brain simultaneously perceives all parts of the *whole* integrating the parts *synthetically* into a gestalt. The majority of images are perceived in an *all-at-once* manner.
>
> Reading words is a different process. When the eye scans distinctive individual letters arranged in a certain *linear sequence*, a word with meaning emerges. The meaning of a sentence, such as the one you are now reading, progresses word by word. Comprehension depends on the sentence's syntax, the particular horizontal sequence in which its grammatical elements appear.

NOTE

Many respected reading experts would disagree with Shlain's explanation of reading as a linear process. My emphasis here is on his point that we experience images differently than we do words, that the immediacy of a powerful image is different from the assembled meaning and subsequent impact of words.

Though I find Shlain's description insightful, it is not useful to me as a teacher in the classroom trying to teach kids to read images. I still need to know how to approach reading an image, just as I need to do more than identify a word, moving into the deeper waters of interpretation and the meanings available to me as a reader of that word, in that sentence, in that text. There is a visual grammar that governs the elements of an image to achieve the same outcome we desire in a written context: successful and powerful communication. Hoffman identifies many of the rules of that grammar in *Visual Intelligence*, saying that we "construct visual worlds from ambiguous images in conformance to visual rules" (1999). In *Reading Images: The Grammar of Visual Design* (1998), Kress and van Leeuwen elaborate on this notion of a visual grammar: "What is expressed in language through the choice between different word classes and semantic structures, is, in visual communication, expressed through the choice between, for instance, different uses of colour, or different compositional structures."

Grammar as they and I use it here is not a set of prescriptive rules that govern words within a sentence but something much more: "It is a means of representing patterns of experience . . . It enables human beings to build a mental picture of reality, to make sense of their experience of what goes on around them and inside them" (Halliday as quoted in Kress and van Leeuwen 1988). This book's guiding principle is that we should teach students to recognize the choices authors (which here include artists, Webmasters, mathematicians, scientists, journalists) make and then realize the consequences of those decisions insofar as they change the meaning of the text or affect the reader. It is through the conscious and unconscious use of this grammatical sense that we convey and, as readers, discern meanings and motivations of not only the author but also the characters within that text, as well as ourselves.

This visual literacy has been defined as follows:

From the beginnings of human culture, visual awareness has been a key element to communication. Just as information conveyed by the written word holds a significance for humanity in the 20th century, the symbols of early cave paintings held a deep significance for the artists and cultures that produced them. Over time these symbols and meanings changed into the alphabets of the world of today, which are the basis for verbal literacy.

To be verbally literate, one must possess and be able to manipulate the basic components of written language: the letters, words, spelling, grammar, syntax. With a mastery of these elements of written communication, the possibilities of verbal expression are endless. Visual literacy must operate within the same boundaries. Just as there are components and common meaning for the elements of verbal literacy, elements and common meaning exist for the elements of visual literacy.

The fundamentals of all visual communication are its basic elements; the compositional source for all kinds of visual materials, messages, objects and experiences . . .

These elements are summarized in the following list:

- *the dot* [the most basic of visual elements], a pointer, marker of space
- *the line*, the restless articulator of form, in the probing loose-ness of the sketch and the tighter technical plan
- *shape*, the basic outlines, circle, triangle, and square
- *direction*, the surge of movement that promotes character of the basic shapes
- *value*, the most basic of all elements, the presence or absence of light
- *hue and saturation*, the make up of color—coordination of value with added component of chroma
- *texture*, optical or tactile, the surface characteristic of visual materials
- *scale*, the relative size and measurement of an image
- *dimension and motion*, both implied through sfumato and other techniques.

These are the visual elements; from them we draw the raw materials for all levels of visual intelligence. It is with the under-standing of these elements that a viewer can come to understand visual syntax. Visual literacy is the ability, through knowledge of the basic visual elements, to understand the meaning and com-ponents of the image. (Pomona College 1999)

Shlain (1998) and others (McLuhan 1997; Stephens 1998) argue that our entire social evolution is moving toward the increased use of images to communicate more efficiently and effectively. We must be able to recognize how someone might be using an image like the one shown in Figure 7–3. As James Gleick writes in *Faster: The Acceleration of Just About Everything* (1999), "As our attention has demanded more stimula-tion, we have gained an ability to process rapid and discontinuous visual images. It seems that we are quicker-witted—but have we, by way of compensation, traded away our capacity for deep concentration?" Gleick goes on to say, "We have learned a visual language made up of images and movements instead of words and syllables. It has its own grammar, abbreviations, clichés, lies, puns, and famous quotations." If you don't believe this, find a copy of *EyeWire*, a publication the Adobe software company puts out. It consists of image banks, all organized into catego-ries: Challenges, Culture, Active Women, Active Vacations. We no longer have time for possible miscommunication, so all images become coded, standardized into pictographs that focus groups chose because the images embody "friendship" or "work." Ironically, such companies are achieving through the increased use of images what E. B. White said—quoting Strunk—we must achieve through written words:

FIGURE 7–3   An image like this flag could be used to symbolize a number of different ideas or emotions. *Photograph by Jim Burke.*

Vigorous writing is concise. A sentence should contain no unnecessary words, a paragraph no unnecessary sentences, for the same reason that a drawing should have no unnecessary lines and a machine no unnecessary parts. This requires not that the writer make all sentences short or avoid all detail and treat subjects only in outline, but that every word tell. (Strunk and White 1999)

Figure 7–4 exemplifies such concise visual language through its use of images and words.

Read the Future: What Do You See?

We are a society that has progressively moved faster and faster. Such movement has challenged us to say more in fewer words until now, in some cases, companies will try to convey everything about themselves through a single image that shows their corporate logo in the bottom

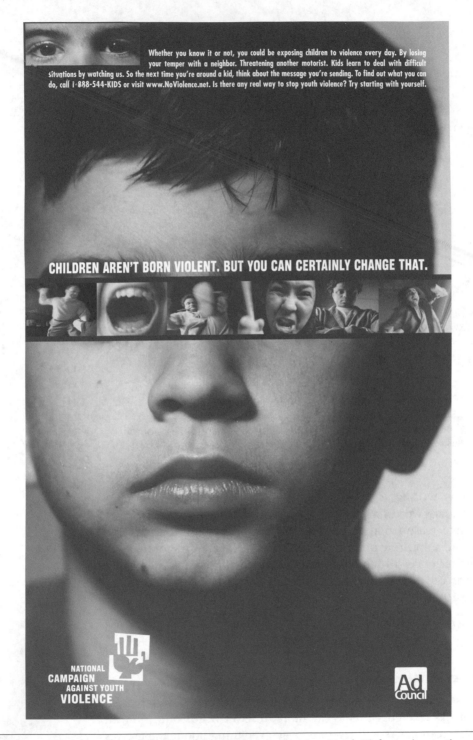

FIGURE 7–4 This ad, produced by the National Campaign Against Youth Violence, is a testimony to the power of images joined with words.

corner. My favorite example of such imagery is an advertisement I saw on television when my wife and I were in Japan. A beautiful Japanese woman reclines in an ancient wooden bath, steam swirling around her peaceful image. No music. No words. Just beauty. As I watch, I'm trying to make sense of it: soap commercial? cosmetics? Then at the last minute, a Honda logo slowly appears in the lower right corner and then the whole image fades out and it's back to the show. In its own way, the commercial embodies Strunk's admonition perfectly in its economy of style and magnitude of detail.

Mitchell Stephens, in *the rise of the image the fall of the word* (1998), identified three main reasons for the continued power and increased use of images: they are concise, compelling, and accessible to the culture at large. Leonard Shlain asserts that two images in the twentieth century began this transition from a verbal to a visual language base in our society: the mushroom cloud rising over Hiroshima and the photograph of Earth as first seen by the astronauts in 1968. Not one to mince words, Shlain writes, "Since the atomic blast in 1945 and the Earth image that followed, not a single book has come close to the degree of impact this one photo [the Earth image] has had. The written word's influence has been declining for the last fifty years, counterbalanced by the increasing power of the image."

I don't entirely agree with Shlain's pronouncement, and neither do others. Don Tapscott, for example, writing about trends in communication, particularly among adolescents and preteens, says just the opposite: "Humanity is turning back to written language. We are undergoing yet another vast and trembling shift from the magic of television to the magic of interactive digital media [which are] based on the written word" (1998). Tapscott proceeds to then describe all the different language-based interactions the Net Generation has, including such obvious venues as e-mail and chat rooms.

NOTE

For more information on the Net Generation, visit <www.growingupdigital.com>.

NOTE

For a wonderful example of the merging of words and images, writing and video, visit Dana Atchley's Web site, <www.nextexit.com>, or the Center for Digital Storytelling at <www.storycenter.org>.

Just as the Internet will not replace books, so images will never replace words. All these competing modes will eventually become yet more tools hanging on a person's tool belt; he will ask himself which he should use—words or images (or both!), page or screen (or both!)—to convey information. I know: I have had such conversations with various technologists since I began this book and decided it would have a multimedia companion to its printed pages.

But just as we have turned to images to say more and to say it faster, we have come to learn that visual truth is fragile. Obviously a painting, because it is created from various impressions, is not intended to be correct in its details, but it should be true to the degree that it conveys its subject's essence. A photograph, however, implies an accuracy it cannot guarantee. Even as far back as the early 1900s, people could buy postcards that showed the Wright brothers flying right down the main street of various little towns. Since then, thanks to computers and programs like Adobe Photoshop, visual truth has only grown more suspect as we try to read what we see.

Types of Images

The word *image* implies a wide range of visual possibilities, only some of which I mean to include in this chapter. While we can certainly use the word to describe graphic charts and other such strictly informational devices, these are addressed in Chapter 6, "Reading Information." For the purposes of this chapter, the word *image* refers to:

- Advertisements
- Collage
- Drawings
- Icons
- Logos
- Mixed media
- Montage
- Monuments
- Paintings
- Photographs
- Posters
- Product packaging

I distinguish between these and the visual explanations by emphasizing the role of aesthetic intent and artistic purpose to which these images are put. While I agree with John Allen Paulos (1999) and Edward Tufte (1990) that statistical data can—even should—be used to explain or narrate ideas, these visual explanations or statistical narratives lack the common features of aesthetic intent I focus on in this chapter. Through the close reading of these different types of images, students reinforce and expand their ability to understand the range of texts they encounter daily. To this list I would add written images as used in literature, for how can we fully understand them if we treat them as just words made of letters instead of images made of words? Consider the opening scene in *The Scarlet Letter*, Romeo looking up at Juliet on the balcony, or the entire town gathered together in Shirley Jackson's story "The Lottery" and the image of her own children stoning their mother.

I don't think it is our responsibility to turn students into art connoisseurs any more than I believe it is our job to crank out literary or film critics. I do, however, want my students to be able to read texts in different ways for various purposes, some of which include:

- Aesthetic
- Existential
- Informational
- Logical
- Narrative

Stop, Look—and Read

I want students to be able to determine the difference between a snapshot and a powerful photograph just as I want them to be able to explain the difference between doggerel and Li Young Lee's poetry, between words and literature, paint and art. Such reading demands that we make time to slow down and look longer at less. In *Art [Objects]: Essays on Ecstasy and Effrontery* (1995), Jeanette Winterson describes this challenge to be a patient reader: "Art takes time. To spend an hour looking at a painting is difficult." If we can achieve this attention to detail, afford our students—and ourselves!—the opportunity to linger and learn from a single image, things begin to happen, perhaps by asking the first question that arises for most of us when we look at an image or read a work of fiction: Do I like this? Once this question is out of the box, regardless of the answer, we have a place to begin: why do or don't I like it? And so the questions keep coming the longer we linger and allow ourselves the time to listen to and learn from the text:

- What does it remind me of?
- How did the artist and the subject(s) feel?
- What was the artist thinking?
- What did the artist see?
- What was going through the subject's mind as the image was made?
- How would I do it differently—that is, what would I change if I could?

NOTE

Repeated reading, a technique discussed at greater length in *Reading Reminders*, is useful in the contexts discussed in this chapter. We often must read a text several times for different purposes to arrive at a more complete understanding. One might begin reading for a literal understanding of what is happening in the short story or the painting, the photograph or the poem.

Here is Winterson's think-aloud, the narrative of her experience as she looks at a painting she has committed herself to study for an hour:

Increasing discomfort. When was the last time you looked at anything, solely, concentratedly, and for its own sake? Ordinary life passes in a near blur. If we go to the theatre or the cinema, the images before us change constantly, and there is the distraction of language. Our loved ones are so well known to us that there is no need to look at them, and one of the gentle jokes of married life is that we do not. Nevertheless, here is a painting and we have agreed to look at it for one hour. We find we are not very good at looking.

Increasing distraction. Is my mind wandering to the day's work, to the football match, to what's for dinner, to sex, to whatever it is that will give me something to do other than looking at the painting?

Increasing invention. After some time spent daydreaming, the guilty or the dutiful might wrench back their attention to the picture.

What is this about? Is it a landscape? Is it figurative? More promisingly, is it a nude? If the picture seems to offer an escape route then this is the moment to take it. I can make up stories about the characters on the canvas much as art-historians like to identify the people in Rembrandt's *The Night Watch*. Now I am beginning to feel more confident because I am truly engaging with the picture. A picture is its subject matter isn't it? Oh dear, mine's an abstract. Never mind, would that pink suit me?

Increasing irritation. Why doesn't the picture *do* something? Why is it hanging there staring at me? What is this picture for? Pictures should give pleasure but this picture is making me very cross. Why should I admire it? Quite clearly it doesn't admire me . . .

Admire *me* is the sub-text of so much of our looking: the demand put on art that it should reflect the reality of the viewer . . . He still has not discovered anything about the painting but the painting has discovered a lot about him. He is inadequate and the painting has told him so.

See Dorothea Lange's photographs, including her famous Nipomo, California, series of a mother and her children. Go to <http://www.museumca.org/global/art/collections_dorothea_lange.html> and pay special attention to what Lange says in her notes about the photograph session.

NOTE

As Winterson says, it takes time to settle down to the task of watching or writing or thinking well about a subject that merits our attention. This is why we must build into our curriculum in the different subject areas opportunity for reflection and close observation over a sustained period of time. One of the most powerful classes I've ever experienced was the day I took my juniors out to the baseball field and told them they could only think about, observe, and write about the area two feet around them on any side. Yes, they wrote well, but what was important was their gratitude: they got calm and focused in a way their busy teen lives do not usually allow. They began to pay attention, to see what was not there before.

How and Why We Should Use Images in the Classroom

Winterson's last comment, that the painting "has told him [he is inadequate]," is a challenging observation—challenging in that it forces readers to confront their limitations and we, as teachers, to realize our responsibility: to help all students develop the capacity to persevere in the face of their own confusion and, using a range of strategies, make sense of the different elements of any visual or written text.

This brings us to the double bonus of studying images: learning to read them develops the skills we need to read all other types of texts, and using them to help students visualize printed or other nonvisual texts helps them see the meaning and the action. To adapt a familiar adage, how do we know what we think unless we see what someone is saying (or writing or thinking)? Judith Langer (1995) calls this technique "building envisionments." Looking at images also reminds us, in part because of their actual frames, that most of what our students read occurs within a larger frame of reference, and that this is just a sample, one square of the larger quilt. To push the point further, visual thinking invites the reader to think outside the frame, to learn to understand the relationship between what they do see and what they cannot see but know is or may be there. Take for example the Vietnam Memorial image (Figure 7–2) in which we can see only the hands of different sizes: to whom do they belong and what information does the image provide to help us draw possible conclusions? Who else might the hands belong to if not the relatives of that soldier? More important: Who was the soldier, the man they have come to remember? What is *his* story?

NOTE

Go to <www.favoritepoem.org> and watch the video based on Kumonyakaa's poem "Facing It."

This very image of the etching reinforces the argument of this chapter: we express our ideas in different forms—etchings, sculpted memorials, engraved names, photographs—to serve different functions: to honor, to remember, to appreciate. Expressed through these different forms, each text tells us different things, things which we learn to see and hear the more we encounter and practice reading them. What's more, they reinforce one another: the use of a painting of the drowned Ophelia or the different film adaptations of *Hamlet* provides windows through which we glimpse the work of literature from a new perspective, thereby helping us better understand and appreciate it. In *The Object Stares Back*, for example, James Elkins (1996) writes about how microphotography of chemical and other processes offers insight into their beauty that can help scientists and mathematicians appreciate them in entirely new and powerful ways. John Briggs' *Fractals: Discovering a New Aesthetic of Art, Science, and Nature* (1992) offers a remarkable portfolio of images based on chaos theory in order to help people build a visual understanding of how this theory applies to math and science.

The study of images connects students to their learning in different ways but also to the world outside the classroom. Such image studies also honor and utilize the skills of students in the class who are not always able to feel successful or recognized when studying texts that are written in words. Because everyone can start at the observable (i.e., objective) level, those students can usually experience quick success in reading the visual text; this gives them the confidence to persevere as they move into deeper encounters with the images and their ideas. Images can also be integrated into all disciplines and used for a wide range of purposes, thus making their use a positive experience for both teachers and students.

Questions to Ask

- Why are we looking at this?
- What are we looking for?
- How should we look at this?
- What choices did the artist make and how did they affect its meaning?
- Is this image in its original state (i.e., no manipulation or doctoring)?
- If this image was altered, who did it and why?

- What are the different components in this image?
- How are they related to one another?
- What is the main idea or argument the image expresses?
- In what context or under what conditions was this image originally created? Displayed?
- Who created it?
- Was it commissioned? If so, by whom? And for what purpose?
- What was the creator trying to do here? (Narrate, explain, describe, persuade—or some combination of these?)
- Can I find any tension or examples of conflict within the image? If so, what are they? What is their source? How are they represented?
- Do I like this image? Regardless of my answer—why?
- How would I describe the artist's technique?
- What conventions govern this image? How do they contribute to or detract from its ability to convey its message?
- Why are parts arranged the way they are?
- What does this image show (i.e., objectively; see Figure 7–2)?
- What does it mean (subjectively; see Figure 7–2)?
- Is this presented as an interpretation? Factual record? Impression?
- What is the larger context of which this image is a part?
- What is it made from?
- Why did the creator choose the materials, medium, and perspective she did?
- What is the place to which my attention is most immediately drawn?
- What is the smallest detail that says the most?
- How would it change the meaning or viewer's experience if different materials, media, or perspectives were used?
- What motivates the creator here?
- What verbs could be used to describe what the components—colors, lines, light, space, objects, characters—are doing in the image?
- What adjectives could be used to best describe the precise details of the objects in the image?
- What nouns most accurately describe the content—colors, lines, light, space, objects, characters—of the image?
- What adverbs most accurately describe how the components—colors, lines, light, space, objects, characters—of the image interact?
- What do we need to know to read the image successfully?
- How did the original artist expect this image to be read (e.g., as an interpretation, a prediction, a documentary)?

- Is the creator working within or against a particular genre or school of expression?
- What are the criteria I am—or should be—using to evaluate this image?
- What are the image's motifs, themes, plot, and characters?
- How would I describe the style of this image and why did the artist make the stylistic choices he did?
- Where should I begin as I try to read this? Why there?
- What questions do I need to ask to read this image successfully?
- What is the best or the prescribed angle from which I should view this image?
- How has the artist used the following elements to communicate with the viewer: light, line, space, time, color?
- Does this image achieve—or is it offered as symbolic or iconic representation (e.g., Dorothea Lange's *Migrant Mother*)?
- Is there an observable pattern used here? If so, what is it and how is it used?
- Does the creator use any devices—repetition, symbols, visual puns? If so, what are they, and how do they work in the image?

Classroom Connection: Cross-Curricular Possibilities

How could anyone teach students about China and Tianamen Square without using such images as the *Goddess of Democracy*, or about Vietnam and the sixties without including such seminal images as the naked Vietnamese girl fleeing down the street, the skin on her back having been burned off from napalm, or Martin Luther King Jr. lying dead at the feet of Jesse Jackson and other men, who all point toward a distant rooftop as fear and desperation distort their faces? Can you teach a process in a science class without giving students the images to study, to help them not only see but also develop the vocabulary? English teachers who do not have students translate the imagery in the opening chapter of *The Scarlet Letter* deprive their students of the opportunity to see and thus understand the novel better.

Health and business classes are no less fortunate when it comes to images worthy of study. Consider how one ad from a magazine could be used for different purposes in the two classes. A Philip Morris Companies, Inc., ad in *Atlantic Monthly* shows a truck driver named Luis who works for United Food Bank in Arizona. Luis is holding a shiny red apple in his right hand and standing in front of all the food he will load in his truck, which we see in the background. Above him appears the caption, "Today I'll deliver enough fresh food to feed 1,400 hungry families." The two-page, full-color advertisement then explains in several paragraphs of text all that Kraft is doing to help people who need food. At the bottom of the page, very discretely placed, is the logo for Philip Morris Companies, Inc., and all its subsidiaries. The health class could spend an entire period reading this image from several different perspectives such as hunger and health in America; the business class could, on the other hand, use it as a case study of a major corporation trying to improve its sullied reputation, which is due to all the negative attention Philip Morris has received from the Joe Camel ad and to antismoking campaigns associating the company with death.

> **T**he companion Web site includes many useful links to Web sites described here or to sites that will complement the ideas discussed in this section.

WEB SITE

Other possible activities include:

- *Museum visit:* Students visit a museum. If they do not have access to one or lack time, a suitable alternative (though not an equivalent replacement) is to take a virtual tour online at any of the world's greatest museums, all of which now offer these. During either visual adventure, they choose a specific number of images (previously assigned) and study them in their context. They first describe them objectively, then follow up with a subjective reflection from their own perspective. Next they write about it from another's perspective, even that of one of the subjects inside the image if they wish. Then, if possible, they compare how we read and respond to this painting today to how those who saw it in its original context would view it.

> **G**o to the companion Web site for a connection to Norman Rockwell's *Four Freedoms* series of paintings done during World War II. You will also find a link to the text of the President Roosevelt speech that inspired the paintings.

WEB SITE

- *Design your own:* This activity can be done with any book, product, CD, or film. In short, students design and critique their own book or CD cover, product advertisement or packaging, using whatever images they feel convey the idea they and the product are trying to express.
- *Walkabout:* Students take paper and pen as they head out for a walk around their town to find images. These images can be buildings or billboards, graffiti or signs, murals or patterns. After focusing on descriptive writing to describe an image itself, they focus on reading it in its local, public context. If, for example, they are looking at the city hall building, they should analyze what the building's architects were

trying to say through its design. On the other hand, if they are looking at a billboard or some other advertisement, they should examine it in light of the neighborhood around it and how the creators are trying to communicate their message to that neighborhood.

- *Personal logo:* According to the Bible's original Greek, in the beginning there was *logos,* meaning the word; now there is *logo,* meaning the image as in the logo on the computer I'm using, on the shirt you are wearing, and on the toys my children are throwing at each other. We might even extend this to include the widespread popularity of tattoos in recent years, these designs signifying something in the mind of the tattooed. With this in mind, students design their own personal logos using a computer or original art. The logo should convey something about the student that is recognizable in the logo itself. Then the student writes an explanation of the logo, first describing it to focus on descriptive writing, then explaining its meaning.

- *Making metaphors, making sense:* Students draw on or develop metaphorical images to help them make sense of an image or a written text. One example, taken from Fran Claggett and Joan Brown's book *Drawing Your Own Conclusions: Graphic Strategies for Reading, Writing, and Thinking* (1992), shows the different sides of Hamlet as represented by an ESL student whose visual vocabulary was much more sophisticated than her spoken or written vocabulary. The image provided an excellent means of helping her expand her written language through her subsequent analysis of the image, during which she not only had to read her image but use the image to show how she had read Shakespeare's play.

- *Image essay:* Students collect or create a set of images organized around an idea or a subject. Each image should, as a paragraph in any essay would, advance the idea and communicate to the reader/viewer. Students give the image essay a title, which they explain in their written explication of their own essay. Excellent examples of such essays can be found on the *DoubleTake Magazine* Web site (<www.doubletake .org>) and the Literacy Through Photography Web site (<http://www -cds.aas.duke.edu/ltp/>).

- *Intertextal unit:* Drawing on images available through the National Archives (<www.nara.gov>), this assignment examines a series of images and the texts that accompany those images. The unit begins with the study of Matthew Brady's Civil War photographs and the letters written by soldiers, then moves into images from and the text of the Gettysburg Address; next is a photo-essay about the construction of the Lincoln Memorial, followed by still images, the performed speech, and written text from Martin Luther King's March on Washington, which was situated on the steps of the Lincoln Memorial.

- *Art and poetry:* Using a book like Edward Hirsch's *Transforming Vision* (1994), which includes poems matched with art, or Naomi Shihab Nye's *The Tree Is Older Than You Are* (1995), which includes a wonderful collection of poetry and art from Mexico, have students read both the poetic and artistic texts and then explain their meaning and the relationship between the two, taking specific details from the texts to support their reading.

- *Three titles:* Put up on the overhead a series of images without any background info, or spread them out across a period of days. The images can be, perhaps even should be, related to some idea or subject you are studying. Have the students create three possible titles for each image and then explain why each title works for that image. In their writing, they should refer to specific aspects or elements of the image to support their reading. They should then discuss these in groups, picking the title they like the most and explaining that one to the class at large. The class might conclude the activity by voting on the title students think best captures the essence of the image, then discussing or writing about why this one works best.

- *Writing the captions:* In a science or history class, give the students a series of images that describe a process or an event. They must then write the captions that go along with the images; these captions should not only explain but summarize the pictures to which they refer.

- *Visual arguments:* Students in history or English, depending on what they are studying, can go to the Library of Congress and find examples of propaganda posters from the two world wars to inspire support in the community and get men to volunteer for duty. They could describe these and then examine the rhetorical devices used to persuade the population to act.

- *Memory Box:* The Center for Digital Storytelling has people gather different artifacts and then assemble them in a box that they decorate according to its purpose, to remember everything that is inside and what it represents.

View a sample of digital storytelling on the companion Web site. "Shipwrecked," by Dana Atchley, offers a powerful example of the use of images mixed with multiple other media to communicate a powerful idea.

WEB SITE

- *Moving images:* In history class, students can use any of Ken Burns' documentary films that depend on still photographs and voiceovers. First, show the film without sound and have each student write his or her own script and voiceover to go along with an image; then play the documentary with the sound on so the class can hear what was actually written. They can also write about or discuss the power of these still images: what is it about them that carries such haunting power? They could, as an extension of this assignment, find their own photograph—of a friend, their family, an event, or someone they don't even know—and write a voiceover to perform for the class or a small group. Then, they should explain why their voiceover went along with their image, and why they chose that image.

- *Draw it:* Students in science or other observation-based classes make careful, precise drawings of what they are studying (e.g., cells, motion) to help train their eyes to read the object more carefully and observe it more closely through the comparison of their own drawings to the subject they are studying. Special attention should be given to the reading of or looking for patterns that might yield information.

- *Integrated unit:* In an English class, students reading Steinbeck's *Grapes of Wrath* write down specific images Steinbeck draws using words. (Chapter 16, for example, is a word painting of a typical diner of that era.) They analyze the use of sensory details to evoke these images, noting sentence structures used to provide emphasis and elements such as color or sound used to animate the image. They then look at a series of photographs from WPA photographer Dorothea Lange and read her commentary on her own photographs.

  Next, they compare Lange's images and explain why the most famous one conveys a power the others cannot. Then they compare Lange's image with several different versions of the Madonna and child by any classical painters. (You can find these easily by going to any museum online and typing in *Madonna and Child* in the search field.)

  Finally, students look at the images of California created in the novel and in the minds of migrants, especially the father of the Joad family. Students discuss the content and origins of these images and how they were used to persuade people to come to California in the wake of the Dust Bowl and the Depression.

Standards Connections

The following standards represent most fields of study. A more complete list of cross-discipline reading standards can be found in Appendix D. The first example, however, comes not from any standards but from the National Council of Teachers of English resolutions.

- RESOLVED, that the National Council of Teachers of English through its publications, conferences, and affiliates support professional development and public awareness of the role that viewing and visually representing our world have as a form of literacy. (NCTE 1997)

- Students make decisions based on observations and inferences they make while reading visual explanations such as tables, symbols, charts, graphs, and images.
- Students develop and use a range of strategies to identify and explain how visual and performing artists use the following to convey meaning and achieve certain effects within the reader:
  - Color
  - Form
  - Images
  - Language
  - Sound
- Students develop and apply aesthetic criteria to different artworks in order to evaluate the quality and success of a given work, using specific examples from that artwork and their rubric to support their interpretation.
- Students infer the possible meanings of an artwork by analyzing the form, function, and relationship between different aesthetic components.
- Students interpret an artwork by examining the artist's intentions, the context in which the work was created, and the work's relationship to past and subsequent works on the same subject by this and other artists.
- Students identify and explain the function of different elements in media productions, including:
  - Arguments
  - Color
  - Images
  - Multiple media
  - Point of view
  - Shape
  - Sound
  - Special effects
  - Stereotypes
  - Stories
  - Symbols
  - Texture
- Students identify and explain the consequences of the author's choices.
- Students interpret and evaluate how visual image makers such as illustrators, documentary filmmakers, and political cartoonists represent meanings.

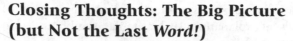

Closing Thoughts: The Big Picture (but Not the Last *Word!*)

I am trying, throughout this chapter and the book itself, to show how we might implement Robert Scholes' ideal of textual skills (1998). Here I have emphasized the skill of reading images (and other types of text); however, we cannot learn to read if we do not have some practice in making images. This constructivist approach recognizes the importance not only of developing these expressive capacities of language but also of the role such activities can play in helping students learn to read better. In short, I am saying that students need to develop their textual intelligence through such reading, and teachers need to use images to help students better understand the written texts they read.

WEB SITE

See the "Maybe I Don't Want a Barbie" ad campaign on the companion Web site. This assignment was done by a group of sophomore girls as part of a unit on visual arguments and war propaganda.

My enthusiasm for such reading is tempered by my concern for the consequences of such reading. Mitchell Stephens himself, after arguing for the importance of the image, writes: "The increasing reliance upon *images*, which began with photography and accelerated with film, certainly seems to have contributed to a decreasing concern with our inner lives and an increasing concern with *image*—with style, possessions and public relations, with surfaces and appearances, and with what Coke commercials are selling" (1998). To develop students' capacities as visual readers, using the questions and techniques I have outlined in this chapter, teachers should focus not on the images themselves, but rather on their content and how they convey meaning. As Eliot Eisner (1998) writes, "the ability to 'make sense' out of forms of representation is not merely a way of securing meaning—as important as that may be—it is also a way of developing cognitive skills." With these cognitive skills, our students can read the images they encounter in the media, images carefully designed to manipulate their attitudes toward themselves and others, and defend themselves against these visual arguments. They can also find their way into what is beautiful, occupying as Maxine Greene (1997) describes it, a world of "hope," one rich in the "prospect of discovery" through which they can learn to see not only themselves but the world around them differently and to understand their role in its creation every time they open their eyes.

Further Studies

Kress, Gunther, and Theo van Leeuwen. 1998. *Reading Images: The Grammar of Visual Design*. London: Routledge.

McCloud, Scott. 1993. *Understanding Comics: The Invisible Art*. New York: Kitchen Sink.

Stephens, Mitchell. 1998. *the rise of the image the fall of the word*. Cambridge: Oxford University Press.

8

Epilogue:
Reading the Future

We must look at the lens through which we see the world as well as at the world we see, and recognize that the lens itself shapes how we interpret the world.
—Stephen Covey, from *The Seven Habits of Highly Effective People*

The development of the faculty of attention forms the real object and almost the sole interest of studies.
—Simone Weil, from *Reflections on the Right Use of School Studies with a View to the Love of God*

These final pages do not conclude this book; indeed, they invite you to become one of the authors of this book, to contribute to the conversation through its companion Web site, through discussions with yourself, your colleagues, your students, and your curriculum. I cannot end this book with the simple declaration that it has reached "the end" because we are only just beginning this next phase of our lives as teachers who are and must be responsible for defining the work we do. The poet W. H. Auden never felt his poems were done; each time he published a new edition of his collected poems, he revised them, changed the sequencing, even altered the titles; he saw them as works in progress.

We and our profession are works in progress, too. This book asks us all to engage in the conversation about what we do, why we do it, and how we should do it. It is also an attempt to remind us that we must take an active role in determining our role in the classroom. The title of this book incorporates not only the historical tradition of illuminating texts through graphic and verbal annotations but also the active role of *illuminating*, of teaching, of performing an act that is responsive, that cannot be scripted given the inherent complexity of students' needs and experiences. The title is also meant to include our very lives and experiences as texts that merit illumination through active reflection in the privacy of our selves and within the community of the classroom, where such essential conversations should take place. Writers as diverse as Simone Weil, Cornell West, Mary Pipher, and Maxine Greene speak about the existential crisis kids face; other writers and thinkers return again and again to the vital role teachers and other mentors can and should play in the lives of these kids who are creating the texts of their lives.

See Lindsay Rosenthal's "annotated life" on the companion Web site. Her work, done in response to Diane McClain's cultural bibliography assignment, shows her thinking about the different experiences that make up her life; through this assignment and the sharing of students' ideas in class, students are encouraged to reflect on what makes for a rich life.

WEB SITE

The best elements of the standards movement serve the interests of all our students in their quest to create balanced, successful lives. The worst aspects of that movement—the push toward standardization of methods, of means, of curriculum—threaten to displace our role as guides and professionals. This book is also a response to that trend, a reminder to us all that we must insist on nothing less than a curriculum as rich in experience as it is in skills, one that develops our intellectual and emotional capacities as much as our aesthetic and existential capacities. I've heard it said that children enter school as question marks and leave as periods. I want my students to know how to use a period, but I also want them to have learned to inquire as to the purpose of the period and whether or not an idea is, in fact, finished just because it has been given a full stop. I want students to resist the neat ending, the quick answer—to say, as Emily Dickinson wrote:

> A word is dead,
> When it is said,
> Some say.
> I say it just
> Begins to live
> That day.

The idea of textual intelligence (TI) explored throughout this book honors the spirit of Dickinson's poem by suggesting we should always examine the life of a word from its many sides to better understand not only what it means but how it works. I have kept the discussion of such aspects of the curriculum as vocabulary and grammar to a minimum, but I cannot end the book without emphasizing their importance. The very notion of grammar is central to the notion of textual intelligence, for it involves the making of structures, the making of sense, the making of meaning.

TI is all about how texts are made and how different grammatical structures create meaning for or affect the reader. Writers use their TI when they decide on everything from the form (poem versus prose versus play) to the purpose (to entertain versus to inform) to the structure (narrative versus expository) to medium (word or image, page or screen). They make TI decisions as they choose the point of view, the tense of the story (past tense, present tense), the use of foreshadowing or flashbacks, the organizational structure (linear or episodic). All these choices come in part from the writer's understanding of how texts and language work. Therefore, the more a student understands these structures, the more options he or she has when he or she writes.

I have asked myself new questions throughout this book, questions I hope have inspired you to ask your own and will lead you to a new and deeper understanding of the work you do, the teacher you are and want to be.

APPENDIX A
Works Cited

American Association of School Librarians and Association for Educational Communications and Technology. 1988. *Information Power: Guidelines for School Library Media Programs.* Chicago and Washington, D.C.: American Library Association and Association for Educational Communications and Technology.

An American Studies Album: Literature, Historical Documents, and Visual Art. 1995. New York: ScottForesman.

Applebee, Arthur. 1996. *Curriculum as Conversation: Transforming Traditions of Teaching and Learning.* Chicago: University of Chicago Press.

Applebee, Arthur, and Judith A. Langer. 1987. *How Writing Shapes Thinking: A Study of Teaching and Learning.* Urbana, IL: National Council of Teachers of English.

Bell, Elizabeth. 1999. "Danville Teen Peeve Headed for Capitol Bill Would Toss Out Dated Texts." *San Francisco Chronicle* 11 November: A12.

Bell, Madison Smartt. 1998. *Narrative Design.* New York: W. W. Norton.

Berring, Robert. 1998. "Extra! Extra. World Wide Web Swallows Whelan's!" *California Monthly* 109(2): 15.

Birkerts, Sven. 1999. "Sense and Semblance." In *Readings.* St. Paul, MN: Graywolf.

Boorstin, Daniel. 1973. *The Americans: The Democratic Experience.* New York: Random House.

Briggs, John. 1992. *Fractals: Discovering a New Aesthetic of Art, Science, and Nature.* New York: Touchstone.

Bringhurst, Robert. 1996. *The Elements of Typographic Style.* 2d ed. Point Roberts, WA: Hartley and Marks.

Brown, John Seely, and Paul Duguid. 2000. *The Social Life of Information.* Cambridge: Harvard Business School Press.

Burke, James. *Connections.* 1995. New York: Little Brown.

———. 1999. *The Knowledge Web: From Electronic Agents to Stonehenge and Back—And Other Journeys Through Knowledge.* New York: Touchstone Books.

Burke, Jim. 1999. *The English Teacher's Companion: A Complete Guide to Classroom, Curriculum, and the Profession.* Portsmouth, NH: Boynton/Cook.

Burke, Jim and Carol Ann Prater. 2000. *I'll Grant You That.* Portsmouth, NH: Heinemann.

Burke, Jim. 2000. *Reading Reminders: Tools, Tips, and Techniques.* Portsmouth, NH: Boynton/Cook.

Butz, Arthur. 1996. "A Short Introduction to Holocaust Revisionism." Home Web Page of Arthur R. Butz. Accessed 12 January 2001. *http:// pubweb.nwu.edu/~abutz/di/intro.html.*

California Department of Education. 1999. *The California Language Arts Content Standards for California Public Schools.* Sacramento: California Department of Education.

Calkins, Lucy, Kate Montgomery, and Donna Santman, with Beverly Falk. 1998. *A Teacher's Guide to Standardized Reading Tests: Knowledge Is Power.* Portsmouth, NH: Heinemann.

Cayton, Andrew, Elisebeth Isreals Perry, Linda Reed, and Allan M. Winkler. 2000. *America: Pathways to the Present.* Needham, MA: Prentice Hall.

Claggett, Fran, and Joan Brown. 1992. *Drawing Your Own Conclusions: Graphic Strategies for Reading, Writing, and Thinking.* Portsmouth, NH: Heinemann.

Cleary, Verne. 1999. Personal correspondence. October.

Cole, K. C. 1999. *The Universe in a Teacup: The Mathematics of Truth and Beauty.* New York: Harcourt Brace.

Cook, Sharon. 1999. "Testing Vocabulary, SAT9 Objectives, and Classroom Activities." Unpublished paper.

Dickinson, Amy. 2000. "Smoke Screen." *Time* 155(10).

Dickinson, Emily. 1960. *Collected Poems of Emily Dickinson.* New York: Back Bay.

Eco, Umberto. 1995. *Six Walks in the Fictional Woods*. New York: Belknap.

Eisner, Eliot. 1998. *The Kind of Schools We Need: Personal Essays*. Portsmouth, NH: Heinemann.

Elkins, James. 1996. *The Object Stares Back*. New York: Harvest.

Faulkner, William. 1950. Nobel prize acceptance speech. 10 December.

Feathers, Karen. 1993. *Infotext: Reading and Learning*. Pippin.

Fish, Stanley. 1982. *Is There a Text in This Class?* Cambridge, MA: Harvard University Press.

FitzGerald, Frances. 1980. *America Revised: History Schoolbooks in the Twentieth Century*. New York: Vintage.

Fox, James. 1998. *Langauge, Media, and Mind*. Urbana, IL: National Council of Teachers of English.

Friedman, Thomas. 2000. *The Lexus and the Olive Tree*. New York: Anchor.

Gardner, Howard. 1983. *Frames of Mind: The Theory of Multiple Intelligences*. New York: Basic.

———. 1996. *Leading Minds: An Anatomy of Leadership*. New York: Basic.

Gleick, James. 1999. *Faster: The Acceleration of Just About Everything*. New York: Pantheon.

Grandin, Temple. 1996. *Thinking in Pictures*. New York: Vintage.

Greene, Maxine. 1997. "Teaching as Possibility: A Light in Dark Times." *The Journal of Pedagogy, Pluralism, & Practice*. 1(1): hypertext. Accessed 21 July 2000. *http://www.lesley.edu/journals/jppp/1/jp3ii1.html*.

Gregory, Marshall. "The Discipline of English and 'The Empty Center of the Field's Sense of Itself'," NCTE, "NCTE to You." 1997. *College English* 59(1): 41–58, 97–104.

Harris, Robert. 1997. "Evaluating Internet Research Sources". Vanguard University of Southern California. Accessed 4 December 1999. *http://www.vanguard.edu/rharris/evalu8it.htm*.

Hirsch, Edward. 1994. *Transforming Vision*. Chicago: Bulfinch.

———. 1999. *How to Read a Poem (and Fall in Love with Poetry)*. New York: Harcourt Brace.

Hobbs, Renee. 1998. "Literacy in the Information Age." In *Handbook of Research on Teaching Literacy Through the Communicative and Visual Arts*, ed. James Flood, Diane Lapp, and Shirley Brice Heath, 7–14. New York: Macmillan.

Hoffman, Donald. 1999. *Visual Intelligence: How We Create What We See*. New York: W. W. Norton.

"How many licks in a tootsie pop?" 1999. *Harper's Magazine* 24.

Jago, Carol. 2000. *With Rigor for All: Teaching the Classics to Contemporary Students.* Portsmouth, NH: Heinemann.

———. 2001. *Beyond Standards.* Portsmouth, NH: Boynton/Cook.

Kafka, Franz. 1904. Letter to Oskar Pollak. 27 January. In *Bartlett's Familiar Quotations,* by John Bartlett, 1992, 651.

Kobrin, David. 1996. *Beyond the Textbook: Teaching History Using Documents and Primary Sources.* Portsmouth, NH: Heinemann.

Kohn, Alfie. 2000. *The Case Against Standardized Testing.* Portsmouth, NH: Heinemann.

Kress, Gunther, and Theo van Leeuwen. 1998. *Reading Images: The Grammar of Visual Design.* London: Routledge.

Kurtz, Howard. 1998. "Outbreak of Fiction Is Alarming News." *Washington Post* 29 June: B01.

Kurzweil, Ray. 1999. *The Age of Spiritual Machines: When Computers Exceed Human Intelligence.* New York: Viking.

Langer, Judith. 1995. *Envisioning Literature: Literary Understanding and Literature Instruction.* New York: Teachers College Press/International Reading Association.

———. 1999. "Beating the Odds: Teaching Middle and High School Students to Read and Write Well." National Research Center on English Learning and Achievement. Accessed 15 July 2001. *http://cela.albany.edu /eie2/index.html.*

Lapham, Lewis. 1997. "Introduction." In *Understanding the Media: Extentions of Man,* by Marshall McLuhan. Cambridge: MIT Press.

Lapp, Diane, James Flood, and Nancy Farnan. 1996. *Content Area Reading and Learning: Instructional Strategies.* Boston, MA: Allyn and Bacon.

Lucas, Greg. 1999. "Gripes Grow over Rampant Textbook Ads: Brand Names Grab Kids' Attention, Publishers Say." *San Francisco Chronicle* (Sacramento Bureau) 26 June: hypertext accessed 11 November, 2000. *http://www.sfgate.com/cgi-bin/article.cgi?file=/chronicle/archive/1999/06/26 /MN107387.DTL.*

Marzano, Robert J., and John S. Kendall. 1997. *Content Knowledge: A Compendium of Standards and Benchmarks for K–12 Education.* 2d ed. Alexandria, VA: Association for Supervisional Curriculum Development.

McCloud, Scott. 1993. *Understanding Comics: The Invisible Art.* New York: Kitchen Sink.

McDermott, Thomas. 2000. Personal correspondence.

McLuhan, Marshall. 1997. *Understanding the Media: Extentions of Man.* Cambridge: MIT Press.

Moffett, James. 1987. *Teaching the Universe of Discourse.* Portsmouth, NH: Boynton/Cook.

Moffett, James, and Betty Jane Wagner. 1992. *Student-Centered Language Arts K–12.* Portsmouth, NH: Boynton/Cook.

Morkes, John, and Jakob Nielsen. 1997. "Concise, SCANNABLE, and Objective: How to Write for the Web." Useit.com: Jakob Nielsen's Web site. Accessed 4 December 1999. *http://www.useit.com/papers/webwriting/writing.html.*

Mukherjee, Bharati. 1999. *Jasmine.* New York: Grove.

Myers, Miles. 1996. *Changing Our Minds: Negotiating English and Literacy.* Urbana, IL: National Council of Teachers of English.

National Council of Teachers of English/International Reading Association. 1994. *Standards for the Assessment of Reading and Writing.* Urbana, IL: International Reading Association and National Council of Teachers of English.

Negroponte, Nicholas. 1995. *Being Digital.* New York: Vintage.

Nielsen, Jakob. 2000. *Designing Web Usability.* Indianapolis, IN: New Riders.

Northwestern Regional Educational Laboratory. 1999. "Traits of an Effective Reader Scoring Guide." Northwestern Regional Educational Laboratory. Accessed 11 November, 2000. *http://www.nwrel.org/eval/reading/scoring.html.*

November, Alan. 1998. "The Web—Teaching Zack to Think." Alan November Presents. Accessed 1 November 1999. *http://www.anovember.com/articles/zack.html.*

Nye, Naomi Shihab, ed. 1995. *The Tree Is Older Than You Are.* New York: Alladin.

O'Brien, Tim. 1996. Speech read at spring convention of the California Association of Teachers of English. Burlingame, CA.

Pauk, Walter. 1997. *How to Study in College.* 6th ed. New York: Houghton-Mifflin.

Paulos, John Allen. 1999. *Once Upon a Number: The Hidden Mathematical Logic of Stories.* New York: Basic.

Pink, Daniel. 1999. "What's Your Story?" *Fast Company.* January (21): hypertext. Accessed 6 December 1999. *http://www.fastcompany.com/online/21/rftf.html.*

Pomona College. "Visual Literacy." Accessed 10 November 1999. *http://www.pomona.edu/visual-lit/intro/intro.html*; 44, September 2000.

Purves, Alan. 1990. *The Scribal Society: An Essay on Literacy and Schooling in the Information Age*. Boston, MA: Longman.

Rosenblatt, Louise. 1978. *The Reader, the Text, and Poem: The Transactional Theory of the Literary Work*. Carbondale, IL: Southern Illinois University Press.

————. 1996. *Literature as Exploration*. 5th ed. New York: Modern Language Association of America.

Rosenblatt, Roger. 1999. "Once upon a Time." Online News Hour. 24 December. Accessed *http://www.pbs.org/newshour/essays/2000_essays /rosenblatt_2000.html*.

Rushkoff, Douglass. 2000. *Coercion: Why We Listen to What "They" Say*. New York: Riverhead.

Schlossberg, Edwin. 1999. "A Question of Trust." *Brills Content* 3(3): 70.

Scholes, Robert. 1982. *Semiotics and Interpretation*. New Haven: Yale University Press.

————. 1989. *Protocols of Reading*. New Haven: Yale University Press.

————. 1998a. "Does English Matter?" *Brown Alumni Magazine*. 99(1): hypertext. Accessed 15 September 2000. *http://www.brown.edu /Administration/Brown_Alumni_Magazine/99/9-98/features/english.html*.

————. 1998b. *The Rise and Fall of English: Reconstructing English as a Discipline*. New Haven: Yale University Press.

Seaton, Edward. 1999. "Newspapers Pause for Reflection." *San Francisco Chronicle* 12 April: A25.

Sewell, Gilbert. 2000. "History 2000: Why the Older Textbooks May Be Better Than the New." *Education Week* 16(39): 52.

Shlain, Leonard. 1993. *Art and Physics: Parallel Visions in Space, Time, and Light*. New York: Quill.

————. 1998. *The Alphabet Versus the Goddess: The Conflict Between Word and Image*. New York: Arkana.

Siegel, Lee. 2000. "Every Sweatshop Has a Silver Lining: Happiness Is a PBS Documentary on New York." *Harper's Magazine* 81–82.

Smith, Frank. 1995. *Between Hope and Havoc: Essays into Human Learning and Education*. Portsmouth, NH: Heinemann.

Stephens, Mitchell. 1998. *the rise of the image the fall of the word*. Cambridge: Oxford University Press.

Stotsky, Sandra. 1999. *Losing Our Language: How Multicultural Classroom Instruction Is Undermining Our Children's Ability to Read, Write, and Reason.* New York: Free Press.

Strunk, William, and E. B. White. 1999. *The Elements of Style.* Boston: Allyn and Bacon.

Tapscott, Don. 1998. *Growing Up Digital: The Rise of the Net Generation.* New York: McGraw Hill.

Time Publications. 1999. *Photographs That Define Our Times*: Time *Great Images of the 20th Century.* New York: Time.

Tufte, Edward. 1990. *Envisioning Information.* Cheshire, CT: Graphics.

———. 1997. *Visual Explanations: Images and Quantities, Evidence and Narrative.* Cheshire, CT: Graphics.

Vendler, Helen. 2000. *Seamus Heaney.* Cambridge: Harvard University Press.

Waldrop, M. Mitchell. 1992. *Complexity: The Emerging Science at the Edge of Order and Science.* New York: Touchstone.

Watson, Larry. 1993. *Montana 1948.* New York: Pocket.

Winters, Clyde. 2000. "History Texts: Who Decides What the Facts Are?" *Education Week* 19(42): 52.

Winterson, Jeanette. 1995. *Art [Objects]: Essays on Ecstasy and Effrontery.* New York: Knopf.

Wolf, Michael. 1999. *The Entertainment Economy: How Mega-Media Forces Are Transforming Our Lives.* New York: Time Warner.

Yellin, Don. 2000. "History, Rated G." *Brill's Content* R(4): 23.

Zuboff, Shoshana. 1989. *In the Age of the Smart Machine: The Future of Work and Power.* Boston, MA: Basic Books.

APPENDIX B

Evaluating a Web Site

Internet Site Evaluation Form

Name _____

Site Address _____

Visiting this site for _____ assignment

Thinking About the Site

a. Has it won any awards?

    1. Yes   2. No   3. It doesn't say

b. If the site has won awards, is there a link where you can go to learn if the award is important?

    1. Yes   2. No

c. If the site has won an award, was it an important one to win? (You might have to check the links given to decide.)

    1. Yes   2. No   3. Can't tell

d. Who is responsible for the content of this site?

    1. _____

    2. Can't tell

e. When was the site last updated?

    1. _____ (date)   2. Can't tell

f. When was the information on the site written?

    1. _____ (date)   2. Can't tell

g. Does the information seem current or out of date?

    1. Current   2. Out of date   3. Don't know

h. Is this site easy to navigate?

    1. Yes   2. No

   May be copied for classroom use. Jim Burke. 2001. Illuminating Texts. Portsmouth, NH: Heinemann.

Thinking About the Author of the Site

a. Who is the author of what you are reading at this site?

   1. _____

   2. Can't tell

b. What information can you find about the author of this site?

   1. _____

   2. No information listed

c. Does that information show you that the author has the authority or knowledge to write about the topic at this site?

   1. Yes   2. No   3. Can't tell

d. Does the site have links to other sites that give you information about the author?

   1. Yes   2. No   3. Can't tell

Thinking About the Audience for the Site

a. Does the author seem to have a specific audience in mind for this site?

   1. Yes   2. No   3. Can't tell

b. Does the site have advertisements?

   1. Yes   2. No

c. If the site has advertisements, do they give you insight into who the audience is supposed to be?

   1. Yes   2. No   3. Can't tell   4. No ads

d. Does the site offer an "About Us" section or an introduction that helps you understand who the audience is supposed to be?

   1. Yes   2. No   3. Can't tell

Thinking About Information Found at Sites

a. Has the information been published anywhere other than just on the Web?

   1. Yes   2. No   3. Can't tell

b. Is the information clear and easy to understand?

   1. Very clear   2. Sometimes confusing   3. Really confusing

c. If the information is about a controversial topic, is more than one side of the topic presented or does the site offer links to sites that would offer the opposing view?

1. Yes   2. No   3. Can't tell

d. Does this site have links to other sites that give you additional information on the topic?

1. Yes   2. No

e. Can you tell when the information at this site is a fact versus an opinion?

1. Yes   2. Some of the time   3. Can't tell at all

f. Does the information have a clearly identified author?

1. Yes   2. No

g. Are there charts and graphs that summarize or explain points?

1. Yes   2. No

h. Is all the quoted information clearly identified and properly cited?

1. Yes   2. No   3. Nothing is quoted in article

Overall, this site:

a. Would help me a lot with my assignment.

1. Yes   2. No   3. Can't tell

b. Links me to other sites that are helpful.

1. Yes   2. No   3. Haven't checked the links yet

c. Looks helpful but the information is too technical or too hard to understand.

1. Yes   2. No

d. Is more an advertisement than information I can use.

1. True—it has too much advertising   2. False—it has enough information

e. Seems to be just one person's opinion without any backing for who that person is or why I should believe that opinion.

1. True—too much opinion   2. False—author's opinion is very well supported

---

Thanks to Kylene Beers for her help in developing this evaluation.

APPENDIX C

Textbook Evaluation

Content

1. Preview the table of contents to get a sense of the book's contents.
2. Find each of the following and write a brief explanation of its purpose:
   - Table of contents
   - Contributors/authors
   - Copyright page
   - Acknowledgments
   - Preface
   - Introduction
   - Foreword
   - Glossary
   - Appendices (all of them)
   - Bibliography
   - Index

Types of Text

3. Skim through the book and make a list of all the different types of documents or types of text you will have to read (include graphic texts like graphs, maps, and so on).

Sidebars and Pull Boxes

4. Find examples of pullout boxes or sidebars. What kind of information appears in these? Are they standardized throughout the book (e.g., "Profiles in History," "Science in the Workplace")?

Features: Typefaces and Styles

5. Find examples of different typefaces and styles. Write down the examples and where they appear (e.g., large, bold type for chapter titles; 18-point font for subheadings throughout the chapter).
6. Look specifically for boldfaced and italicized words. How does this book use boldfaced type? What does it mean when the author uses italicized words?

Features: Color

7. Does the textbook use color to convey information? If so, how (e.g., what does it mean when you see words in red ink on the page)?

Features: Symbols and Icons

8. Does the textbook use symbols or icons to convey information? If so, how? For example, if you see an icon with a question mark in it, what does that mean? Are you supposed to do something, like ask a question? Does it mean this is a potential test question? Or is it a link to a theme running throughout the book?

Features: Images and Graphics

9. What kind of information accompanies illustrations or images? Find examples of a map, a chart, and a photograph and then look for captions or sidebars that explain or discuss the images. How is the image identified (e.g., Figure 2.6)?

Organization

10. Create an outline that describes how chapters are organized. Here is an oversimplified example to get you started:

   a. Unit title

      1) Overview

      2) Objectives

      3) Terms to know

      4) Time line

   b. Section header (24-point bold)

      1) Introduction

      2) Subheadings

   c. End-of-chapter review

      1) Section review questions

      2) Unit review

      3) Study questions

      4) Etc.

Navigation: Headers and Footers

11. Look at the words at the very top and bottom of the pages of the book. These are called the header and the footer. What kind of information is contained in this space? What do you notice as you flip through fifty consecutive pages? For example, does the content of the header or the footer change? If so, in what way and for what purpose?

Testing! Testing!

12. Imagine you must now prepare for a big test. What features of this book would help you prepare for that test? (Hint: Do not limit your answer to the practice of study questions.)

Note-Making Strategies

13. Cornell notes or outline notes would probably help you the most while reading this book. Read a page and create an example for yourself of what good notes for this book will look like.

Necessary Skills

14. Identify the skills needed to read this book. Make a list, beginning with the section in the book that provides different skills workshops.

Reading Speed

15. While your teacher times you, read one page of the book, taking notes as you normally would while reading it for homework. How long did that take you? Now do the math: Your teacher tells you to read the opening section for tomorrow and this section is thirteen pages long. How much time do you need to allot for your homework in this class?

Concerns

16. After familiarizing yourself with this textbook, you may have concerns or questions. Getting these answered up front might help you read the textbook with greater success and confidence. Take this time to list any concerns you might have (e.g., reading speed, vocabulary).

Solutions

17. Create a table like the following one to identify some strategies you can use if you get stuck when reading:

If	Then	So
You get stuck	Reread the passage	You can clear up confusion or identify the source of your confusion
You get confused	Identify the source of the confusion	You know what to ask for help with or where to focus your attention

APPENDIX D

Reading Standards Across Disciplines

English Language Arts

1. Students develop and use a range of strategies to identify and explain how authors use the following to convey meaning and achieve certain effects within the reader:
   - The different devices available to them in each genre
   - The elements of language: grammar, semantics, syntax, diction
   - The elements of story: plot, character, setting, theme, point of view
   - The senses: color, sound, texture, taste

2. Students improve their capacity by expanding their study of literary and expository texts to include the study of:
   - The author's philosophies, culture, and biases as they relate to the text
   - The characteristics and constraints of each genre
   - The elements of a writer's style
   - The text in its original historical context versus its current context

3. Students identify and analyze the form and the functions that characterize literary, expository, media, procedural, and functional texts, which include, but are not limited to:
   - Elements of design
   - Rhetorical devices

4. Students develop and use a range of strategies to help them read a range of literary, expository, media, procedural, and functional texts, which include, but are not limited to:
   - Asking (the author, the text, the teacher, and peers) questions as they read
   - Making predictions
   - Skimming for essential information
   - Using those note-taking, organizing, and reflective techniques they find helpful
   - Visualizing abstract ideas

5. Students search for and choose texts appropriate to their purpose and ability from all genres.

6. Students determine why they are reading a particular text and decide how they should read it, adjusting their approach as needed. During the course of the school year, they read to:
   - Answer a question
   - Enjoy
   - Know
   - Learn
   - Reflect
   - Understand

7. Students develop and learn when to use different strategies to define and extend understanding of new and specialized vocabulary encountered while reading. These strategies include, but are not limited to:
   - Applying knowledge of word origins and derivations
   - Learning to use the dictionary
   - Semantic mapping
   - Word study

8. Students reflect on what has been learned after reading and formulate ideas, opinions, and personal responses to texts.

9. Students draw conclusions and make inferences based on explicit and implicit information in texts, which they use to support their claims.

10. Students differentiate between fact and opinion when reading a text.

11. Students distinguish between essential and superficial information when reading a text.

12. Students scan a passage to determine whether it relevant information and thus should be read.

Home Economics

1. Students determine the quality and appropriate use of products and information based on:
   - Consumer reviews
   - Labels
   - Observation of performance
   - Product information (print and online editions)
   - Product package information
   - Warranties

2. Students successfully complete a procedure or answer questions in order to demonstrate their ability to read:
   - Diagrams
   - Directions
   - Recipes

3. Students learn the crucial terms necessary to reading in this domain.

Health

1. Students make decisions based on observations and inferences they make while reading:
   - Contextual cues in various social situations
   - Informational and procedural documents
   - Nonverbal signs such as facial and bodily gestures
   - Observable patterns of behavior in people, products, or processes

- Persuasive texts in different media
- Statistical and factual information found in informational documents, including labels, directions, and warnings
- Visual explanations such as tables, symbols, charts, graphs, and images

2. Students explain their decisions using evidence from the texts to support their reasoning and interpretation.

3. Students evaluate the effectiveness of different media and the messages they communicate.

4. Students develop and learn to apply appropriate strategies to help them determine the credibility of an idea or a text they read.

5. Students know how to determine the credibility of a particular idea or text before acting on or passing on health-related information.

Visual and Performing Arts

1. Students read, critique, analyze, and interpret the following:
   - Critical reviews and analyses of visual and performing arts productions
   - Dramatic performances of plays from different cultures, eras, and authors
   - Informal and formal theatre, film, television, and electronic media productions
   - Instrumental or vocal scores

2. Students explain how the elements of a text—that is, a musical score, a painting, or a play—function and relate to one another in order to affect the audience for that production.

3. Students know the meaning and the function of symbols, terms, and conventions common to each of the visual and performing arts.

4. Students identify and explain the political, cultural, and historical influences on a particular artwork.

5. Students develop and use a range of strategies to identify and explain how visual and performing artists use the following to convey meaning and achieve certain effects within the reader:
   - Color
   - Form
   - Images
   - Language
   - Sound

6. Students develop and apply aesthetic criteria to different artworks in order to evaluate the quality and success of a given work, using specific examples from that artwork and their rubric to support their interpretation.

7. Students infer the possible meanings of an artwork by analyzing the form of, the function of, and relationship between different aesthetic components.

8. Students interpret an artwork by examining the artist's intentions, the context in which the work was created, and the work's relationship to past and subsequent works on the same subject by this and other artists.

Business

1. Students develop and use a range of strategies to identify and explain how the following types of text convey meaning and affect the reader:
   - Commercial advertisements
   - Contracts
   - Functional documents (maps, directions)
   - Graphic texts (diagrams, charts, graphs)
   - Laws
   - Product packaging
   - Reports
   - Web sites

2. Students identify and make predictions based on important information in different texts, supporting their predictions and interpretations with evidence from these texts.

3. Students learn the appropriate concepts and terminology of the discipline.

4. Students develop and use a range of appropriate strategies to interpret the message conveyed by different media.

5. Students identify and synthesize the ethical, ideological, and psychological positions advanced in the text, drawing examples from these texts to support their analysis.

6. Students read, identify, and draw meaningful conclusions about different types of information and raw data to help them make informed decisions.

7. Students identify and analyze the forms and the functions that characterize financial, commercial, legal, media, procedural, and functional texts, which include, but are not limited to:
   - Brochures
   - Commercial advertisements (print, online, and television)
   - Letters
   - Newsletters
   - Product packaging
   - Product support materials
   - Résumés
   - Statements

8. Students evaluate and make decisions about the validity and the credibility of information contained in different texts in different media.

9. Students develop and use appropriate strategies to read the contextual and behavioral clues that will help them successfully complete a business transaction.

10. Students know and ask the appropriate questions needed to make sense of different texts in different media.

Science

1. Students evaluate and make decisions about the validity and credibility of information contained in different texts in different media.

2. Students know and ask the appropriate questions to help them make sense of different texts in different media.

3. Students identify and analyze the forms and the functions that characterize scientific, expository, media, procedural, and functional texts, which include, but are not limited to:
   - Directions
   - Elements of design
   - Equations
   - Experiments
   - Observable behaviors and features
   - Pattern formations
   - Systems

4. Students know and use the appropriate concepts, symbols, and terminology for this subject.

5. Students develop and use different strategies to help them read and interpret such devices as computer-linked probes, spreadsheets, and graphing calculators, maps, or computerized simulations while performing tests, collecting data, analyzing relationships, and displaying information.

6. Students call upon and use strategies from different branches of science to analyze situations and solve problems encountered while interpreting incoming data in different forms (i.e., visual, statistical, behavioral).

7. Students develop and apply logic and skepticism in order to determine what is important and what is insignificant, what is fact and what is opinion.

8. Students identify and analyze the relationship between the individual elements that make up an experiment, an observable formation, or other phenomena they are studying, using inferences to support their interpretations.

9. Students read data and other texts to determine what is known as well as what is not known.

10. Students read expository essays about the field as a supplement to their more formal scientific or procedural texts in order to expand their scientific thinking.

Mathematics

1. Students develop and use a range of strategies to analyze and make sense of the following:
   - Arguments
   - Charts
   - Diagrams
   - Equations
   - Geometrical shapes
   - Graphs
   - Patterns
   - Probabilities
   - Statements
   - Symbolic expressions
   - Tables
   - Theorems
   - Word problems

2. Students develop and use the concepts, the terminology, and the symbolic language of mathematics and the sciences so they can read in this discipline.

3. Students develop and use appropriate strategies to help them make sense of mathematical texts, including:
   - Inductive and deductive reasoning
   - Prediction
   - Spatial and algebraic reasoning
   - Speculation
   - Testing hypotheses
   - Trial and error

4. Students use these strategies in order to:
   - Determine mathematical hypotheses
   - Determine the validity of arguments and data
   - Develop sound arguments
   - Perceive logical subtleties
   - Solve a range of problems

5. Students learn to perceive logical subtleties and develop sound mathematical arguments before making conclusions.

6. Students learn to identify and explain the flaws in an argument and any errors in reasoning by analyzing the components of the argument.

7. Students know how to judge the validity of an argument by analyzing its components and testing it against various reliable sources.

8. Students demonstrate understanding by identifying and giving examples of undefined terms, axioms, theorems, and inductive and deductive reasoning.

9. Students develop an appreciation for the beauty and the power of mathematics.

10. Students read and apply their mathematical thinking to real-world problems.

11. Students develop and ask appropriate questions to help them make sense of the various mathematical texts they read.

History/Social Sciences

1. Students develop and use a range of strategies to analyze and make sense of the following texts common to the history/social sciences curriculum:
   - Demographic and statistical information
   - Expository texts
   - Historical documents
   - Historical patterns and trends
   - Maps
   - Primary source documents (letters, diaries)
   - Stock market reports
   - Textbooks
   - Visual explanations (charts, graphs, time lines)

2. Students develop and use a variety of strategies to help them read and analyze different texts; these strategies include, but are not limited to:
   - Comparing and contrasting
   - Evaluating
   - Predicting
   - Questioning
   - Speculating

3. Students know and use the concepts and the terminology appropriate to the discipline to read various texts in different media.

4. Students evaluate the validity of information, the probability of events, and the rhetorical content of different arguments throughout history, taking into consideration such contextual factors as culture and the era.

5. Students analyze and explain historical trends and other observable patterns using such tools as maps, graphs, and charts to organize their information and convey their understanding.

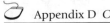

6. Students identify and explain the flaws in arguments, interpretations, and documents, taking into consideration such factors as bias and the original context.

7. Students analyze historical texts for examples of bias, motivation, validity, philosophical influences, and alternative explanations.

8. Students compare and contrast different explanations of historical events in light of their original context and their current explanation.

9. Students read analytically in order to determine the influences on and the cause and effect of different historical events and trends.

10. Students develop and apply different strategies to analyze financial, economic, philosophical, and historical trends and patterns throughout history.

11. Students read and critique those primary source documents by which the world was organized and governed, focusing on their influence, structure, argument, philosophical principles, cultural values, and historical effect on the world and its people.

12. Students identify the structural design and elements of different documents and are able to explain their effect on the reader and the text.

13. Students recognize the difference between and can identify rumor, opinion, truth, and fact in a variety of texts in different media.

Media Literacy

1. Students develop and use a range of strategies to analyze and make sense of the following types of text:
   - Commercial advertisements (print, online, and broadcast)
   - Film
   - Magazines
   - Multimedia presentations
   - Multimedia productions
   - Music
   - Newspapers
   - Television
   - Video
   - Visual images
   - Web sites

2. Students know and use the concepts and the terminology appropriate to the medium when reading it.

3. Students identify and explain the function of different elements in media productions, including:
   - Arguments
   - Color

May be copied for classroom use. Jim Burke. 2001. Illuminating Texts. Portsmouth, NH: Heinemann.

- Images
- Multiple media
- Point of view
- Shape
- Sound
- Special effects
- Stereotypes
- Stories
- Symbols
- Texture

4. Students identify and explain the consequences of the author's choices.

5. Students distinguish between superficial and significant information in a media production, supporting their analysis with examples and data from credible sources.

6. Students interpret and evaluate how visual image makers such as illustrators, documentary filmmakers, and political cartoonists represent meanings.

7. Students compare and contrast the same story or idea and its treatment in different media, explaining how effectively each one conveys the central ideas.

8. Students assess how language, medium, and presentation contribute to the message.

9. Students explain how meanings are communicated through elements of design, including shape, line, color, and texture.

10. Students identify and explain the purpose of various media forms such as informative texts, entertaining texts, and advertisements.

11. Students recognize and explain those strategies used by media to inform, persuade, entertain, and transmit culture through advertising, perpetuation of stereotypes, use of visual representations, special effects, and language.

12. Students learn the basic techniques used to create different media texts so that they can deconstruct the products of such techniques and be informed readers of such texts.

13. Students develop and ask the right questions of texts and their authors in order to determine bias, credibility, and validity.

APPENDIX E
Literacy Time Line

This time line was created by Leonard Shlain, author of *The Alphabet Versus the Goddess: The Conflict Between Word and Image* (1998). You can find it and more information, including sample chapters, on Shlain's Web site (<http://www.alphabetvsgoddess.com/>). The following passage from Shlain's book offers a bit more context to the time line; the book is not a narrative of history but an argument about literacy that draws examples from history to illustrate and support Shlain's idea that we are returning to a predominantly image-based society:

> Long before there was Hammurabi's stela or the Rosetta stone, there were the images of Lascaux and Altamira. In the beginning was the image. Then came five millennia dominated by the written word. The iconic symbol is now returning. Women, the half of the human equation who have for so long been denied, will increasingly have opportunities to achieve their potential. This will not happen everywhere at once, but the trend is toward equilibrium. My hope is that this book will initiate a conversation about the issues I have raised and inspire others to examine the thesis further. (432)

3,000,000–2,900,000 years ago
- Hominids differentiate away from other primates by becoming meat eaters instead of vegetarians.
- Extended childhoods of hominid babies require prolonged attention from hominid mothers.

- Males of the species predominately engage in hunting and killing.
- Females primarily engage in nurturing and gathering.
- Hominids become the first species of social predators in which the females do not participate in hunting and killing.

200,000–90,000 years ago

- Language develops.
- Homo sapiens differentiate away from hominids.
- Language requires complete rewiring of human brains.
- Over 90% of language modules placed in the left hemisphere of right-handed humans, who comprise 92% of the population.
- Split-brain phenomenon becomes highly exaggerated only in humans.
- Most hunting and killing strategies placed in left hemisphere.
- Most nurturing and gathering strategies placed in the right side.

40,000–10,000 years ago

- Homo sapiens organize into highly effective hunter/gatherer societies.
- Division of labor between sexes diverges more than in any other species.
- Males hunt and females nurture.
- Each sex develops predominate modes of perception and survival strategies to deal with the exigencies of life.
- Left-hemispheric specialization leads to an increased appreciation of time.
- Humans become first animals to realize they will personally die.
- Awareness of death leads to formation of supernatural beliefs.
- Societies in which hunting is a more reliable source of protein than gathering elevate hunting gods over vegetative goddesses.
- Societies in which gathering is a more reliable source of protein than hunting elevate vegetative goddesses over hunting gods.
- In general, hunter/gatherer tribes worship a mixture of both spirits.

10,000–5,000 years ago

- Agriculture discovered/domestication of animals discovered.
- Crops need to be tended/flocks need to be nurtured.
- Female survival strategy of gathering and nurturing supersedes male hunting and killing one.

- All early agrarian peoples begin to pray to an earth goddess responsible for the bountifulness of the land and fertility of the herds.
- She awakens the land in springtime and metaphorically resurrects her weaker, smaller dead son/lover.

5,000–3,000 years ago

- Writing invented.
- Left-hemispheric modes of perception, the hunting/killing side, reinforced.
- Literacy depends on linear, sequential, abstract, and reductionist ways of thinking—the same as hunting and killing.
- Early forms of cuneiform and hieroglyphics difficult to master.
- Less than 2% literate.
- Scribes become priests and new religions emerge in which the god begins to supercede the goddess.

45,000–3,000 years ago

- Alphabet invented.
- Extremely easy to use.
- Near universal literacy possible.
- Semites—Canaanites, Phoenicians, and Israelites—become first peoples to become substantially literate.
- First alphabetic book is the Hebrew Bible.
- Goddess harshly rejected from Israelite belief system.
- God loses his image.
- To know him, a worshipper must read what he wrote.
- Images of any kind proscribed in first culture to worship written words.

3,000–2,500 years ago

- Greeks become the second literate culture.
- While not rejecting images, they suppress women's rights.
- Athens and Sparta were two societies that shared the same language, gods, and culture and were in close proximity.
- Women had few rights in Athens; women wielded considerable power in Sparta.
- Athenians glorified the written word; Spartans cared little about literacy.
- Socrates disdained writing and wrote nothing down. He held egalitarian views.

- Plato wrote extensively of what Socrates said. Not as generous toward women as Socrates.
- Aristotle represents Greek passage from an oral society to a literate one. He taught that women were an inferior subspecies of man.

2,500 years ago

- Buddha becomes enlightened in India.
- Buddha, though literate, writes nothing down.
- Teaches love, equality, kindness, and compassion.
- His words are canonized in an alphabetic book five hundred years later.
- Book purports to show the Buddha had negative opinions about women, sexuality, and birth.
- Taoism and Confucianism arise in China.
- Taoism embodies feminine values: no attempt to control others, promotes Mother Nature as a guide.
- Confucianism touts masculine values: structures patriarchal society, touts Father Culture.
- Two systems of belief coexist in relative equilibrium until the Chinese invent the printing press in 923 A.D. Literacy rates soar.
- Soon after, Taoism declines and Confucianism becomes China's dominant belief system.
- Women's foot binding begins in 970 A.D. and becomes a common practice.
- Taoism transmutes into a hierarchy with sacred texts and temple priests.
- Taoist priests expected to be celibate. Women's rights plummet.
- In nearby Asian cultures that do not embrace literacy, women's rights remain high.

2,000–1,500 years ago

- Roman Empire achieves near universal alphabetic literacy rates due to the stability of Pax Romana, tutors from Greece, papyrus from Egypt, and an easy-to-use Greek and Latin alphabet.
- New religion emerges based on the sayings of a gentle prophet named Jesus.
- His oral teachings embody feminine values of freewill, love, compassion, nonviolence, and equality.
- Jesus writes nothing down.
- Women play prominent role in new religion.
- Paul commits to writing what he interprets to be the meaning of the Christ event.

- Subsequent Gospel writers detail Christ's crucifixion, death, and resurrection.
- Creed that evolves increasingly emphasizes masculine values of obedience, suffering, pain, death, and hierarchy.
- Alphabetic text becomes canonized in 367 A.D. Women banned from baptizing or conducting sacraments.
- Women ordered to back of the church and ejected from the choir.
- Christians destroy Roman images.

1,500–1,000 years ago

- Rome falls to barbarian invasions.
- Literacy lost in secular society.
- Dark Ages begin.
- When stage of history reilluminated in the tenth century, women enjoy high status.
- Age suffused with love of Mary.
- People know her through her image, not her written words.
- Women mystics revered.
- Women Cathars and Waldensians baptize.
- Abbesses lead major monasteries.
- Chivalric code instructs men to honor and protect women.
- Courtly love becomes all the fashion.
- Cathedrals dedicated to Notre Dame.
- Religious art flourishes.
- Few outside the Church can read and write.

1000–1453 A.D.

- High Middle Ages characterized by a renewed interest in literacy.
- Commerce demands literate clerks. Literacy rates climb.
- Masculine values begin to reassert dominance over feminine ones.
- Renaissance begins. Cult of the individual encourages male artists, male thinkers, and macho themes in art.

1454–1820

- Gutenberg's printing press makes available alphabet literacy to the masses.
- Books become affordable.
- Literacy rates soar in those countries affected by the printing press.

- Tremendous surge in science, art, philosophy, logic, and imperialism.
- Women's rights suffer decline.
- Women mystics now called witches.

1517–1820

- Protestant reformation breaks out, fueled by many who can now read scripture.
- Protestants demand the repudiation of the veneration of Mary, the destruction of images.
- Protestant movement becomes very patriarchal.
- Ferocious religious wars break out, fought over minor doctrinal disputes.
- Torture and burning at the stake become commonplace.
- Hunter/killer values in steep ascendance only in those countries impacted by rapidly rising alphabetic literacy rates.

1465–1820

- After the Bible, the next best-selling book is the *Witch's Hammer*, a how-to book for the rooting out, torture, and burning of witches.
- Witch craze breaks out only in those countries impacted by the printing press.
- Germany, Switzerland, France, and England have severe witch-hunts. All boast steadily rising literacy rates.
- Russia, Norway, Iceland, and the Islamic countries bordering Europe do not experience witch-hunts. The printing press has a negligible impact on these societies.
- Estimates range that between 100,000 women to the millions were murdered during the witch-hunts.
- There is no parallel in any other culture in the world in which the men of the culture suffered a psychosis so extreme that they believed that their wise women were so dangerous that they had to be eliminated.

1820–1900

- Invention of photography and the discovery of the electromagnetic field combine to bring about the return of the image.
- Photography does for images what the printing press had accomplished for written words: it made reproduction of images inexpensive, easy, and ubiquitous.
- Right hemisphere called upon to decipher images more than the left.
- Egalitarianism becomes a motif in philosophy.

- Protestantism softens its stance toward women.
- Mary declared born of Immaculate Conception by the Church, elevating her status.
- Nietzsche declares "god is dead."
- Suffragette movement coalesces in 1848.

1900–1950

- Photography and electromagnetism combine to introduce many new technologies of information transfer.
- Telegraph, radio, film, and telephone reconfigure the world.
- Communists demand redistribution of wealth.
- Capitalists demand less government interference.
- Natives restless, servants surly; everywhere paternalism is in retreat.
- Women receive the vote in 1920 in the United States and in 1936 in England.
- Russia, an oral society, recently becomes literate in the nineteenth century.
- Great burst of male creativity.
- Outbreak of religious intolerance against the Jews.
- Russian Communism repeats all the madness of Europe's first brush with alphabet literacy.
- Hitler, armed with a microphone and a radio, hypnotizes Germany, one of the most literate countries of the world.
- Mother Russia, an oral society, is bedeviled by literacy.
- Germany, the fatherland, becomes susceptible to madness by oral technology.

1950–2000

- Popularity of television explodes after the end of WWII.
- Television requires different mode of perception than radio.
- Iconic information begins to supersede text information.
- Image of the atomic bomb blast and Earth beamed back from space change the consciousness of the world more than any written books.
- Society begins to elevate feminine values of childcare, welfare, healthcare, and concern for the environment.
- Feminist movement of the '60s occurs in the first television generation.
- World wars abate among the literate countries affected by television image.

- Invention of personal computer greatly changes the way people interact. Graphic icons increasingly replace text commands.
- Internet and World Wide Web based on feminine images of nets and webs. Iconic revolution begins.
- Everywhere alphabets come into usage, religions based on sacred alphabetic books come into being.
- These all share certain characteristics.
- Women banned from conducting religious ceremonies.
- Goddesses declared abominations.
- Representative art in the form of images declared idolatry.

APPENDIX F

Table of Contents for *Reading Reminders: Tools, Tips, and Techniques*

I have included the complete table of contents for my book *Reading Reminders* because it serves as a practical companion to this book. Moreover, the following list of reminders serves as a useful checklist for what we and our students should know and be able to do. I often begin workshops by asking people to go through and identify those reminders they use or want to and those they do not or have never heard of. This establishes a helpful starting place that ensures each individual learns what he or she most needs to know.

What Teachers Must Do
Establish a Reading Culture

Teach and Support Students

18. Develop Guidelines for Group Discussion

19. Use Questions to Support Reading

20. Teach Vocabulary Strategies

21. Teach Students How to Ask for Help

22. Challenge and Support Students While They Are Reading

23. Provide Good Directions

24. Create and Use Study Guides

25. Support Students with Special Needs

26. Support English-Language Learners

27. Support Students with Learning Difficulties

Evaluate Your Own Teaching

28. Remember *Why* We Read

29. Consider Richard Allington's Ten Principles of Good Instruction

30. Teach by Design

31. Stop and Reflect Periodically

32. Consult the Standards

33. Revisit the Six Features of Effective English Instruction

Evaluate Your Students

34. Use Reading Surveys

35. Develop Portfolio Guidelines

36. Compare Effective and Ineffective Readers

37. Have Them Use the Reading Scale

38. Troubleshoot Reading Difficulties

39. Check for Understanding and Growth

What Students Must Be Able to Do

Read a Variety of Texts for Different Purposes

40. Textbooks

41. Poems

42. Web Pages

43. Narrative Texts

44. Expository Texts

45. Images

46. Tests

47. Primary Source Documents

48. Plays

49. Essays

50. Read in Different Ways: To Think, to Study, to Gather

51. Read for Style, Argument, Form, and Genre

52. Ask Different Types of Questions

53. Self-Selected Books

Use Various Strategies

54. Question the Author (Q & A)

55. ReQuest (Reciprocal Questioning)

56. Concept Cards

57. Repeated Reading

58. PreReading Plan (PreP)

59. Directed Reading and Thinking Activity (DRTA)

60. SQ3R

61. KWL

62. CRITICS Procedure

63. Anticipation Guides

64. Think-Aloud

65. Reciprocal Teaching

66. Ask Questions to Understand Stories

67. Make Predictions

68. Keep a Journal

69. Annotate Texts

70. Take Good Notes

71. Retell the Text

72. Perform the Text

73. Draw the Action

74. Chunk the Text

Develop Their Own Reading Capacity

75. Read Different Types of Texts

76. Write to Improve Reading

77. Develop Textual Intelligence

78. Read at Different Levels

79. Read from a Variety of Perspectives

80. Develop Prior Knowledge

81. Use Written Conversations

82. Use Shared Inquiry

83. Outline What They Read

84. Summarize and Paraphrase

85. Expand Vocabulary

86. Make the Foreign Familiar

87. Know the Difference Between Fact and Opinion

88. Understand Narrative Design

89. Discuss the Role of Character

90. Know the Organizational Structures of Information

91. Improve Speed, Fluency, and Stamina

92. Determine What Is Important

93. Explain Their Thinking: Elaboration Strategies

94. Discuss Their Reading: Reporting Strategies

95. Make the Abstract Concrete

96. Develop Confidence

Evaluate and Monitor Their Understanding, Performance, and Progress

97. Review, Reflect, and Reinforce

98. Develop Reading Goals

May be copied for classroom use. Jim Burke. 2001. Illuminating Texts. Portsmouth, NH: Heinemann.
(From Jim Burke, Reading Reminders. Portsmouth, NH: Heinemann. 2000.)

99. Recast the Text

100. Keep a Learning Log

Appendices

1. Works Cited

2. Further Information: Recommended Reading

Graphic Organizers

3. Categorical Thinking

4. Conversational Roundtable

5. Cornell Notes I

6. Cornell Notes II

7. Cornell Notes III

8. Feature Analysis

9. Idea Cards

10. Interactive Reading (CRITICS Procedure)

11. KWL (What I Know/What I Want to Know/What I Learned) Organizer

12. Linear Array

13. On Target

14. Outline Template

15. Plot the Action

16. Reading an Argument

17. Reading to Compare

18. Semantic Map

19. Story Board

20. Story Structure

21. Think in Threes

22. Three-Column Organizer

23. Time Line Organizer

24. Venn Diagram

25. Vocabulary Square

26. What Confuses Me Most

27. What's the Big Idea?

Additional Resources

28. Independent Reading Follow-up Essay Assignment

29. Rhetorical Modes

30. Bookmark—Reading: Think About It!

31. Bookmark—Reading Reminders

32. Reading the World of Standards Across Disciplines

33. Reading Survey

34. The Elements of a Text

35. California Language Arts Content Standards Checklist (Grades 9–10)

36. California Language Arts Content Standards Checklist (Grades 11–12)

37. Sample Rationale for Teaching a Text

38. The Northwest Regional Educational Laboratory "Traits of an Effective Reader Reading an Informational Text Scoring Guide"

39. The Northwest Regional Educational Laboratory "Traits of an Effective Reader Reading a Literary Text Scoring Guide"

40. Glossary of Literary Terms

41. 103 Things to Do in the Classroom to Improve Student Reading Performance Before/ During/After

42. Dear Sophomores: The Last Word on Learning and Reading

43. Types of Text

APPENDIX G

California Language Arts Content Standards Checklist (Grades 9–10)*

Student Name: _____   Spring/Fall of _____

Course Title: _____   Freshman or Sophomore _____

.0 WORD ANALYSIS, FLUENCY, AND SYSTEMATIC VOCABULARY DEVELOPMENT

- ❑ ❑ Apply their knowledge of word origins both to determine the meaning of new words

Vocabulary and Concept Development

- ❑ ❑ Identify and use the literal and figurative meanings of words
- ❑ ❑ Distinguish between the denotative and connotative meanings of words
- ❑ ❑ Identify and use origins of Greek, Roman, and Norse mythology to understand new word

.0. READING COMPREHENSION (FOCUS ON INFORMATIONAL MATERIALS)

- ❑ ❑ Analyze the organizational patterns, arguments, and positions advanced
- ❑ ❑ Students read two million words in different genres annually on their own

Structural Features of Informational Materials

- ❑ ❑ Analyze the structure, format, and textual features of workplace documents
- ❑ ❑ Analyze how authors use these features to achieve their purposes
- ❑ ❑ Prepare a bibliography using a variety of consumer, workplace, and public documents

Comprehension and Analysis of Grade-Level-Appropriate Text

- ❑ ❑ Generate relevant questions about readings that can be researched
- ❑ ❑ Synthesize the content and ideas from multiple sources/documents
- ❑ ❑ Paraphrase and connect ideas to other sources or ideas to demonstrate understanding
- ❑ ❑ Extend ideas through analysis, evaluation, and elaboration
- ❑ ❑ Demonstrate ability to use sophisticated learning tools by following technical directions

Expository Critique

- ❑ ❑ Analyze the organizational structure of documents by evaluating sequence and possible misreadings
- ❑ ❑ Evaluate the credibility of an author's argument
- ❑ ❑ Critique the relationship between generalizations and evidence
- ❑ ❑ Evaluate an author's intent and how that affects the text's structure, tone, and meaning

.0. LITERARY RESPONSE AND ANALYSIS

- ❑ ❑ Analyze recurring patterns and themes in historically or culturally significant works of literature
- ❑ ❑ Analyze the form, function, and characteristics or different forms of dramatic literature
- ❑ ❑ Compare and contrast a thesis or topic across genres to show how genre shapes the text and ideas

Narrative Analysis of Grade-Level-Appropriate Text

- ❑ ❑ Analyze how internal and external conflicts, motivations, relationships, and influences affect the plot
- ❑ ❑ Examine how characters reveal themselves through what they say and how they say it
- ❑ ❑ Compare and contrast literary works' universal themes using examples and ideas found in the text
- ❑ ❑ Analyze and trace an author's development of time and sequence in a story
- ❑ ❑ Examine literary devices, techniques, and elements and how they function within different texts
- ❑ ❑ Explain how voice, persona, and narrator affect tone, characterization, plot, and credibility

Literary Criticism

- ❑ ❑ Evaluate the impact of diction and figurative language on tone, mood, and theme using literary terms
- ❑ ❑ Analyze how a work of literature reflects and is influenced by its historical period

*Note: These are not actual standards—this is a checklist I made based on the standards.

.0 WRITING STRATEGIES

- ❏ ❏ Demonstrate an awareness of audience and purpose, and use of the stages of the writing process

Organization and Focus

- ❏ ❏ Establish and maintain a controlling idea or coherent thesis through a piece of writing
- ❏ ❏ Use precise language, action verbs, sensory details, and appropriate modifiers instead of a passive voice

Research and Technology

- ❏ ❏ Formulate and guide their writing using clear research questions and effective research methods
- ❏ ❏ Synthesize ideas from multiple sources, examining how the different perspectives affect meaning
- ❏ ❏ Integrate quotations and citations into written text, while maintaining the flow of ideas
- ❏ ❏ Use appropriate conventions to document sources when writing in any medium or genre
- ❏ ❏ Design and publish multi-page documents in different media to a range of audiences

Revising and Evaluating Strategies

- ❏ ❏ Use the writing process to evaluate the needs and improve the logic and coherence of the text
- ❏ ❏ Evaluate use of word choice and tone as they relate to the writer's audience, purpose, and context

WRITING APPLICATIONS (GENRES AND THEIR CHARACTERISTICS)

- ❏ ❏ Know when/how to use the rhetorical strategies of narration, exposition, persuasion, and description
- ❏ ❏ Write biographical and autobiographical narratives or short stories
- ❏ ❏ Use sensory details to evoke or describe the people or events in a scene
- ❏ ❏ Use appropriate devices and techniques to develop character, plot, and setting in a scene
- ❏ ❏ Recognize the decisions that writers face and understand how those decisions affect the story

Writing Responses to Literature

- ❏ ❏ Use examples from the text to support and illustrate the ideas their writing tries to convey
- ❏ ❏ Write expository compositions, including analytical essays and research reports
- ❏ ❏ Convey the significance of ideas by using various rhetorical and grammatical devices
- ❏ ❏ Use visual aids to organize and record information on charts, maps, and graphs
- ❏ ❏ Anticipate and address readers' potential misunderstandings, biases, and expectations
- ❏ ❏ Structure ideas and arguments in a sustained and logical fashion using examples to support
- ❏ ❏ Write a business letter and various other types of functional documents
- ❏ ❏ Write a technical document that follows the criteria appropriate for that audience

WRITTEN AND ORAL ENGLISH LANGUAGE CONVENTIONS: GRAMMAR AND MECHANICS

- ❏ ❏ Identify and use clauses, phrases, and punctuation for effect and clarity
- ❏ ❏ Identify and use different types of sentences structures
- ❏ ❏ Know how words, sentences, and paragraphs are used to convey different effects and meanings

LISTENING AND SPEAKING STRATEGIES

- ❏ ❏ Deliver speeches and presentations in various contexts for different purposes
- ❏ ❏ Compare and contrast how the media cover the same event
- ❏ ❏ Structure and provide emphasis within their speeches to achieve the desired effect
- ❏ ❏ Analyze historically significant speeches (e.g., Lincoln's "Gettysburg" or King's "Dream")
- ❏ ❏ Analyze and employ the different types of arguments including causation, analogy, authority, and logic
- ❏ ❏ Evaluate the aesthetic effects used in speeches (in films, campaigns, and other contexts)

SPEAKING APPLICATIONS (GENRES AND THEIR CHARACTERISTICS)

- ❏ ❏ Deliver extemporaneous presentations that combine different rhetorical strategies
- ❏ ❏ Interview a range of people for different purposes
- ❏ ❏ Participate in class discussions about literature using appropriate vocabulary and examples for support
- ❏ ❏ Deliver informational and procedural speeches using appropriate aids to convey your ideas
- ❏ ❏ Use multimedia tools to support your presentation of information

APPENDIX H

California Language Arts Content Standards Checklist (Grades 11–12)*

Student Name: _____   Spring/Fall of _____

Course Title: _____   Freshman or Sophomore _____

.0 WORD ANALYSIS, FLUENCY, AND SYSTEMATIC VOCABULARY DEVELOPMENT

❑ ❑ Applies knowledge of word origins to determine meaning of words

❑ ❑ Knows etymology of terms from political science and history

❑ ❑ Knows Greek, Latin, and Anglo-Saxon roots/affixes for scientific and mathematical terms

❑ ❑ Knows how to make sense of metaphorical/figurative language

.0 READING COMPREHENSION (INFORMATIONAL MATERIALS)

❑ ❑ Recognizes and comprehends use of different types of public documents

Comprehension and Analysis of Grade-Level-Appropriate Text

❑ ❑ Identifies and analyzes different types of rhetorical devices in public documents

❑ ❑ Explains how various techniques affect meaning

❑ ❑ Examines and clarifies facts used in a variety of public documents

❑ ❑ Recognizes and demonstrates the difference between fact and opinion

❑ ❑ Makes reasonable assertions about the author's arguments

❑ ❑ Supports assertions using effective examples, quotes, and conclusions

Expository Critique

❑ ❑ Critique the power, validity, and truthfulness of arguments set forth in public documents

.0 LITERARY RESPONSE AND ANALYSIS

❑ ❑ Reads significant works of literature that complement studies in history

❑ ❑ Identifies and analyzes recurring themes

Structural Features of Literature

❑ ❑ Reads and knows characteristics of subgenres (e.g., satire, parody, allegory) used in various genres

❑ ❑ Reads and understands the structure of novels.

❑ ❑ Reads and understands the devices used in short fiction.

❑ ❑ Reads and understands the devices used in drama.

❑ ❑ Reads and understands the devices used in poetry.

❑ ❑ Reads and understands the devices used in literary essays.

Narrative Analysis of Grade-Level-Appropriate Text

❑ ❑ Uses textual evidence to support claims.

❑ ❑ Knows and uses literary terms when responding to literary texts

❑ ❑ Explains use of various literary techniques and how they affect the text

❑ ❑ Traces the development of American literature across time

❑ ❑ Compares works—i.e., themes and styles—from one period to another

❑ ❑ Explains the historical/philosophical influences of a historical period on a text and its writer

❑ ❑ Understands and uses archetypes from myth and literary tradition to examine literature

Literary Criticism

❑ ❑ Examines literary texts using philosophical arguments (e.g., feminism, existentialism)

*Note: These are not actual standards—this is a checklist I made based on the standards.

1.0 WRITING STRATEGIES (ORGANIZATION AND FOCUS)

❏ ❏ Knows and uses different elements of discourse when writing

❏ ❏ Uses variety of stylistic and rhetorical devices when writing

❏ ❏ Supports ideas and arguments with precise and relevant examples

Research and Technology

❏ ❏ Develops and uses surveys and interviews to generate data

❏ ❏ Uses a variety of sources from different media for research

❏ ❏ Organizes information during research using appropriate strategies (e.g., outlining)

❏ ❏ Integrates databases, graphics, and spreadsheets into word-processed documents

❏ ❏ Revises documents to improve voice, style, and meaning

Writing Applications (Genres and Their Characteristics)

❏ ❏ Writes documents at least 1500 words each

❏ ❏ Demonstrates a command of Standard American English

❏ ❏ Writes a variety of narratives

❏ ❏ Writes a literary response essay

❏ ❏ Writes a reflective essay

❏ ❏ Writes a historical investigation report (research project)

❏ ❏ Writes a job application and resume

❏ ❏ Delivers multimedia presentations

❏ ❏ Demonstrates master of business letter by writing one

❏ ❏ Writes letters of complaint, inquiry, and intent

❏ ❏ Writes a proposal

❏ ❏ Writes a precis

.0 WRITTEN AND ORAL ENGLISH LANGUAGE CONVENTIONS

❏ ❏ Knows and uses proper formatting in all documents

❏ ❏ Produces work that is legible

❏ ❏ Writes a paragraph that is focused, organized, and developed

❏ ❏ Writes a variety of types of sentence patterns

❏ ❏ Uses a variety of grammatical structures and modifiers in sentences

.0 LISTENING AND SPEAKING STRATEGIES

❏ ❏ Identifies and evaluates strategies used by media to inform, persuade, and entertain

❏ ❏ Explains the impact of media on the political process

❏ ❏ Compares and interprets various ways in which events are presented by visual media

Organization and Delivery of Oral Communication

❏ ❏ Uses different rhetorical devices to achieve clarity, force, and effect

❏ ❏ Identifies and evaluates use of logical, ethical, and emotional appeals in presentations

❏ ❏ Uses language, imagery, metaphor to create effective presentations

Analysis and Evaluation of Oral and Media Communications

❏ ❏ Analyzes techniques used by media to convey meaning

❏ ❏ Analyzes four basic types of persuasive speech

.0 SPEAKING APPLICATIONS (GENRES AND THEIR CHARACTERISTICS)

❏ ❏ Delivers effective presentations

❏ ❏ Delivers reports on historical investigations

❏ ❏ Delivers oral responses to literature

❏ ❏ Delivers multimedia presentations

❏ ❏ Performs a variety of literary texts (e.g., from plays, poems, speeches)

Index